ARAB CHRISTIANS IN BRITISH MANDATE PALESTINE

ARAB CHRISTIANS IN BRITISH MANDATE PALESTINE

COMMUNALISM AND NATIONALISM, 1917–1948

Noah Haiduc-Dale

EDINBURGH
University Press

© Noah Haiduc-Dale, 2013, 2015

Transferred to digital print 2015

Edinburgh University Press Ltd
The Tun – Holyrood Road
12 (2f) Jackson's Entry
Edinburgh EH8 8PJ

www.euppublishing.com

First published in hardback by Edinburgh University Press 2013

This paperback edition 2015

Typeset in 11/13 JaghbUni Regular by
Servis Filmsetting Ltd, Stockport, Cheshire, and
printed and bound in Great Britain by
CPI Group (UK) Ltd, Croydon CRO 4YY

A CIP record for this book is available from the British Library

ISBN 978 0 7486 7603 3 (hardback)
ISBN 978 1 4744 0924 7 (paperback)
ISBN 978 0 7486 7604 0 (webready PDF)
ISBN 978 0 7486 7606 4 (epub)

Contents

Illustrations

Acknowledgements

A series of experiences led me to study Middle East history, and without the Revd John Patterson, Elias Jabbour, Larry Penrose and Steve Tamari I would never have become interested in the Palestinian–Israeli conflict; without Jeff Tyler, I probably would not have become a historian. Thank you. My studies at the University of Arizona and New York University prepared me for the task of writing this book, and a number of professors guided me through those years. Charles D. Smith at the University of Arizona, and Zachary Lockman, Khalid Fahmy and Fred Cooper at NYU deserve special thanks, as well as Ellen Fleischmann. Funding from NYU and the Fulbright–Hayes programme made my travels possible, while the actual research was facilitated by assistance from numerous librarians and archivists. Various scholars in Palestine helped me to ask the right questions and guided me towards the best sources, among them Hillel Cohen, Adnan Musallam, Bernard Sabella and Salim Tamari. Thanks to the participants in the scholarship group at Waynesburg for keeping me motivated, Jill Sunday for polishing my writing, and Cori Schiplani for assisting with images and creating the wonderful maps. Other colleagues helped indirectly at various stages: without Jonathan Gribetz and On Barak, my research would have been far less enjoyable. Nicola Ramsey, Rebecca Mackenzie and Michelle Houston at Edinburgh University Press have been both patient and helpful answering my many questions along the way.

My family has been wonderfully supportive. Thank you to my parents, Steve and Wendy Dale, and my in-laws, George and Violet Haiduc, for their love and encouragement. Most important has been the patience and support of my wife, Michelle, who accompanied me across the world and back and has supported me in so many ways. She and our children, Maia, Asher and Ethan, who arrived at various points along the way, have kept me motivated through long days of research and writing.

Introduction:
Nationalism and Religious Identification

I am not Christian, nor Buddhist, nor Muslim, nor Jewish. I am not Arab, or English, or French, or German, or Russian, or Turkish, but I am one of the human race.[1]

Khalil al-Sakakini, 26 March 1915

If I enjoy any position in this land, if the people love me and respect me, it is because they think that I am nearer to Islam than to Christianity, because I am wealthy in the Arabic language, because they fancy that I am a conservative and will not depart from Oriental customs under any circumstances.[2]

Khalil al-Sakakini, 12 December 1932

My first exposure to the Palestinian–Israeli conflict came in high school when I travelled with a group of American teenagers for a month-long stay with Elias Jabbour, founder of the House of Hope in Shefaᶜamr, an Arab–Israeli village near Haifa. Jabbour, a Melkite Christian, framed his approach to the conflict through his religious beliefs, describing himself as 'a Christian, Palestinian, Arab, Israeli'.[3] Two years later, while living and studying the conflict in Jerusalem as a college student, I was confused when the programme director insisted that the conflict was not about religion at all, but about land, economics and politics. This academic argument did not match up with the explanation I had been given while living in Shefaᶜamr. How could religion not be integral to the conflict, when those who were living in it insisted it was essential?

The academic explanation has a lot to offer, since a religious explanation often hides more than it illuminates. In its simplest formulation, the Palestinian–Israeli conflict is a conflict between two groups of people, Palestinians and Israelis, who claim nationhood and collective ownership over the same piece of land. Many commentators, as well as many Palestinians and Israelis themselves, couch this nationalistic conflict in religious terms, as a clash between Jews and Muslims. But like all people, individual Israelis and Palestinians fall along a broad spectrum between secular and religious. Both sides utilise nationalist reasoning in their

1

political struggles, though the relationship between religious and national-ist ideology is complex. A third issue is that minorities are often pushed out of the conversation by this polarising approach. Arab Jews, Palestinians in Israel, Messianic Jews and other groups fail to fit the narrow categories often ascribed to the conflict.

A question emerged between these historiographical poles: where did Arab Christians fit in Palestinian history, since they were so often left out of the standard narrative? Though their relative population has shrunk to under 2 per cent in recent years, Christians constituted a sizeable 10 per cent minority in the early decades of the twentieth century when the Palestinian national movement was in its formative stage. The disjuncture between nationalist and religious explanations demands a closer examina-tion of Arab Christians' place in society during the period of British rule (1917–48) in an effort to understand the meaning of religious identifica-tion and relationship of Christians to the nationalist movement. Such an examination also uncovers sharp disagreements between Christians, exposes debates about communal identification and illuminates reasons for Christians' divergent views.

The Palestinian Arab community was fundamentally reshaped by political developments of the late nineteenth and early twentieth centuries. The fall of the Ottoman Empire reverberated throughout the Middle East, perhaps more so in Palestine than elsewhere due to the British occupation and support for a Jewish homeland there. The transitional moment between Ottoman and British rule has recently captured the attention of scholars for other reasons, too. They suggest that the period calls into question tradi-tional historical divisions and provides a fascinating look at the impor-tance of local issues before the region was fully beset by the Arab–Zionist conflict.[4] The upheaval also contributed to the reshaping of the Arab identification. Arabs residing in Palestine were stripped of their Ottoman labels, and the community underwent a process of redefining itself in the light of the new political circumstances. Modern forms of national-ism were beginning to take root throughout much of the world, and the Middle East was no different. The loss of the Ottoman option meant that belonging would be determined by shared ethnicity or geography (either as Arabs or specifically Palestinians, depending on the particular histori-cal moment). Yet nationalism is rarely 'pure'. That is, alternative forms of identification remained, such as factional and religious groupings. These ways of identifying oneself and others were more or less important for various groups and individuals, but the balance between them was always contested. Historians now widely accept that both nation and religious community (as a political grouping) are historically created or 'invented' ideas. In this context, Arab Christians, both as a minority community and as individuals, negotiated, debated and struggled to define their place in a rapidly changing society.

The reason for concentrating on this minority is threefold. First, despite their important role in the Palestinian national movement since its inception, Arab Christians have been largely overlooked in modern Palestinian history, lost in a rift often summarised as between Muslims and Jews.[5] Secondly, focusing on a minority group illuminates much about the nationalist movement itself, and offers an alternative perspective that cannot be understood from the vantage point of the majority. Finally, interreligious conflict continues throughout the Middle East and much of the Islamic world, and understanding how Arab Christians responded at one point in history can help to more accurately interpret contemporary conflicts. By elucidating the historical relationship between Palestinian Arab Christians and the Palestinian nationalist movement, I demonstrate Christians' refusal to accept the standard nationalist–communalist dichotomy. Instead, in the name of both national and self-interest, Christians sought to navigate between those two seemingly exclusive modes of identification as the shifting political balance and specific events shaped and reshaped their options.

In agreement with scholars of sectarianism and communalism who focus on conflicts throughout Africa and Asia, the Palestinian case demonstrates how a combination of internal and external factors contributed to a growing conflict between Muslim and Christian communities.[6] The advent of British rule, the influx of Zionist settlement and the strengthening of that movement's call for an ethnic homeland, and the interests of other international powers in the 'Holy Land' all enhanced changes taking place throughout Palestinian society. Islam's role shifted as well, both directly and indirectly due to British policies, a trend that changed the options available to Christians within the community.

The British government developed organisational and political structures based on the assumption that religion was the primary element of Arab identification. Such efforts often enhanced religious boundaries, but it would be simplistic to label communalism as solely a colonial creation. Rather, Arab Christians struggled among themselves and in public to define the meaning of religious identification and their role as a religious minority. For some, responding to political upheaval by embracing a politicised religious identification was the best way to protect themselves and their community; others sought to distance themselves from such claims. Such debates and the varying level of participation in the national movement among Arab Christians reflect Christians' agency in determining

3

their own space in society, though their options were limited by historical circumstances. Disunity among Christians also highlights the diversity of that community along denominational, class and regional lines.

This examination of religious identification fits squarely between two opposing trends in literature about the British Mandate: insistence on religion as a primary identifier for Palestinian Christians, and ignoring religion altogether. Many scholars have accepted the belief held by British Mandate officials who assumed that religious identification was primordial and unchanging, what scholars refer to as a 'strong' or 'immutable' identity.[7] That is, Arab Christians were, first and foremost, Christians, while Arab Muslims were identified primarily as Muslims (and, the theory continued, identified themselves primarily as such). British obsession with this feature of Arab life can be found in official correspondence, where marginal notes highlight the religious affiliation of important Arabs and official memoirs dwell on religious conflicts.[8] Jerusalem district commissioner Edward Keith-Roach, recalls that 'the country was beset by a strange form of nationalism based not so much on race as on religion, for the criterion of nationality was normally creed'.[9] As a result, the colonial leadership often misread and was slow to accept the nationalist claims of Arab Christians.

The British were not the only ones to assume such religiously driven identification. After discovering that the Christians were not amenable to the Zionist cause, one Zionist lamented that 'Christians are, from the first to the last, our deadly enemies ... Catholic or Greek Orthodox or Protestant, they have one [thing in] common: a fanatical religious hatred of the Jews.'[10] This was not fully true, of course, especially by the mid-1920s, though a small group of Christians had spearheaded the anti-Zionist movement in the first decades of the century. Regardless of their inaccuracy, such opinions help to shaped a society defined along religious lines.

For many years scholars accepted this version of Christian identification, privileging both Christian and Muslim communalism over all other options. Yehoshua Porath stands out among those who perpetuated the notion of an immutable Arab Christian identity. Porath's understanding of Arab Christians is essential because his two-volume history of the British Mandate was among the first to examine seriously Palestinian nationalism during that period.[11] As the first in the field, many of Porath's conclusions have been challenged by other scholars, yet his conclusions concerning the Arab Christian population remain unchallenged and are often quoted by even the most revisionist scholars.[12] Porath's argument is fundamentally problematic because he assumes the accuracy of British sources without accounting for their colonial interpretation of Arab society. Porath accepts British assumptions that Muslims and Christians existed as two separate groups, rather than as two parts of a single community. He also overstates Muslim–Christian discord, while downplaying or overlooking simultaneous episodes of intercommunal cooperation, a practice leading to the conclusion that tension was always at the heart of Muslim–Christian relations. Finally, he always describes Muslim–Christian conflict as religious in nature and ignores other possible motives, such as class divisions or factionalism.

Daphne Tsimhoni, whose study of Palestinian Christians focuses on the first five years of the British Mandate, maintains the primacy of religious identification. While she does recognise that Christians had strong connections to Arab Muslims, she argues that such a relationship was possible only because Palestinian Christians 'accept[ed] their marginal and secondary position to which they were doomed as a religious minority group'.[13] On the contrary, Arab Christians did not acquiesce to an inferior position, but constantly strived to re-imagine their place in Palestinian society. Assuming an immutable religious identification allowed Porath and Tsimhoni to downplay other elements of Arab Christians' political lives; nothing could trump identification by religious community.

A different group of historians, focusing on religious history, presents Christians as isolated and divided minority communities. Such scholarship is heavily influenced by interest in Palestine as a Christian holy land and addresses the specifics of Christian subcommunities at the expense of a broader understanding of the relationship of Christians to Palestinian Arab society, culture and politics.[14] Religion is the primary category of interest, and edited volumes often devote much attention to very small minorities, such as Armenians, Copts, Ethiopians and Anglican missionary women.[15] Even when issues of religious and political identity are addressed, they are tackled with little or no reference to Christians' wider Palestinian Arab context.[16] While such studies are important in their own right, they often fail to situate their subjects within Palestinian society as a whole.

The 'nationalist response' in Israel–Palestine scholarship not only denied religion as a primary identification, but almost entirely neglected religion as a salient feature of Palestinian Arab life during the Mandate. This narrow focus on nationalism can be explained with both political and academic reasoning, but such explanations cannot conceal the flaws of that interpretation. The resurgence of Palestinian nationalism in the 1960s, like movements throughout much of the decolonising world, meant that national identification became the primary way many Palestinians described themselves. As a result, Palestinians have often described themselves as united by national identity, denying the importance of religious identification in their own history.[17] Scholars responded to this political trend by reading 1960s nationalism into the early twentieth century as well. The study of religion as a basis of historical enquiry also declined during the 1960s, while categories of gender, race and social class became the most prominent tools in academic discourse. While this trend has reversed somewhat in recent years due to new historical and political realities, for a time nationalism provided a new and powerful lens through which to interpret the past.

Among historians of the Mandate, the nationalist narrative is most clearly employed by Rashid Khalidi and Muhammad Muslih, two of the first scholars to elucidate the history of Palestinian nationalism. Both argue that religious identification diminished in importance throughout the late Ottoman and Mandate periods in favour of secular national identification, failing to see the role that religious identification played in political decision-making and societal relations. Khalidi's *Palestinian Identity: The Construction of Modern National Conscious* was a groundbreaking study of Palestinian nationalism, and acknowledges the multiplicity of possible identities available to an Ottoman Arab, but his narrative focuses on the growing tendency to identify primarily as Palestinian.[18] The extent of Khalidi's focus on religious affiliation is his argument that the importance of Palestine as a holy land for both Christians and Muslims helped to establish Palestine's informal boundaries during the Ottoman era.[19] Beyond that, religion plays a role of decreasing importance in his narrative, and there is no discussion of how Christians understood their place in the nationalist movement. Muslih focuses on class, education and employment status in describing Christians' political activities. While these are important elements, religious communities receive scant mention in his assessment of national development. Some nationalist figures may have been Christian, but that label means little in his assessment.[20] Many scholars have accepted this narrative as comprehensive and have likewise ignored the role that religion played in this process.[21]

Both schools of thought discussed above make the same error: they ignore the process of identification. Neither religious nor national identity is primordial; rather, both are products of a particular historical moment. It is true that for some Palestinian Christians, at some times, religious community was paramount. It is equally true that religion played an insubstantial role in the self-identification of other Christians at other times. The important questions are when and why did one aspect of Christians' many levels of belonging become more important than others? And how did various Christians at various times understand their role in the nationalist movement? Christians held diverse opinions, complicating generalisations, but one thing is certain: trends within the Christian community reflected changes in political circumstances.

While histories of Israel/Palestine often fail to go beyond colonial policies and relationships with elite leaders in the Zionist and Arab communities, recent scholarship has begun to illuminate British–Palestinian interactions. Drawing conceptually from studies of African and Asian history, historians have begun to paint a picture of Mandate Palestine's social history, as well as offering new interpretations of Palestinian history as a site of colonial encounter. Zachary Lockman's *Comrades and Enemies* argues against the standard narrative that Jewish and Arab communities developed independently from one another and looks instead at the relationships and interactions between Jewish and Arab workers, in particular. Other recent publications focus on Palestinian collaborators with Zionism, the involvement of Palestinian women in the nationalism movement, and the rise of the political party *al-Istiqlal* as a major force in creating a popular, rather than elite-led, national movement.[22]

The role of religion during the Mandate had until recently been limited to a few studies of Muslim elites and organisations, such as Hajj Amin al-Husayni, often considered the leader of the Palestinian nationalist movement, and the Supreme Muslim Council, a British-established organisation headed by Husayni.[23] Finally, Nels Johnson's *Islam and the Politics of Meaning in Palestinian Nationalism* briefly examines the role of Islam in the origins of Palestinian nationalism, but the book devotes more time to Islam in later periods of nationalist development.[24] Only one book, very recently published, addresses this topic, though from a different angle. In *Colonialism and Christianity in Mandate Palestine*, Laura Robson's goals are twofold: to explain how sectarianism became prominent in twentieth-century Palestine; and how that shift led to the marginalisation of Palestinian Arab Christians.[25] While Robson's study is closely related to the subject of this book, my primary goal is to examine Christian actions in response to the circumstances created by the onset of British rule as a way of understanding the process of identification. While I will address the creation of those circumstances, the emphasis here is on the variety and meaning of Christian responses.

The Arab Christian Communities in Palestine

'People ask me,' Elias Jabbour once told me, 'when my family converted to Christianity. I tell them that Jesus was the first missionary to Palestine.' Indeed, Christians have been in Palestine for centuries, perhaps throughout all of Christian history. The region was almost wholly Christian until the

Arab conquests of the 600s, after which a long, slow process of conversion eventually established a Muslim majority. Perhaps because of the longevity of their presence in Palestine, Arab Christians are a heterogeneous group. In some regards, it makes little sense to write of them as a single unit. What follows is an introduction to the Arab Christian communities in Palestine, focusing on their position in the late Ottoman Empire during the second half of the nineteenth and early twentieth centuries, covering the lead-up to the British occupation.

The best estimate of the Arab Christian population of Palestine in 1914 is 81,000, just over 11 per cent of the population.[26] Because Christians did not consider themselves to be part of a single religious community, this statistic must be broken down further in recognition of denominational divisions that varied in importance at different times throughout the Mandate. Such statistics are available from the 1931 census: at that time the Christian population reached nearly 92,000 (remaining steady at 11 per cent of the Arab population) of which 43 per cent were Greek Orthodox, 20 per cent Latin (Roman Catholic), 14 per cent Melkite, 5 per cent Anglican and 4 per cent Maronite, with Armenian Orthodox, Syrian Orthodox, Presbyterian, Lutheran, Abyssinian, Coptic, Gregorian, Syrian Catholic and 'unclassified' Christians constituting the remainder.[27] The denominational divisions complicate analysis of the 'Christian community' because each denomination was pulled in different directions by different societal forces. Still, particularly among local Christians (that is, excluding non-Palestinians, such as Armenians, Syrians, Copts and the like) there were many shared experiences, and at times the denominations presented a semi-unified front. Furthermore, denominational affiliation is not always clear because of inconsistent labelling in Mandate-era documentation. Despite British and Zionist awareness of the differences between, for example, Orthodox and Latin Christians, they often grouped all Christians into a single category.

While recognising the variety of denominations represented in Palestine, four are central to the role of Christians in British Mandate history: Greek Orthodox, Latin (Roman Catholic), Melkite (Greek Catholic) and Protestant (largely Anglican at that time). While central to Lebanese history, the Maronites, who were congregated in the Galilee, comprised only 4 per cent of the Christian population in Mandate Palestine, and were not as involved as their Melkite neighbours (who were also concentrated in the north) in national politics. Likewise, Copts, who are very important in Egypt, comprised only a tiny percentage of Christians in Palestine, and Armenians did not consider themselves Arab, nor did they participate in the national movement (although a few did join in the 1936 revolt).

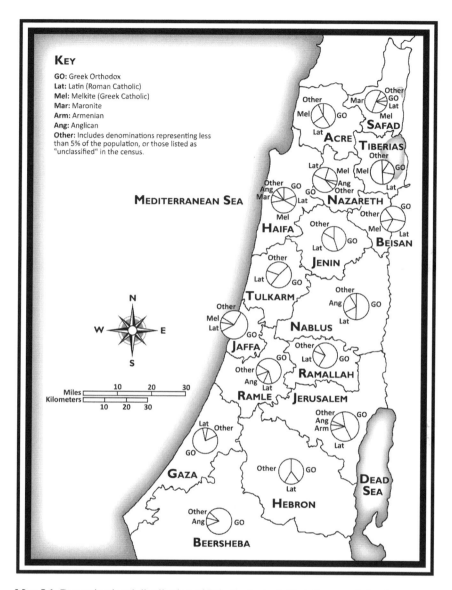

Map I.1 Denominational distribution of Palestine's Arab Christian population by subdistrict. Note that seven districts held 92% of Christians in Palestine: Jerusalem (34%); Haifa (18%); Jaffa (11%); Ramallah (8%); Nazareth (8%); Acre (8%); Ramle (5%). The Christian populations of the other districts are each 2% or less of the total number of Christians. Data compiled from E. Mills (ed.), *Census of Palestine 1931*, vol. II (Alexandria: Whitehead Morris, 1933).

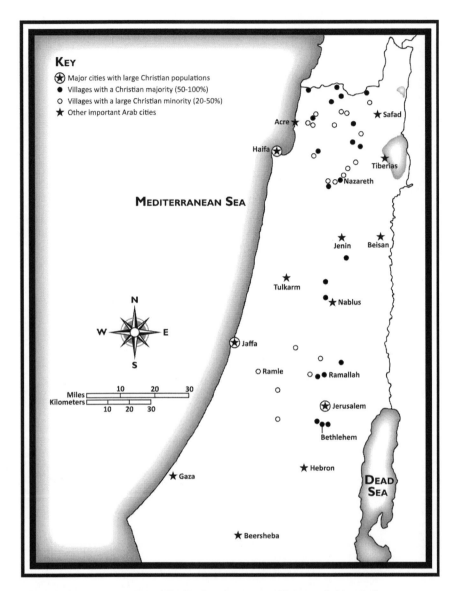

Map I.2 Christian population distribution: important villages and cities during the Mandate. Data compiled from Yaacov Shimoni, *Arabs of Israel* (Tel Aviv: Davar Printing Press, 1947) and www.palestineremembered.com (last accessed 19 July 2012).

The most important denomination, both in terms of numbers and its members' roles in national politics, was Greek Orthodox. Its members also held the most diverse views on the place of Christians in Palestinian Arab politics, so generalising is particularly difficult. Orthodox Christians in Palestine had an additional story unfolding in their community, prompted by the changes wrought by late-Ottoman reforms and European, particularly Greek, nationalism. Over the centuries of Ottoman rule, a small group of Greek monks called the Brotherhood of the Holy Sepulchre consolidated power in its own hands, appointing the Patriarch of Jerusalem from their ranks and creating strong ties to the church hierarchy in Greece. The Brotherhood's efforts to maintain a fully Greek hierarchy were successful, but the laity in Palestine was constituted largely of Arabs who understood 'Greek Orthodox' as an historical or theological term rather than as an ethnic or linguistic descriptor.[28] The distinction between Greek and Arab Orthodox Christians became more apparent after the struggle for Greek independence in the 1820s, a development that tied church identification to a nation. Still, it was not until the latter half of the nineteenth century that Orthodox Arabs in Jerusalem and the surrounding area began lobbying for greater Arabisation of the patriarchate. The 1898 election of an Arab patriarch in the Antioch patriarchate provided a stronger impetus for the Arab laity in Jerusalem to demand the same, although they were unsuccessful in gaining much traction in these early efforts.[29] This controversy appears repeatedly throughout Mandate history (and beyond), re-emerging again and again as an important influence on Arab Orthodox political perspective.

The Latin Church (that is, Roman Catholic) has usually been overshadowed in Palestine by the Orthodox patriarchate, with the exception of the relatively brief crusader period in which the Catholic Church took full control of religious institutions in the region. The comparatively small size of the Latin population (about half that of the Orthodox) is half the reason; also, after Catholic involvement in the Crusades, Muslim leaders were hesitant to allow the Latin patriarch back in to Jerusalem. For centuries he served in name only, living in Europe while Franciscan monks managed Latin interests in the Holy Land. It was not until 1847 that Pope Pius IX received permission from the Ottoman government to re-establish a Latin patriarch in Jerusalem. While the Orthodox patriarchate was interested in securing institutional advantages, the mission of the Latin patriarch was to 'serve Christians in the land of Jesus'.[30] Of course, the Vatican was interested in expanding its regional authority at the expense of the Orthodox Church, but in the absence of a strong leadership it did so through strengthening the local Arab Catholic community. Louis Barlassina was appointed patriarch at the outset of the British Mandate and presided over the church in Palestine until his death in September 1947. Barlassina led the local Arab laity directly, unlike his Orthodox counterpart, but his political activity was heavily influenced by shifting Vatican policies. Under his strong leadership, Latin Arabs were encouraged to be less active in national issues and more involved in strictly Catholic endeavours, a trend more fully described in Chapter 1.

The only notable exception to the foreign leadership of the major denominations was the Melkite, or Greek Catholic, Church.[31] Melkites have been in communion with Rome since 1724, and members of the church are spread throughout Palestine, Lebanon and Syria, with a particularly large number in the Galilee (what is today northern Israel).[32] Despite its connection to the papacy, the denomination maintained considerable autonomy, particularly concerning local politics. When Arab nationalism emerged as a powerful force, Melkites looked to their Arab hierarchy (with a patriarch in Antioch and an archbishop, Grigorios Hajjar, in Haifa) with particular pride. They did not have to fight against their hierarchy in order to receive nationalist direction. Thus, despite its small size, the Melkite community occasionally played an outsize role in national politics.

One final denomination of note is the Anglican Church. While the Arab Anglican population was not particularly large (numbering just 1,800 Arab Anglicans in 1931), the denomination's importance was enhanced by the British occupation.[33] The church in Palestine was divided into three parts: a British church to serve the needs of the English; an indigenous Arab congregation; and a church for Christian Jews converted through the work of an Anglican mission called the London Society for Promoting Christianity among the Jews.[34] Though few in number, Anglicans played an important role despite a government pledge not to grant the church special treatment.

Beyond denominational differences, the Christian community was diverse in other ways, too. While most Christians lived in the larger cities of Jerusalem, Jaffa and Haifa, important towns, such as Bethlehem, Nazareth and Ramallah, were either exclusively, or at least mostly, Christian. Other Christians lived in villages scattered throughout the region. Such geographic diversity led to a difference in approach to that of Arab Muslims, since those in mixed urban areas were more likely to have friends and colleagues of the other faith. Social class, too, played a role in determining individual Christian perspectives, and the elite class from the Ottoman period held very different views from those of the younger generation of Palestinian Arabs who rose in prominence later in the Mandate. Such variations in Christian experience shaped individuals' approaches to the nationalist movement and became important at specific periods during the Mandate.

Despite the variety of differences within the Christian community, it is true that, particularly during the earliest years of the Mandate, when the Arab *ayan*, or notables, sought to maintain a central political position, Christians held important roles in many nascent nationalist organisations as well as in the new Mandate government. Higher levels of education and personal connections to Europe among Christians provided them with opportunities not afforded to Arab Muslims. As a result, the British sought out Christians for civil service posts, the Arab nationalist leadership often sent Christian envoys to Britain to serve as spokesmen for the Arab cause in Palestine, and, in the early Mandate period, Arab Christians controlled nearly every major newspaper in Palestine. As a whole, then, Christians were an important and sizeable segment of the Palestinian population, even if members of that community held divergent, even opposing, views at times. Despite that diversity, the effect of Christians on the national movement, and the movement's impact on Christians, were important dimensions of Palestinian nationalism.

The book is organised chronologically, and each chapter examines the most pressing issues facing the Christian community, as well as Christians' responses to those issues. The three major themes in Chapter 1 (1917–23) are: the British role in redefining the meaning of religious identification; the rise of the Muslim Christian Association (MCA), an elite-run political organisation that emerged immediately following the British occupation; and the role played by the foreign clergy of the Orthodox and Latin denominations. Chapter 2 (1923–9) examines two trends from the late 1920s: first, new British policies placed a great deal of power in the hands of Muslim religious authorities; in addition, when vying for power within the new British system, the Arab leadership splintered, sometimes using religious differentiation to drive a wedge between various political and familial factions. Christians responded to both the 'Islamicisation' and factionalisation of Palestinian nationalism in a variety of ways. Chapter 3 (1929–36) and Chapter 4 (1936–9) focus on a period in which interreligious tensions threatened national unity. In the first half of the decade, a series of religiously charged events occurred: the 1929 Wailing Wall violence, which recast the Arab–Jewish conflict in a religious light; the 1930 murder of an Arab Christian newspaper editor in Haifa by a group of Muslims; and a pan-Islamic Congress held in Jerusalem in 1931. These three case studies suggest the continued politicisation of religion. Chapter 4 examines the role of Christians in the Great Revolt, and the increase in interreligious tensions as the revolt foundered at the end of the decade.

Challenging scholarship that points to Christian inaction in the uprising, I argue that while Christians were fully engaged, they simultaneously became increasingly aware of their tenuous place in the Palestinian social order. Finally, Chapter 5 explores Christian efforts in the 1940s to adopt both nationalism and communalism, defining the two non-exclusively. Whereas Christians once sought recognition as Arabs who happened to be Christian, political realities forced many to reassess that identification and to seek protection by coalescing in stronger communal groupings. Evidence for this is found everywhere: from the communalisation of Palestinian sports, to the documents of the Union of Arab Orthodox Clubs, to Christian responses to the 1948 war. Despite this trend, Christians also remained unabashedly nationalistic.

Communalism is most often studied in locations where religious tension has led to violence or at least political controversy. While Muslim–Christian relations in Mandate Palestine were occasionally tense, this period provides an example of interreligious relations and minority identification where Arab Christians developed a unique understanding of communalism. The struggle of the Christian minority to identify its role in the national movement continues to this day. The ongoing conflict presents many of the same difficulties and options, while various upheavals and ideological shifts have led to further changes in Palestinian Christian identification. Elias Jabbour seems quite typical, however. Like most Palestinian Christians he remains firmly committed to a variety of religious, ethnic and national forms of identification.

Notes

1. Akram Musallam (ed.), *Yawmiyat Khalil al-Sakakini: yawmiyat, rasaʾil wa-taʿammulat*, vols 1–8 (Ramallah: Markaz Khalil al-Sakakini al-Thaqafi, 2003–2008), vol. 2, pp. 157–8. Entry for 26 March 1915.
2. ISA P356/7, a letter from Khalil al-Sakakini to his son, Sari al-Sakakini, 12 December 1932.
3. The terminology used when writing about Palestinian history can make a political statement. I use 'the Arab Christians of Palestine' or simply 'Arab Christians' in recognition of the ethnic and religious identification of the population, as well as their specific geographic location and, eventually, nationalism.
4. Recent scholarship has closely examined the shift from Ottoman to British rule. See, for instance, Roberto Mazza, *Jerusalem: From the Ottomans to the British* (New York: I. B. Tauris, 2009) and Abigail Jacobson, *From Empire to Empire: Jerusalem between Ottoman and British Rule* (Syracuse, NY: Syracuse University Press, 2011). For a closer look at Muslim–Christian rela-

tions in the late Ottoman period, see Michelle Campos, *Ottoman Brothers: Muslims, Christians, and Jews in Early Twentieth-Century Palestine* (Stanford, CA: Stanford University Press, 2001).

5. Christians receive scant mention in most of the most basic works on Palestinian history, such as Baruch Kimmerling and Joel S. Migdal, *Palestinians: The Making of a People* (Cambridge, MA: Harvard University Press, 1993) and Mark Tessler, *A History of the Israeli–Palestinian Conflict* (Bloomington, IN: Indiana University Press, 1994), though each does briefly point to Christians' high level of importance and tensions in Christian–Muslim relations.

6. Some of the most important works include Eric Hobsbawm and Terrence Ranger (eds), *The Invention of Tradition* (New York: Cambridge University Press, 1983); Louis Dumont, *Religion, Politics and History in India: Collected Papers in Indian Sociology* (Paris: Mouton, 1970); Ussama Makdisi, *The Culture of Sectarianism: Community, History, and Violence in Nineteenth-Century Ottoman Lebanon* (Berkeley, CA: University of California Press, 2000).

7. Phillip E. Hammond, 'Religion and the Persistence of Identity', *Journal for the Scientific Study of Religion*, 27(1) (1988), p. 2.

8. See, for example, Samuel to Colonial Office, 14 December 1923, in Robert L. Jarman (ed.), *Political Diaries of the Arab World, vols 1–3: Palestine & Jordan* (Slough: Archive Editions, 2001), vol. 1, pp. 725–32.

9. Edward Keith-Roach, *Pasha of Jerusalem: Memoirs of a District Commissioner under the British Mandate* (London: Radcliffe Press, 1994), p. 78. The memoirs were written in the 1950s, although not published until much later.

10. CZA S25/665/4, following a letter dated 30 January 1925, although it is not clear if the two are attached.

11. Yehoshua Porath, *The Emergence of the Palestinian-Arab National Movement, 1918–1929* (London: Frank Cass, 1974) and *The Palestinian Arab National Movement: From Riots to Rebellion, vol. 2: 1929–1939* (London: Frank Cass, 1977).

12. Daphne Tsimhoni conducted a detailed study of Arab Christians for her 1976 dissertation, 'The British Mandate and the Arab Christians in Palestine, 1920–1925', Ph.D. dissertation, University of London, 1976. While that manuscript remains unpublished, she has published articles about Arab Christians in Mandate Palestine, as well as a book about Arab Christians in Israel and Jordan following the 1948 war. The dissertation, however, remains her most complete study of the mandate. See also, Daphne Tsimhoni, 'The Status of the Arab Christians under the British Mandate in Palestine', *Middle Eastern Studies*, 20(4) (1984), pp. 166–92; *Christian Communities in Jerusalem and the West Bank Since 1948: An Historical, Social, and Political Study* (Westport, CT: Praeger, 1993); and 'The Arab Christians and the Palestinian Arab National Movement During the Formative Stage', in

Gabriel Ben-Dor (ed.), *The Palestinians and the Middle East Conflict* (Forest Grove, OR: Turtledove, 1979).

13. Tsimhoni, 'The British Mandate', p. 338.

14. Some examples of edited volumes on Christianity in Palestine include Bryan F. Le Beau and Menachem Mor (eds), *Pilgrims and Travelers to the Holy Land* (Omaha, NE: Creighton University Press, 1996); Anthony O'Mahony (ed.), *The Christian Communities of Jerusalem and the Holy Land: Studies in History, Religion and Politics* (Cardiff: University of Wales Press, 2003); Anthony O'Mahony (ed.), *Palestinian Christians: Religion, Politics and Society in the Holy Land* (London: Melisende, 1999); Anthony O'Mahony, Göran Gunner and Kevork Hintlian (eds), *The Christian Heritage in the Holy Land* (London: Scorpion Cavendish, 1995); and Andrea Pacini, *Christian Communities in the Arab Middle East: The Challenge of the Future* (New York: Clarendon Press, 1998).

15. O'Mahony, *Palestinian Christians*, does provide a more well-rounded historical account of the role of Christians in Palestine. With the exception of O'Mahony's introduction, however, all subsequent chapters focus on the post-1948 period. Certainly, some of the work here has influenced my own research (such as Nur Masalha's piece on 'Operation Yohanan' to rid the Galilee of Christians), but the dearth of Mandate-period history is notable.

16. Sotiris Roussos, 'The Greek Orthodox Patriarchate and Community of Jerusalem: Church, State and Identity', in O'Mahony, *The Christian Communities*, pp. 38–56.

17. Ted Swedenburg, *Memories of Revolt: The 1936–1939 Rebellion and the Palestinian National Past* (Fayetteville, AR: University of Arkansas Press, 2003), p. 89.

18. Rashid Khalidi, *Palestinian Identity: The Construction of Modern National Consciousness* (New York: Columbia University Press, 1997) and 'The Formation of Palestinian Identity: The Critical Years, 1917–1923', in Israel Gershoni and James Jankowski (eds), *Rethinking Nationalism in the Arab Middle East* (New York: Columbia University Press, 1997), p. 171.

19. R. Khalidi, 'Formation of Palestinian Identity', pp. 173–5.

20. Muhammad Y. Muslih, *The Origins of Palestinian Nationalism* (New York: Columbia University Press, 1988), p. 158.

21. Religion has played an important role in contemporary discussions of Palestinian nationalism as Hamas and Islamic jihad have vied for national authority. Yet during the Mandate religion is overlooked because such overt political Islam was not present. Instead, for instance, Adnan Abu-Ghazaleh focuses on 'cultural nationalism', or the integration of national themes with literature in his study of Mandate-era nationalism (*Arab Cultural Nationalism in Palestine During the British Mandate* (Beirut: Institute of Palestine Studies, 1973)), while Zachary Foster implies that secular nationalism is the focus of most studies because that is the type of nationalism that eventually became the most powerful nationalist voice ('The Emergence of a Palestinian

National Identity: A Theory-Driven Approach', *Michigan Journal of History* (Winter 2007)).

22. Hillel Cohen, *Army of Shadows: Palestinian Collaboration with Zionism, 1917–1948*, trans. Haim Watzman (Berkeley, CA: University of California Press, 2008); Ellen Fleischmann, *The Nation and its 'New' Women: The Palestinian Women's Movement, 1920–1948* (Berkeley, CA: University of California Press, 2003); and Weldon C. Matthews, *Confronting an Empire, Constructing a Nation: Arab Nationalists and Popular Politics in Mandate Palestine* (New York: I. B. Tauris, 2006).

23. For biographies of Hajj Amin al-Husayni, see Philip Mattar, *The Mufti of Jerusalem: Al-Hajj Amin al-Husayni and the Palestinian National Movement*, 2nd edn (New York: Columbia University Press, 1992) and Taysir Jabarah, *Palestinian Leader, Hajj Amin al-Husayni, Mufti of Jerusalem* (London: Kingston Press, 1985). The only complete history of the Supreme Muslim Council is Uri M. Kupferschmidt, *The Supreme Muslim Council: Islam Under the British Mandate for Palestine* (Boston, MA: Brill, 1987).

24. Nels Johnson, *Islam and the Politics of Meaning in Palestinian Nationalism* (Boston, MA: Kegan Paul, 1982).

25. Laura Robson, *Colonialism and Christianity in Mandate Palestine* (Austin, TX: University of Texas Press, 2011), p. 1.

26. Justin McCarthy, *The Population of Palestine: Population History and Statistics of the Late Ottoman Period and the Mandate* (New York: Columbia University Press, 1990), p. 10.

27. Eric Mills, *Census of Palestine* (Alexandria: Whitehead Morris, 1933), pp. 21–43. McCarthy, *Population of Palestine*, pp. 78–9.

28. Anton Bertram and Harry Luke, Palestine Commission on the Affairs of the Orthodox Patriarchate of Jerusalem, *Report of the Commission Appointed by Government of Palestine to Inquire into the Affairs of the Orthodox Patriarchate of Jerusalem* (Oxford: Oxford University Press, 1921), p. 13.

29. See Phillip C. Allen, 'The Last Despot: Ethnic Consciousness, Power Politics, and the Orthodox Church in Late Ottoman Syria', Doctoral dissertation, Princeton University, 2000, for an excellent account of this fascinating story, which included various levels of Ottoman intervention, international pressure and an undisputable rise of Arab ethnic consciousness.

30. 'History and Activities of the Latin Patriarch of Jerusalem', available at: www.lpj.org/newsite2006/patriarch/history_patriarchate.html, accessed 11 July 2012.

31. For a reasonably comprehensive history of the Melkite Church in Jerusalem and its relationship to other Jerusalem denominations, see The Metropolitan Lutfi Lihaam, *Kitaab al-youbeel al-tadhkaari* (Jerusalem: Amerzian Print Foundation, 1998).

32. A small group of Melkites in northern Syria remains unaffiliated with the Vatican until the present time. Joseph Chammas, *The Melkite Church* (Jerusalem: Emerezian, 1992), p. 89.

33. Mills, *1931 Census*, p. 31.
34. Lester Groves Pittman, 'Missionaries and Emissaries: The Anglican Church in Palestine 1841–1948', Ph.D. dissertation, University of Virginia, 1998, p. 2.

1917–1923: Balancing Religion and National Unity

We the inhabitants of Palestine, 700,000, representing and acting for 800 million Christians and Moslems in this Holy Land, shall [raise] our voice and say: 'After the blood we have shed and after that which was shed for us, is it permissible for the existing conscience of the world to give our land to a mixture of emigrants, called the Zionists, coming from the five continents of the world and wanting to appropriate our land . . .? They hardly amount to one eighth of us, we the inhabitants of the land.'[1]

> F. Beiruti, on Behalf of the Muslim Christian Association,
> 25 October 1919

Serious difficulty [for British rule] arises from the political division of the community into three sections, based upon religion. If the municipal electoral law paid no regard to these divisions, they would, nevertheless, be found to operate in practice.[2]

> Edward Keith-Roach, 14 February 1921

In March 1920 ᶜArif al-ᶜArif, Arab nationalist leader and editor of the newspaper *Suriyah al-Janubiyah* (southern Syria), extolled some since-forgotten show of religious unity:

> Never in all its later history have Palestine and ancient Jerusalem witnessed so great a day as last Friday. On that day the national feeling swayed Arabs, Christians and Moslems – on that day an end was put to religious strife. These two religions will henceforth live in peace. Until this historic day Europe has not inclined an attentive ear to the words of the Palestinians because they were not united, and did not have the means of making their pleadings known to the European nations and the democratic public.[3]

Many Palestinian Arabs agreed with this sentiment and pushed forward a vision of a unified Arab society. Yet even as elite Arabs from across the political and religious spectrum joined in calls for Arab independence, the British mandatory government, as well as a variety of other political forces, worked against that ideal.

Britain denied Arab Christians' nationalism as a legitimate form of identification because, from its colonial perspective, Arabs were tightly bound to their religious community in a way that Europeans were not. In

19

reality, late Ottoman Arab society underwent a transformation between the 1830s and the early 1900s as the empire sought to recast imperial attachment along modern, nationalistic lines. In Palestine, the transformations of the nineteenth century triggered a rise in Arab nationalism that dominated the political discourse among the elite leadership at the beginning of the British Mandate. It should have come as no surprise that in 1918, shortly after the British occupation of Jerusalem, Arab notables who had been powerful during Ottoman times coalesced in an effort to influence the political trajectory of their country and organised the Muslim Christian Association (MCA), which was, for a few years at least, the most important Arab organisation in British-ruled Palestine.

Yet the nationalism espoused by the MCA and other like-minded organisations was unfamiliar to the British. Unlike strictly secular nationalist movements, the MCA's goal was not secularisation, but greater influence with their new British rulers. Religious unity and equality were a by-product of that goal rather than the result of some ideological secularism.[4]

The MCA emerged within a complex political atmosphere created by the combination of late Ottoman reforms and constitutionalism, the advent of British rule in Palestine, the influences of foreign clergy on local Christian populations, and the arrival and early success of Zionists in the region. And while the Association presented interreligious unity as well-established fact, in reality such unity was more a goal or a method, rather than a reality. The nature and meaning of religious identification was a matter of much debate, and intercommunal tensions did surface behind the scenes, particularly when political differences between elite factions fractured the national movement. Such conflicts among the leadership were present immediately, but until the official ratification (1922) and imposition of the British Mandate (1923) the MCA remained largely united around a pro-Arab, anti-Zionist platform. By the time Britain received international recognition of its rule in Palestine, imperial policies, Zionist plans for a Jewish homeland and Arab factionalism succeeded in undermining the MCA, and the explicit dialogue of religious unity along with it.

Religious Identification between Ottoman and British Palestine

The relationship of Arab Christians to the broader Palestinian Arab community has always been influenced by the meaning of religious identification at a particular historical moment. At times religious groupings divided the community, while at others such categories were overshadowed by imperial or national notions of belonging. Mid-nineteenth-century reforms overhauled an older system of Ottoman religious differentiation, and the rise of nationalism later in the century also triggered a shift in the way Ottoman Arabs identified themselves. Britain ignored these trends and managed its newly mandated territories based on colonial assumptions rather than on decades of societal restructuring.

From the earliest years of Ottoman rule, the authorities dealt with the presence of large and numerous minorities, both ethnic and religious, in various parts of the empire. Like other imperial powers, the Ottoman Empire developed a system to stabilise an empire with the presence of ethnic, religious, geographic and linguistic variation. Both due to doctrinal Islamic tolerance for other monotheistic faiths (historically practised to varying degrees), and for pragmatic reasons relating to governing a large and multi-ethnic, multi-religious empire, the Ottoman state offered substantial communal autonomy to religious minority populations, or *millets*, a word derived from the Arabic *millah*, meaning religious community.[5] The *millet* system developed over a lengthy period, beginning in the 1400s but not spreading empire-wide until the early nineteenth century.[6] Within the *millet* system, communal leaders operated religious courts, maintained their own religious traditions and managed their own holy sites, with assistance from Istanbul when conflicts arose between various *millets*. The *millet* system provided the empire with a legal method of toleration and inclusion, allowing people of various religions to live together peacefully.[7] Regardless of their religious community, Ottoman subjects were able to participate in the economic, social and political life of the empire, albeit with some limitations for non-Muslims.[8] Some scholars even credit the *millet* system for preserving the very existence of minority religious communities throughout the long period of Ottoman rule in the Middle East.[9]

A combination of internal changes and external influences during the eighteenth century challenged the *millet* structure and produced a nationalities crisis for the Ottoman regime. First, the Ottoman government triggered a restructuring of the social order by relying more and more on local notables for collection of taxes and management of state lands, creating a powerful local elite class with strong ties to the government.[10] Christian notables benefited at the local level since there were limitations on upward social mobility for non-Muslims at the imperial level.[11] In addition, European states were adopting new formulations of national identification as the structure of traditional early modern empires was called into question. The rise of Greek national identification in the nineteenth century complicated the meaning of 'Greek Orthodox', and overshadowed the primary religious connotation with a secondary division reflecting ethnic and linguistic divisions.[12] Nationalism spread throughout the Balkans, perhaps encouraged by the autonomy that Christian communities there had traditionally maintained through the *millet* system.[13] Ottoman reformists countered demands for greater independence by re-legitimising the Ottoman Empire as a multi-ethnic entity, but failed to quash the rising tide of religious-ethnic identification. Europeans interested in influencing or even dismembering the Ottoman Empire encouraged the nationalist trend by sponsoring minority communities, particularly various Christian denominations, as a way to intervene in Ottoman affairs. By the 1800s, France and Russia, in particular, claimed guardianship of minority Catholic and Orthodox Christian populations, respectively, as part of the capitulations arrangement.[14] These governments gathered information 'regarding the perceived oppression of the native Christians',[15] and advocated in Istanbul on behalf of minority communities, provided economic and educational opportunities, and offered minority groups quasi-legal protections.

In the mid-1800s the empire struck back, instigating the *tanzimat*, or restructuring, in an effort to maintain territorial integrity in the face of increasing European dominance. The 1839 Gulhane Decree, which marked the beginning of the *tanzimat*, redefined the meaning of imperial belonging. One method was by propagating the notion of Ottomanism, which granted Christians and Jews the right of full citizenship beyond the confines of the *millet* system, overcoming religious and ethnic differentiation by focusing on shared imperial belonging.[16] The long-standing method of communal governance was difficult to undo, and some Muslims challenged the notion that non-Muslims could truly be equal in an Islamic empire. Many Christians were equally wary because equality included conscription. Europeans continued to intervene on the part of minority groups, contradicting Ottoman efforts to create a community of imperial citizens. Even some Ottoman rulers worked against the new social structure. One of the last sultans, Abdulhamid II (r. 1876–1909), reversed the secularisation of the empire and reclaimed legitimacy as the Muslim caliph, advocating pan-Islamism out of fear that ethnic nationalism was tearing apart his large, multi-ethnic empire.[17] Abdulhamid did not fully abandon the reform efforts of the *tanzimat*, but he clearly tried to reassert a deeper sense of religious identification among Ottoman subjects.

Unlike non-Arab Ottoman Christians, Arabs Christian throughout greater Syria were inclined to support the secularising tendencies of the *tanzimat* period.[18] While the Balkans were populated by various ethnic groups comprising Christian majorities, Arab Christians comprised a small minority in the empire's Middle Eastern territories and were of the same ethnic group as the Muslim population in the Arab lands. For both Muslims and Christians following the 1908 revolution, the growth of Arab ethnic identification was not seen as contrary to Ottoman citizenship: one could be a good Arab by participating fully in the empire. Even the growth of ethnic social and literary groups in the late nineteenth century was cultural in nature, with no nationalistic implications, though such organisations did help to set the stage for fully-fledged Arab nationalism that emerged in the First World War period.[19]

Until the nineteenth century, Palestine was formed by the same processes that shaped the rest of the Ottoman Empire. Jerusalem's importance as a holy city for the three major monotheistic faiths drew some attention from European missionaries and foreign governments, but missionaries were sent throughout the Muslim world. This changed in the early nineteenth century due to new Protestant interpretations of the Bible and the rise of Christian Zionism. The Zionist movement that emerged among Jews in Europe in the last decade of the nineteenth century was even more important. Driven by European and Russian anti-Semitism and the failure of European nations to fully accept Jews as citizens, Jewish activists founded the Zionist Organization in 1897 to pursue the goal of an independent state for the Jews. The Zionist Organization quickly focused its efforts on Palestine because of the region's historical and religious importance to the Jews, and began lobbying the Ottoman Empire for permission to establish a Jewish presence there. In addition, a small immigration of Eastern European Jews to Palestine began in the 1880s, followed by organised Zionist efforts to encourage Jews to settle there.

Rashid Khalidi and Muhammad Muslih have both rightly pointed to tendencies among Palestinians towards the development of a regional identity before the emergence of Zionism. Still, Zionism was an important catalyst for the growth of Arab nationalist sentiment, and throughout the first decade of the twentieth century Arabs developed a strong sense of anti-Zionism and supported any ideology that countered Jewish encroachment.[20] Christians were among the first to raise the alarm: as early as 1908 the Palestinian newspaper *al-Karmil*, edited by Najib Nassar, a Christian, wrote about the Zionist threat.[21] Orthodox Christian ʿIsa al-ʿIsa founded *Filastin* in 1911, primarily as a tool to attack Zionism.[22]

Societal organisation shifted as the empire crumbled. The *millet* system was a work in progress, but had provided stability in the multi-religious empire. What would be better, Christians wondered: a continuation of official communal representation or negotiating space within a non-sectarian polity? William Ochenwald writes:

The emergence of various Christian communal ethnic-religious nationalisms, the spread of nationalism to several Ottoman Muslim ethnic groups, and the rise of Pan-Islamic ideology as sponsored by the state all contributed to a confused, inchoate, and occasionally contradictory political atmosphere in the Ottoman Empire during its last decades. This uncertainty about the identity and nature of the political community and its relationship to religion was matched later by similar problems that continued to bedevil many of the independent successor states following the end of the empire.[23]

Add to this the fear of Zionist settlement in Palestine, and the complex position of the Arab Christian population in Palestine begins to become clear. Yet ethnicity remained essential for Arab Christians, and rather than seek independence as a national-religious minority as was common in the Balkans, Arab Christians sought to enhance their position as a religious minority.[24]

As Ottoman subjects in Palestine and elsewhere struggled to understand the new basis for imperial belonging, tensions rose in Europe that would soon lead to the First World War, the collapse of the Ottoman Empire and the British occupation of Palestine. The Ottomans sided with Germany in the war, and Britain took Palestine both to prevent other imperial powers from doing so first and to safeguard its protectorate in Egypt. Britain's rule in Palestine was complicated by a series of wartime agreements promised in an effort to garner support during its campaign against Germany and the Ottomans. Britain had offered France imperial control of Syria and Lebanon; Arab independence in exchange for an internal revolt against Ottoman authority; and, in the Balfour Declaration, a Jewish homeland in Palestine. In addition, the world was war-weary and sought new and more effective forms of international organisation in a concerted effort to prevent such devastation in the future. Unchecked imperialism had lost much of its former lustre, and US President Woodrow Wilson openly called for the right of self-determination, although such demands were balanced by his recognition of European imperial demands.[25] Still, Palestine did not become just another part of the British Empire, but was instead offered as a 'mandate' by the newly established League of Nations, meaning that it was supposed to prepare the local population for independent nationhood.[26] The system worked according to plan in Iraq, for instance, which received formal independence from Britain in 1932, even while retaining close ties to its former imperial ruler until 1958. Yet in Palestine, the British promise of a Jewish homeland was enshrined in the Mandate, causing Palestinians to reject it as a threat to their national rights.[27]

While Britain's dedication to the Balfour Declaration brought hope to the Zionist leadership, it also confirmed Palestinian Arabs' worst fears and served as a catalyst for political action. While isolated instances of anti-Jewish violence occurred prior to the British occupation, elite Arabs, who had been politically important in the Ottoman period, believed their best chance to alter British policy was before the British solidified power and achieved international recognition. It was within this context that Palestinian Arab notables from various factions of society joined to form the MCA in 1918, hoping a successful show of Arab political unity would turn the British away from the Balfour Declaration and towards support for some form of Arab autonomy. Muslims and Christians were 'converging on several different levels, not least of which was in joint opposition to Zionism and the changing Palestinian landscape'.[28]

When British troops, led by Edmund Allenby, commander-in-chief of the Egyptian Expeditionary force, arrived in Jerusalem on 11 December 1917, they carried preconceived notions of what religion meant to Arabs and ignored more than seventy years of debate and negotiation triggered by Ottoman reforms.[29] Colonial suppositions about religious identification pervade government documents, intelligence reports, British and Zionist officials' personal correspondence, and have also influenced many historians. For most British officers of the early twentieth century, religion was considered an immovable identity: rather than simply denoting one's belonging to a particular religious group, they believed that religious affiliations explained political and social behaviour. With India, Egypt and other colonies as examples, the British were convinced of inherent differences between Muslims and Christians, as well as between Christians of different denominations. When Christian–Muslim relations proved to be different to British presuppositions, officials redefined religious stereotypes but always insisted that an Arab's religious community was essential to understanding his or her personality and beliefs.

Since European involvement in the Ottoman Middle East was often predicated on the assumption of beleaguered and ill-treated religious minorities, British observers were shocked to find that Christian and Muslim Arabs were not hostile towards one another. In 1921, a British official wrote back to London and expressed amazement that a joint funeral had been conducted: 'The Mufti went into the Greek Church and the Greek Priest went into the mosque, an occurrence which I should think is absolutely unique in a country which saw the Crusades.'[30] The veracity of this particular event was later questioned, but British amazement over sharing religious spaces is telling. In fact, Christians in mosques and Muslims in churches were common occurrences during political rallies at this time.

Despite witnessing interreligious cooperation among Palestinian Arabs, the British were still convinced that Christians and Muslims could not possibly adopt a common identifying feature on which to base a national movement. Edward Keith-Roach, the district governor of Jerusalem during the early Mandate, explained in his memoirs that 'the country was beset by a strange form of nationalism based not so much on race as on religion, for the criterion of nationality was normally creed'.[31] The assumption that Islam was the basis for national belonging categorically excluded Christians, and convinced the British that Christians and Muslims were not part of the same ethno-national movement.

In the light of intercommunal tensions that British observers assumed were lurking beneath all Muslim–Christian ventures, the British constantly divided the Arab population into religious categories. British officials usually referred to 'the Moslems and Christians', and specified the religious affiliation of those present or wounded at protests.[32] Keith-Roach expressed concern that, in a mixed religious city, no members of minority communities would be elected to Jerusalem municipal office without specifically allotted posts. As a remedy he suggested 'proportional representation', even while acknowledging that such a policy 'would have the effect of perpetuating existing divisions and of preventing the development of a movement, such as is already beginning, towards co-operation between groups of the different communities, a movement which it is most desirable to promote'.[33] Herbert Samuel, the first British high commissioner, ignored Arab efforts at intercommunal cooperation and accepted Keith-Roach's advice, appointing ten local men – four Muslims, three Christians and three Jews – to the Jerusalem municipal council.[34]

In their speculations about the differences between Christians and Muslims, British observers, and later historians as well, assumed that Christians friendly with Muslims were unfaithful to their own religious heritage. For example, Tsimhoni, who tends to accept the British interpretation of communal tendencies, laments that 'Christians had become accustomed to using Muslim law, whereas their own religious law was in many cases unknown'.[35] She describes Nakhleh Surayq, a Protestant who converted from Orthodoxy, as 'assimilated into the Muslim environment to such an extent that he was regarded by some Muslims to be secretly one of them'.[36] Assimilation made the British uncomfortable, and some officers could accept such unity only as a façade. One wrote, 'I suppose, the Nablus Moslems dislike the Xtians as much as the Jews, but they have produced at least a good semblance of Moslem–Xtian unity.'[37]

During the first years of the Mandate, it became clear to the British that Arab Christians were fully invested in the national movement. The British eventually seemed to accept the presence of Christians in the Palestinian

Arab national movement, though they still analysed social differences along religious lines. 'It is interesting to note,' wrote the Ramallah sub-district governor, 'that the five Christian (and largely Orthodox) villages in the Sub District are far more progressive than the Moslem, but at the same time are the most difficult to handle.'[38] This focus on the level of 'progressiveness', brought about by higher literacy rates among Christians and their contact with European cultures, is a generalisation based on the measurable fact that Christians did regularly obtain higher levels of education.

British rule also permitted Zionists to gain influence in Palestine, and they sought to capitalise on even the smallest communal disagreement in an effort to earn Arab allies or at least create dissention among the Arab population. In 1922, a member of the Palestine Zionist Executive wrote to the office of the Zionist Organization in London suggesting that, 'we should try to bring the Protestant and Orthodox Arabs to our side, as anti-Semitism in Christian circles was mainly originating from Rome'.[39] Another Zionist leader offered an economic, rather than religious, explanation for Latin anti-Zionism: Arab Latins 'caus[ed] a rift between . . . the Jews and the Moslems, because it is this rift that has given them the possibility of remaining in their [governmental] positions'.[40] In his understanding, the Latin community encouraged Muslims and Jews to be hostile towards one another and towards government policy, providing themselves with the opportunity to fill the government's needs. The argument that some Christians were anti-Zionist because they feared personal economic loss as a result of Jewish immigration to Palestine was sometimes expanded to include all Christians, and was predicated on the argument that Christians would have been supporters of Jewish immigration were it not for economic concerns. Mordechai (David) Miller, a Zionist living in Nablus, was a proponent of this argument. In 1923, he reported that some of the most virulent anti-Zionists, such as Bulus Shihada (a Protestant), could be swayed by economic means, since that was really the only reason he fought against the Jews.[41] This theory has been maintained as a valid explanation for Christian anti-Zionism, though there is little evidence that many Christians were actually swayed strictly by the promise of economic gain.

By mid-decade the Zionists were showing frustration with their efforts to find friendly Christians communities. In November 1923, Frederick Kisch, head of the Palestine Zionist Executive, wrote to the high commissioner claiming that Christians were 'intensely hostile' and decrying 'their undue influence over administrative machinery', even while recognising that their anti-Zionist attitudes and administrative strength were due to education rather than religion.[42] And in a memorandum from some time in 1925, a Zionist writer concurred:

> Christians are, from the first to the last, our deadly enemies ... Catholic or Greek Orthodox or Protestant, they have one [thing in] common: a fanatical religious hatred of the Jews ...
>
> With Muslims, indeed, matters are quite different. In the first instance they generally do not hate the Jew to the extent to which the Christians hate him; in fact, outspoken, real hatred of the Jew is to be found with them only in moments of excitement ... But apart from such occasions, the Moslem's behavior towards the Jew is incomparably better than that of the Christian; and, whereas it would be hard to find a case of real friendship between a Christian and a Jew, sincere friendship between a Moslem and a Jew is far from being a rare thing. The Moslem, moreover, has in the depth of his heart more confidence in the righteousness of the Jew than in that of the Christian.[43]

The writer further argued that Christians were manipulating the Muslim population in their effort to rule all of Palestine.

British views concerning the Muslim community were equally based on erroneous stereotypes about Arabs and their religions, and they based policy on these ideas. Over the course of the first decade of British rule, the government created new religious offices and organisations that structured Palestine along communal lines (see Chapter 2). Palestinians, both Muslim and Christian, did not necessarily reject such divisions, although religious differentiation did not exclude simultaneously belonging to a single national group. Their acceptance of religious and national identification coexisting confused the British, Zionists and many historians since.[44] Many Palestinian Arabs, both Christian and Muslim, adopted a different view of religion, race and nationality altogether, arguing that diverse religious communities could easily fit together in a united national movement. Such identification was not paradoxical at all, but made perfect sense within the new atmosphere in which nationality trumped religious identification. It was the marriage of the *millet* legacy with the reality of new national boundaries. Variations on this mainstream view were not uncommon, but, in the 1920s, the debate was monopolised by a nationalist elite devoted to this goal.

British and Zionist officials varied in their view of the minority Christian community, but they shared the assumption that Christians could be accurately identified primarily as members of their religious community and distinct from Arab Muslims. In effect, the colonial mentality assumed that religion and nation were two separate things, and that Arabs, Christian and Muslim alike, belonged solely to their religious community.

The Foreign Leadership of Palestinian Churches

While British and Zionist views of Arab religious identification were inaccurate, those views still shaped government policy and even influenced the way in which Arab Christians understood society. Beyond governmental policy, a wider range of pressures specifically influenced Arab Christians. The tendency of Arab Christians to reside in urban areas, to enjoy higher levels of economic prosperity and academic achievement, and to maintain closer contacts with European merchants and consuls were all important. Denomination was also a salient factor in shaping political views, although individual affiliation is sometimes unclear since Mandate-era records often label people as 'Christian' without further distinction. Still, in the early 1920s denominational leadership had an important impact on a community's political outlook and behaviour. Official politics for each religious body were determined by the hierarchy of clergy, monks and missionaries who, with the exception of the Melkites, were governed by foreigners. Their political goals were orchestrated from abroad, implemented through the foreign ecclesiastical leadership in Jerusalem, and passed on to the local laity in a variety of ways. As Mazza points out, religious institutions, foreign or not, 'were part of the social fabric . . . [and] the church were also involved in local issues'.[45] Arabs did serve as local priests in both the Orthodox and Latin communities, but they had no input in the governing bodies or official politics of the church. This setup provided the leaders of different denominations the opportunity to foster drastically different relationships with their indigenous followers.

For Orthodox Christians, the entire hierarchy was tainted by the ongoing dispute between the laity and the patriarchate.[46] Arab Orthodox Christians were disgruntled by their inability to participate in church decision-making and frustrated by the lack of social services, diminishing educational standards (the Orthodox College in Jerusalem closed during the war), fewer opportunities in Orthodox institutions, and little, if any, Arab representation in church matters. Demands for changes in patriarchal leadership following re-implementation of the Ottoman Constitution in 1908 never disappeared completely, and Arab Orthodox leaders interpreted President Wilson's call for the right of self-determination (part of his famous Fourteen Points speech) as applicable in denominational as well as national disputes. The Ottoman government supported the patriarchate, and Arabs hoped the British administration would back their cause instead. The British did intervene in the dispute and established a commission to examine the Orthodox problem, led by Judge Sir Anton Bertram and Harry Charles Luke, assistant governor of Jerusalem. To the laity's dismay, the commission focused only on the severe wartime debt incurred by the patriarchate, pushing the Arab congregants towards more direct political action.[47]

In 1923, Arab Orthodox leaders organised the First Arab Orthodox Congress in Haifa to formulate a community-wide response to the patriarchate, the British government, Zionism and nationalism.[48] The immediate impetus for the congress was a controversy surrounding the appointment of a new bishop of Nazareth who could not speak Arabic and was rejected by the majority of the community, though this latest appointment was only the tipping point: the laity had already shifted closer to the Arab/ Palestinian nationalist camp.[49] As Bertram and Luke explained in their 1921 report, the *millet* system had unified Orthodox, Greek and Arab alike. It was only in the nineteenth century that 'the Greek Ecclesiastics and Monks had acquired a new national consciousness or, rather, had retained their old national consciousness under a new name. They conceived of themselves no longer as "Romans" but as "Hellenes".'[50] This definition of Greek Orthodox excluded Arabs from their own religious community and led to an increased reliance on Arabness rather than on Orthodoxy and full Arab Orthodox support for nationalism.[51]

As a result, at the 1923 congress Arab Orthodox leaders pushed for full Arabisation of their church. In addition to demanding a mixed council (of Arab laity and Greek monks, as established during the Ottoman period and confirmed by Bertram and Luke) with a two-thirds majority of 'native learned men', they also asked for an Arabic language test for priests and deacons, dismissal of all non-Arabic-speaking spiritual heads, the appointment of native archbishops throughout Palestine and Transjordan, and translation of church laws into Arabic.[52] Even an Orthodox 'Moderate Party', which produced its own set of demands shortly thereafter, agreed with the Arabising trend, differing only in their acceptance of phased implementation of their demands.[53] Despite the strong effort by the lay community, the British government refused to pressure the patriarchate to accept Arab demands, due largely to Cypriot, Greek and Cairene patriarchal resistance.[54]

At this point, some Christians turned away from Orthodoxy by converting to Protestantism, but the more common trend was to pursue Orthodoxy with an Arab twist.[55] Two reasons contributed to this approach. Some Christians were playing the odds, strengthening their position in two possible communities of belonging. Others understood their religious community to be an integral part of their nationality and desired to strengthen all elements of their personal identification. Like the Arab Orthodox in Syria who had succeeded in Arabising the Antiochian patriarchate, Palestinian

Arab Orthodox Christians highlighted their Arabness in the controversy with the church, an act which brought together Arab Orthodox in an activist cause. Religious and national elements of their identification were merged in response to an unhelpful patriarch and a new British government that failed to support their denominational cause.

The Latin community, however, was led by an anti-Zionist, anti-British patriarch who received praise from Arabs throughout the Mandate for his political views.[56] Initially, Latin Patriarch Louis Barlassina's two most important supporters, France and the Vatican, gave him free reign to antagonise the British while lobbying for French rule over Palestine, or at least Latin rule over the holy sites. Both entities stood behind the Latin patriarch, although at times his confrontational attitude made such support difficult.[57] After the Mandate came into effect in 1923, and his supporters sought to repair relations with the British, Barlassina maintained his provocative demeanour in spite of repeated warnings from the Vatican.

Despite his anti-Zionist and anti-British stance, Barlassina was ultimately more pro-Latin than pro-Arab. Tsimhoni notes that Arab Latin Christians avoided the nationalist movement because they were protected by Barlassina, and that later, as Barlassina's confrontationalism waned, so did the laity's.[58] This assessment is valid, but Barlassina's impact went deeper still: he deflated Arab Latin political movements by encouraging the Latin laity to focus on its Latinness and to distance itself from the wider Arab community. In 1920, Barlassina 'warmly exhort[ed] all our Brethren and Children in Christ to take no part in political excitements',[59] suggesting that it was better to focus on personal moral behaviour and faith in God. He later issued a patriarchal order forbidding Arab Latins to join the British-run Girl Guides (a Scout troop) and the Protestant-founded YMCA.[60] In a similarly exclusionary vein, Catholic dignitaries demanded guaranteed seats on the Jerusalem municipal council for Catholics, as opposed to simply asking that seats be allocated for Christians.[61] Barlassina also refused government oversight of Latin schools,[62] complained about Zionist morals in the Holy City,[63] and refused to attend the king's birthday celebrations because the service was in a non-Catholic church.[64] The message from the patriarch was clear: the Latin Church was a community unto itself, and support of Arab rights was important only when they paralleled specifically Latin rights. While some Arab Latins did emerge as important nationalist figures, they did so as individuals rather than as denominational representatives.

This patriarchal influence meant that Arab Latins played a very different political role from that of Orthodox Christians in the national leadership. Like their Orthodox counterparts, Latin Christians participated in the MCA.

Figure 1.1 Louis Barlassina (on right), Latin Patriarch of Jerusalem, 1920–47 with Lord Plumer and the Archbishop of Naples, 1926. *Library of Congress*

Yet, in line with patriarchal demands, they remained a community apart. For example, at an MCA meeting in 1919, Khalil al-Sakakini described the Association's decision to recognise Arab Independence Day in conjunction with the anniversary of the Great Arab Revolt. The Muslims and Orthodox members were easily convinced, but the Latins insisted on speaking among themselves before agreeing. Al-Sakakini vented in his journal that the Catholics were interested only in their own sect for four reasons:

> first, they don't believe the country is able to be independent by itself, and second, they don't believe the Muslims' perspective, and third, because they are weak nationalists, small in spirit and short in vision, and fourth, because they act for their personal benefit over the general benefit of the country, and they aren't going to be kept waiting for the general benefit to become clear while on their way toward personal benefit.[65]

Al-Sakakini's concerns about the Latin community's relationship to the greater national good were shared by others, and tensions between Arab Orthodox and Latin Christians arose periodically throughout the Mandate. In later years, however, after Barlassina's radicalism was quieted by the Vatican, the Latin laity occasionally opposed his leadership.

Denominational separatism remained important, however, particularly in the 1930s when a murder in Haifa led to serious interreligious tension.[66]

Arab Orthodox notables also debated how much emphasis should be placed on their specific Christianness, but came to a very different conclusion from that of the Latin leaders. When Francis Khayyali and Hanna al-ʿIsa proposed a Christian political party in 1914, al-Sakakini, already a pre-eminent nationalist leader, refused. He was an Arab, he said, and would only support joint Muslim–Christian efforts such as clubs and societies that pursued nationalist goals. Some allocated seats to Christians, such as the Jerusalem MCA, while others, like *al-Nadi al-ʿArabi*, were composed almost entirely of Muslim notables. When the Arab Orthodox held a denominational congress in 1923, they held it at the same time as the Sixth Palestinian Arab Congress, and the two congresses sent delegations to visit each other in a show of nationalist solidarity.[67] Thus, in the early years of the Mandate, Orthodox lay leaders formulated a balance between Arabness and Christianness by including religion in the ethno-national identification they shared with Arab Muslims. The Latin community, on the other hand, accepted the separatist attitude espoused by its leadership, arguing that participation in the nationalist movement should be as a recognised and protected minority.

The Melkite Church provides a very different example of church structure and relation to the nationalist movement. While the Melkite Church was officially under Vatican authority, it was overseen in Palestine by Bishop Grigorios Hajjar of Haifa. The British distrusted Hajjar, whom they believed (perhaps rightly) to be a French agent with Vatican protection. Early in the Mandate he was active in uniting Christians and Muslims against British policy, and became a symbol for Christians of other denominations since he was the highest ranking Arab clergyman in all of Palestine.[68] Due in part to the small size of his community, centred particularly in the northern areas (Melkites were almost non-existent in Jerusalem), his authority was limited. Still, when the nationalist leadership sent a delegation to the Vatican in 1922 it chose Bishop Hajjar and Fuʿad Saʿd, another Melkite, rather than representatives of the Latin Church.[69] The relative importance of Melkite over Latin is notable, showing that the Arab leadership privileged Christians who embraced their Arabness most fully, even if their denomination was smaller or internationally less important.

The debate concerning the relationship between communalism and nationalism was dominated by a small number of elite Orthodox leaders who became active through the Orthodox issue, but were also early advocates of anti-Zionism. For them, a secularised Arab state held tremendous

Figure 1.2 Melkite Bishop Grigorios Hajjar. *Source unknown*

promise. Barlassina's efforts to retain Latin distinctiveness, and the call of some Orthodox leaders for a specifically Christian party, suggest that others believed more strongly in returning to a *millet*-like system of protected minorities. This debate emerged periodically throughout the Mandate as the intercommunal unity of the early Mandate waned, the political situation became more dire, the Arab Muslim majority came to rely more heavily on its religious identification, and a shift in the leadership allowed alternative voices to emerge on all sides of the debate.

Three Christian Perspectives

Lumping Christians into unwieldy stereotypes was a common practice among British and Zionist leaders, and the tendency has carried into academic writing on Palestinian history. Like their Muslim counterparts, Christians were individuals who were influenced by particular circumstances, some of which were shared at the national level, while others were shaped by regional, local or personal experiences. Christians participated in politics with their own interpretation of what was best for the nation, their specific denominational community and themselves. As with Palestinian Arabs as a whole, Christians were unified only in their opposition to Zionism. The views and activities of three Orthodox Christian figures, Khalil al-Sakakini, Najib Nassar and ʿIsa Bandak, clearly exhibit the problem with sweeping generalisations about Arab Christians.

Khalil al-Sakakini, by virtue of his published diary as well as his historical importance, has become a favourite of historians, who often overlook
other important actors from the period.[70] He was well-educated, mingled
freely with British officials and espoused views that struck British officials
as 'modern' and 'Western' – he was a nationalist, interested only in creating a nation built on Arab ethnicity. To this end, al-Sakakini established
an Arabic language journal, *al-Dustur*, in 1910 and founded a school in
which Arabic was the language of instruction at a time when Ottoman
Turkish was the official language of the empire.[71] And when a Jewish spy,
Alter Levin, knocked on his door during the First World War looking for
refuge from the Ottoman authorities, al-Sakakini cited his cultural heritage
and Arab hospitality rather than a Christian ethic in justifying his decision
to allow Levin into his home.[72]

Frustration with the Orthodox Church resulted in detachment from the
religious community of his birth. After the 1908 Ottoman Constitution
and the uprising of the Greek Orthodox lay community against the patriarchate, a revolt in which al-Sakakini himself was a leader, he distanced
himself from the church: 'I am not Orthodox! I am not Orthodox!' he
wrote in frustration.[73] In formally leaving the church, he sought to create
a new identity for himself in the Arabic *umma*, or nation,[74] and he even
considered converting to Protestantism.[75] More than any other figure from
this period, al-Sakakini sought to replace his religious identification with
a strictly national one. Despite this attempted shift, al-Sakakini remained
known to others as an Orthodox Christian and personally continued to
devote attention to the Arab Orthodox issue. Even later in life he persisted
in referring to himself as an Orthodox Christian.

An elite upbringing also coloured al-Sakakini's political views: he
was educated in the Anglican school in Jerusalem and he travelled to
New York in 1907–8.[76] Later on, living in Jerusalem, home to the British
government of Palestine, meant that he was close to the political centre
of Mandate Palestine. He was friendly with British officials, particularly
General Waters-Taylor, the chief political officer in Palestine, and visited
him daily during the early Mandate. He had cordial, if not friendly, relations with Muslim leaders as well. His ability to cross social boundaries
that were difficult for others was perhaps his most unique trait.[77]

Al-Sakakini recognised himself as distinctive in his advocacy of fully
non-sectarian nationalism, and his diary reveals frustration with what he
saw as the true state of interreligious relations. In describing the Arab
Congress in Damascus in 1919, he lamented that 'the Muslims came
to be Muslims, and the Christians came to be Christians . . . Each party
returned to its old racial or national position, and no wonder, for this

party-centredness is not the offspring of the hour, but the offspring of generations.'[78] He described the 'old-fashioned Muslims' in harsh terms, lamenting that 'they don't trust a Sakakini or any other Christian. They're not for Palestine, only for their friends and families.'[79] His radical secular vision was, he feared, unattainable in such an atmosphere.

Participation in various congresses, the MCA, *al-Nadi al-ʿArabi* and other nationalist organisations confirms al-Sakakini's importance. Yet it is essential that al-Sakakini should not be the only Palestinian Arab Christian voice heard, since he held rare, radical views on the nature of religious identification. Rather than flee the religious community of their birth, most Arab Christians sought to transform the community to fit the rapidly developing sense of themselves as Arabs, anti-Zionists and nationalists.

Najib Nassar distinguished himself by being the first Arab in Palestine to publicly warn of the dangers of Zionism. His newspaper, *al-Karmil*, was the most important of the nineteen newspapers founded in Palestine in 1908 following the restoration of the Ottoman Constitution.[80] Nassar, an Orthodox Christian, used the pages of his paper to press for Arab unity, to raise awareness of Zionism and its goals, and to encourage the formation of an Arab political party to counter the Zionist congresses taking place in Europe.[81] Twice during the Ottoman period his paper was suspended, the first time for 'agitating public opinion' and the second, in 1910, for calling for a suspension of land sales to Jews.[82] In 1911 he published many of his columns in a book about Zionism's goals.[83] To Nassar, the message was more important than the financial success of his paper, and in addition to distributing hundreds of papers without receiving payment, he encouraged Muslim-run papers to spread the message of anti-Zionism as well.[84]

When *al-Karmil* began publication again in 1920 after suspending operations during the war, Nassar adopted a new political tone, remaining anti-Zionist while accepting British rule and arguing for increased cooperation with the government.[85] He even helped with the formation of the Farmers' Parties, organisations of rural Arabs that were considered Zionist creations by most nationalists.[86] Yet despite Nassar's sympathies for the British, he never reduced his animosity towards the Zionists. He spoke at a 1920 rally in Haifa, a rally that was, the Jewish Committee at Haifa informed the government, 'not purely peaceable'. In particular, Nassar's speech was 'noted for [its] provocative nature in propagating a regular campaign of boycotting to be led against the Jews, and furthermore in exhorting the populace to sacrifices, which does not content itself with simple manifestations'.[87] In the same year, he signed a petition from the Muslim and Christian Committees of Haifa demanding reunification with Syria.[88]

Nassar's politics were unique: not only did he differ from the main-stream nationalist programme, but he was open and honest about the reason for his divergence from that track. Nassar's one goal, to end Zionist expansion in Palestine, was in line with other nationalist voices of the period, while his advocacy of strong relations with the British was antithetical to national aims. Naturally, he was criticised by other Arab leaders, but his unceasing anti-Zionism helped to offset the criticism. In addition to working through the British, Nassar was also an advocate of utilising the international Christian community. In 1924, he published an open letter to the pope in which he criticised the Christian community at large and called on the pope do all he could to redeem Palestine 'by sub-scribing a million pounds for this purpose'.[89]

Nassar offered a much more sectarian picture of Palestinian Arab nationalism than al-Sakakini. In his letter to the pope, as elsewhere, Nassar acknowledged the supremacy of the Muslim majority: 'Some Christian societies demand that the defence of Christianity be entrusted to them, but they ignore the fact that the Christians are a minority in Palestine and they cannot live without their Moslem brothers who are in the majority. Christian efforts in this respect cannot baffle the Zionist design.'[90] This statement can be read in two ways. First, it can be seen as a continuation of the recognition of Muslim–Christian unity displayed throughout the rest of the letter. Alternatively, it can be read as Nassar's acknowledge-ment that Christians had to accept their position as a minority. Nassar wrote in the negative: it was not that Christians desired good relations with Muslims, but that they could not survive without them. Such an attitude was contrary to al-Sakakini's ethno-cultural Arab nationalism.

Like al-Sakakini and Nassar, Bandak was Orthodox: in fact, his father was a Greek Orthodox priest. The most notable difference about ʿIsa Bandak is that he was from Bethlehem, a small Christian village with less than 7,000 inhabitants. Even with the neighbouring cities of Beit Jala and Beit Sahour included, the population barely reached 10,000.[91] Bandak's opportunities were significantly limited in comparison as well. Educated in the Orthodox elementary school in Bethlehem and a Christian second-ary school in Jerusalem, the war began before he could seek higher educa-tion. Instead, he went to work for the Ottoman telegraph service, travelling throughout the Levant.[92] In 1919, at the age of 21, Bandak, along with his friend and co-ideologue Yuhnan Dakart, founded a monthly review, simply titled *Bayt Lahm* (*Bethlehem*). The journal was a by-product of *al-Muntada al-Adabi*, the Literary Society, a non-religious nationalist organ-isation prominent during the war years. Bandak explained later that the journal was established in response to the tendency towards 'communal pride' that was common at that time, in an attempt to provide people with political and literary knowledge.[93]

Because of geographical differences, the issues important to Bandak differed from those raised by al-Sakakini and Nassar. He devoted much of his time and many pages of his journal and newspaper, *Sawt al-Sha°b* (founded in 1922), to emigration, a chief concern for Bethlehem residents at the time. The issue was particularly salient to Dakart, who was born in Bethlehem but raised in Argentina before returning to Palestine after his secondary education.[94] Bandak did raise awareness about issues of national importance (such as advocating unity with Syria), and was as anti-Zionist as other nationalist leaders, but national issues competed for space with issues of local concern.

Bandak's social and political circles differed from those of the elite class of Jerusalem, Jaffa and Haifa. He maintained an important relationship with the Palestinian Arab community abroad through *Bayt Lahm*'s subscribers in South America.[95] The Christian community in which he operated allowed him to take on religious issues unselfconsciously, with no concern that he would be labelled sectarian or polarising. To that end, Orthodox issues maintained a prominent place in *Sawt al-Sha°b* throughout the mandate.

These three men, all Orthodox Christians and self-described nationalists, represented three subtly different approaches to politics. All were nationalists, but one was willing to work with the British, one was strictly secular and the third engaged fully in Orthodox issues. Their individual interpretations of communal and national identification were different because of their unique experiences and ideological and political concerns. The diversity among these three figures is notable, though so is the fact that the MCA brought them together with Muslims from across factional lines and from throughout Palestine.

The Rise and Fall of the Muslim Christian Association

Arab leaders founded the Muslim Christian Association in this complex political climate where the meaning of religious identification was the focus of much debate. As the self-proclaimed representative of 'the Muslims and Christians' of Palestine, the organisation left behind a thick trail of memoranda, protests and correspondence with the British government both in Palestine and London. British and Zionist intelligence reports often highlight internal disputes that do not appear in documents produced by the image-conscious MCA. As the following account of the MCA explains, the organisation was not the spearhead of secular nationalism,[96] but rather an organisation that recognised the participation of Christians and Muslims within the same ethno-national movement. There was no erasure of religious identification.

The earliest mentions of the organisation were in 1918, and an undated memo, probably from 1919, tallying society membership in Palestine counted 650 members of the MCA between the Jerusalem, Samaria, Gaza and Galilee subdistricts.[97] The head of the Criminal Investigation Department (CID) concluded in December 1920: 'On the whole it may be stated that for practical purposes the Moslem Christian Society has been the only really active [society] during the past year.'[98] Such discrepancies in when, exactly, the MCA became an important political force do not mask the fact that Arab politics during the earliest years of British rule was dominated by the organisation.

The MCA was comprised of 'older and more representative Moslems and Christians',[99] and was remarkable for its success, albeit partial and short-lived, in unifying disparate notable families (both across the Muslim–Christian divide, and between families of the same religious community) in a single political cause. The association was coordinated on a national level from an office in Jerusalem, and Jaffa, Gaza, Nablus, Tiberias, Tulkarm and Hebron all had independent branches.[100] Arabs from towns and villages were often involved in MCA efforts even if they did not have a local organisation.[101] Haifa, which is often cited as an example of the failure of interreligious unity because Muslims and Christians formed separate organisations, was simply organised in a different way. May Seikaly suggests that the large population of Christians in Haifa led to the division, and she cites unsuccessful efforts to join the two groups into an official MCA branch.[102] Despite never officially merging, in practice the two groups functioned in a similar fashion to the standard MCA societies, co-signing petitions and holding joint rallies. In fact, it is not uncommon to find reference to the 'Haifa MCA' in British and Zionist documents.[103]

In an effort to claim legitimate leadership of the national movement, the MCA sponsored a series of national congresses which gathered members from around Palestine to officially protest against British policies. The most important outcome of these national MCA gatherings was the election of the Arab Executive (AE), a body designated to petition the government on behalf of the congress and, so they claimed, the entire Arab population of Palestine. The first congress held in Palestine was actually titled the 'Third Arab Congress', in order to 'stress continuity with the first (1919) and second (1920) [Arab nationalists] congresses held in Damascus'.[104] Palestinian delegates had attended these two congresses in support of the pan-Arab demands still believed to be viable before the French defeated the Arab government in Syria in July 1920. Additional Palestinian congresses were held in May 1921, August 1922 and June 1923. The congresses sponsored delegations to London, reaffirmed their rejection of a Jewish–Arab legislative council and other British proposals, and generally advocated a policy of non-cooperation with the government.[105] While remaining dedicated to the notion of Muslim–Christian unity, the AE dropped explicit reference to religion, focusing attention on ethnicity instead. Despite this difference, the congresses, the AE and the MCA were all organised and controlled by the same circle of elite, educated Arabs (led by the Husayni family), and all perpetuated similar official views.

The MCA's main goal was to convince the British government, both locally and in London, that a united Arab front proved Arab ability to govern an independent Palestine. At its most basic, Muslim–Christian unity was a way of demanding European attention. Arab notables knew of President Wilson's Fourteen Points speech, which included a call for

> a free, open-minded, and absolutely impartial adjustment of all colonial claims, based upon a strict observance of the principle that in determining all such questions of sovereignty the interests of the population concerned must have equal weight with the equitable claims of the government whose title is to be determined.[106]

Arab leaders also understood the theory of imperial tutelage enshrined in mandate theory. The League of Nations categorised Palestine as a class A mandate: not quite ready for independence, but requiring only a short period of Western tutelage. In the absence of an official timetable, the Arab elite wanted to prove itself immediately capable of independent rule. The MCA sought to portray itself as the only legitimate national body and suggest to the government that it controlled the masses, even warning the government when specific policies would push the public beyond MCA control and towards violence.[107]

Secondly, the MCA sought to garner international support among Christians, mostly British and American, by calling on them to display solidarity with their Arab Christian co-religionists in the face of Zionist aggression.[108] The MCA also sent delegations to the Vatican, fostered relations with the Archbishop of Canterbury and even utilised a British Christian adviser on an early trip to London.[109] British officials in Palestine were reminded that while serving as colonial rulers, they were also co-religionists. All of these efforts were designed to convince the British government and public alike, as well as other important international Christian groups, that international Christians had religious and cultural connections to Palestinian Arabs.

The MCA limited its political agenda to three basic demands: forbidding land sales to the Jews; limiting or ceasing Zionist immigration; and British recognition of full Arab independence, either as part of reunification with Syria or independently. These topics were mentioned in nearly every protest sent to the government, and remained consistent from town to town and year to year. Some local branches addressed other issues as well, such as agricultural loans, tobacco prices and port policies, but these were of local and secondary importance, while the primary goals were agreed upon by all members allowing the MCA to maintain political unity despite disagreement on other issues. One such area of disagreement prior to the ratification of the League of Nations mandate was which European country should gain permanent rule over Palestine. As one British official described the Jerusalem branch:

> The Latins in it are pro-French; the Greek Orthodox are nearly all pro-British; the Moslems are out for independence, though if they cannot have it some prefer Britain and others America as [the] Mandatory Power. The Moslems want nothing to do with France. But Latin, Greek Orthodox and Moslem are all equally opposed to Zionism and Jewish immigration . . . In brief, practically all Moslems and Christians of any importance in Palestine are anti-Zionist, and bitterly so.[110]

Foreign observers claimed that this show of intercommunal unity was something new. Former missionary and the MCA's unofficial adviser, Miss Francis Newton, wrote that the MCA adopted 'a striking symbol of unity – a picture of the crescent and the cross'.[111] In his diary, even Khalil al-Sakakini stressed the uniqueness of the MCA as an intercommunal organisation.[112] More important than the presence of Christians and Muslims was the overt language of intercommunal cooperation that the MCA used to present a unified Arab community, as well as the deliberate efforts to include Muslim and Christian representatives at all times. For instance, at an early meeting of the Jaffa MCA chapter in 1919, a Christian speaker gave the keynote address, while three Muslims also gave speeches that presented a message of unity.[113]

Yet interreligious unity is different to secularisation. The MCA highlighted its members' religious communities and claimed to speak on behalf of both religions. For instance, in the Basic Law of the Jerusalem MCA, membership was composed of, 'every person of Jerusalem as well as of its districts, both Moslem and Christian'.[114] Likewise, Musa Kazim al-Husayni, former mayor of Jerusalem, appealed to the British government not in the name of Arabs, but rather 'in the name of the two Religions of Islam and Christianity'.[115] In MCA efforts to present inter-communal unity, Islam and Christianity were presented as equal partners in the Arab national movement. While understandable as a way to bolster MCA claims, such posturing ensured that the organisation carried both ethnic and religious meaning. Tom Segev's assessment of the MCA as an organisation in which 'Muslims and Christians were united in one religion, the religion of the homeland, which granted equal rights to all', is too simplistic.[116] With a few notable exceptions, such as Khalil al-Sakakini, most members were dedicated to being Arab as well as Muslim or Christian; ethnic and religious identification coexisted. Still, as opposed to Ottoman-era councils based in Muslim privilege and Christian protections under the *millet* system, the MCA's conscious focus on religious unity did represent an important shift.

Despite rhetoric about religious unity, it is difficult to determine exactly what role Christians played in the MCA. The Jerusalem branch was the only one with pre-determined leadership roles for Muslims and Christians: ten Muslims, five Latins, five Orthodox and an additional ten village *mukhtars* (village leaders, who appear initially to have been all Muslim).[117] Therefore, Christians held 33 per cent of the communally designated seats on the organisation's leadership committee, despite comprising less than 25 per cent of the population in Jerusalem and just over 10 per cent of the national population.[118] Yet in al-Sakakini's account of MCA meetings Christian denominational delineations retained importance, weakening the potential importance of such a large Christian presence.[119] At times Christians served in important leadership roles, such as when Michel Beiruti of Jaffa held the position of temporary president of the AE for a time in 1919. He and Christian Khalil Sahimi were also elected as special representatives of the Christian community on the AE at the Sixth Palestinian Arab Congress in 1923. In addition to these specifi-cally Christian representatives, other Christians, including ʿIsa Bandak of Bethlehem, were also elected to the AE.[120] Other important Christians, such as Yaʿcoub Farraj, Yusef al-ʿIsa, ʿIsa al-ʿIsa and Shukhri al-Karmi, as well as certain Christian clergy, such as Protestant Asad Mansur and the Melkite Bishop Hajjar, were also affiliated with the MCA.[121] Two con-clusions may be drawn: first, Christians did indeed hold important posi-tions in the MCA and AE; and, secondly, it must be noted that the actual number of Christian members was not large, with a small number of the political elite participating in the name of the wider community.

More important than specific levels of Christian participation was how MCA ideology pervaded public political action of the day. For example,

Nazareth did not have a local MCA, but village leaders sent a protest to the military governor in 1920, with a letter signed by the heads of five Christian churches as well as Muslim religious leaders, *mukhtars* and other village notables.[122] In Safad, 6,000 demonstrators proceeded first to the mosque and then to a church: the local mufti, the mayor, Christian *mukhtars* and other notables followed the protest by meeting with the military governor of Galilee.[123] Measuring levels of non-elite participation in the MCA is impossible, but Arab commoners, Muslim and Christian alike, were certainly involved in such gatherings, even though elite Muslims and Christians fully controlled public dissemination of their message. Arab women also took an active role the movement, telling the government that it was the first time the 'Moslem and Christian ladies' had joined a political movement: 'Had not the matter been serious, you would not have seen us disobeying our oriental habits that do not entitle us to appear in such a manner.'[124] Until this point, most women's involvement in social organisations had been through charitable and educational organisations.[125]

While Arab efforts at intercommunal cooperation were often peaceful, protests did occasionally turn violent: anti-Zionist violence that occurred in conjunction with the Muslim festival of *Nebi Musa* (Prophet Moses) on 4 April 1920 was the most dramatic case during this period. A combination of politicised speeches opposing Zionism and a pilgrimage route through Jerusalem's Jewish Quarter provided the impetus for the violent outburst. Over the course of four days, five Jews and four Arabs were killed and more than 200 Jews were wounded.[126] In recent years Christians had joined in the procession in increasing numbers because of the nationalist overtones of *Nebi Musa*, but Christian participation in the actual violence was apparently quite insignificant, despite the presence of thousands of Christian pilgrims in Jerusalem for the Easter holidays. Khalil al-Sakakini left the festival-turned-riot in disgust, lamenting that 'the religion of Muhammad was founded by the sword'.[127] The following year at *Nebi Musa*, with Hajj Amin al-Husayni (soon to become the mufti) at the helm, the politicisation of the festival continued. Signs reading 'Moslems and Christians are brothers' were held high, and a Christian, Jubran Kosma, spoke in favour of Arab farmers and against Zionism.[128] Christian shopkeepers prepared for the worst by marking their doors with crosses to prevent rioters from looting their stores, a measure repeated during the 1929 uprising.[129]

On 3 May 1921, High Commissioner Samuel wrote to Colonial Secretary Winston Churchill describing the outbreak of fresh violence in Jaffa. The initial disturbance, he claimed, stemmed from a confrontation between Jewish groups, but spread to a mixed Muslim–Jewish neighbourhood where the real violence began. By the time the violence had subsided, British officials reported forty people dead, thirty Jews and ten Muslims.[130] That evening a meeting of Muslim notables was held to discuss ways of restoring calm to Jaffa.[131] Samuel later published casualty reports confirming eighty-five dead, two of whom were Christian. Two other Christians were among the 315 wounded in the conflict.

Even if Christian participation in the actual violence was minimal, Christians were active in the aftermath by verbally protesting against what they interpreted to be Jewish violence against Arabs. Some Christians, at least, did not want to be left completely out of the hostilities. The inhabitants of Tulkarm sent a letter to the British government in which they decried the Jewish attack on 'the Moslem and Christian inhabitants of Jaffa': the petition was signed by a variety of village leaders, including representatives of the Orthodox, Latin and Melkite Communities.[132] And when it came to assigning a commission to look into the incident, Samuel appointed a Muslim, a Christian and a Jew to be members in recognition of the impact of such violence on all segments of the population.[133]

One of the most successful protests spearheaded by the MCA and the AE was the 1923 boycott of the British proposal for a legislative council. The British wanted to create a council composed of set numbers of Jews, Muslims, Christians, and British officials, of which the combined number of Jewish and British members would comprise a majority. The AE demanded a fully representative council to ensure an Arab majority, but the British refused.[134] Nationalists were caught in a dilemma, since they did not want to miss the chance to be officially recognised representatives in a government council, but they also feared that by participating in mandate programmes they would implicitly be accepting the Balfour Declaration.[135] Many moderate politicians considered participating in the elections, but the risk of being labelled a traitor and losing support was enough to trigger their withdrawal.[136]

It is tempting to read the historical record as suggesting that Christians were more inclined towards accepting the legislative council. When British officials met the Palestinian Arab delegation in London in January of that year, a British official remarked that the two Christian members of the committee, Shibley Jamal (a Jerusalem Protestant) and Wadi al-Bustani, 'showed some disposition to adopt a more accommodating attitude and it's believed that some at least of them would have liked to come to an understanding with the Government'.[137] The two Muslim members took an uncompromising stance. Two other Christian notables also appear to have leaned towards participation in the elections. Sulaiman Nasif of Haifa met with Samuel on behalf of a small committee comprising himself and seven Haifa Muslims where they agreed to start a moderate party that would accept British rule and ignore the Balfour Declaration.[138] Bulus Shihada, soon to join the Nashashibi-led opposition National Party, wrote about the election in his newspaper *Mirat al-Sharq*. He recognised the legitimacy of Palestinian Arab concerns over government policy, but called on Arabs to show their anger against the government through the council, rather than by boycotting it.[139]

In his election report, the high commissioner described the failure of the legislative council project. Problems were reported even prior to the actual election: Muslims had nominees for only 16 per cent of their potential seats, while Christians had filled only 32 per cent of the spots on the ballot. In the actual election, 18 per cent of potential Muslim voters appeared at the ballot box in comparison with only 5.5 per cent of Christian voters.[140] Arab Executive president ʿAbd al-Qadir al-Muzaffar praised the demonstration of national unity and declared 14 March (election day) a national holiday. He closed his statement by declaring, 'Long live the free and independent Palestine. Long live the union of Moslems and Christians.'[141] Despite a handful of elite Christians appearing conciliatory to the British, the Christian community at large maintained its national unity and obedience to MCA demands for a nationwide boycott.

Intercommunal unity was not simply a façade, as many British observers believed, nor was it the only Arab position. Yet, although other opinions did exist, opposition to this chief aim of the MCA was silenced in public forums. The Fourth Arab Congress of 1921, however, provides a window into the presence of intercommunal tensions in nationalist circles during this period. The notes of the meeting were, a British official acknowledged, given to the government by 'Mr Myers, which explains the distinctively Jewish tone of the comments'.[142] But despite the overtly Zionist perspective of the report, the tensions seem plausible. In his opening address Musa Kazim al-Husayni reaffirmed the importance of intercommunal unity:

> On the occasion of the opening of the congress, we declare ourselves all united and our eyes have to be turned on the future. Our signal must be union between Moslem and Christian. The purpose of this Fourth Arab Congress and its sittings is not only to discuss the recent Jaffa events, which are a result of the enemy immigration into Palestine, and the declarations made by Churchill during his stay in Palestine. We have to resist everything which others will want to make of our country in the future.[143]

Despite his plea for Muslim–Christian unity, the conversation quickly turned sour. Najib Nassar, ardent anti-Zionist and editor of the *al-Karmil* newspaper, suggested that the vice-president of the congress be a Christian, 'so that the Christians might be satisfied and be inspired with confidence in the [Congress]'. ᶜAbdullah Salah of Nablus replied, 'The numbers of Christians in this country are so comparatively few that in reality there ought not to be more than one of their members at this Congress.'[144] Even statistically speaking, Salah was only partially correct: Christians comprised approximately 15 per cent of the membership, not a great deal higher than the 9 per cent of Christian residents of Palestine at the time.[145] For proportional communal representation, there should have been only seven Christians instead of twelve. The foundation of Salah's argument was that Muslims were the great majority of Palestinians and should be represented as such. And while Salah may have exaggerated in his state-ment, it is true that Christians comprised 33 per cent of the executive com-mittee elected to represent the Fourth Congress, the highest percentage of Christian representation in any such committee.[146] Ibrahim Shammas, an Orthodox Christian known for moderation in his approach to the British, tried to diffuse the argument concerning the vice-president's religion by stating that it did not matter if a Christian or Muslim was elected. The representatives then voted for ᶜArif al-Dajani, a Muslim from Jerusalem. Fuᶜad Saᶜd, a Melkite from Haifa who also ran for vice-president, received only fourteen of seventy-six votes, the same as the number of Christians at the Congress.[147] Nassar was correct that without an allotted position for a Christian executive one would not be voted into power.

On the fifth day of the congress, religious tensions rose again as the delegates tried to determine who to nominate for the planned delegation to Europe. The previous day Nassar had proposed five names, including three Christians. Other Christians demanded that all six delegates be Christian and insisted that one of them be Melkite Bishop Hajjar. The account of the congress claims that 'the Muslims' opposed Hajjar's nomination, and Saᶜid Abu Khadra of Jaffa 'asked whether the delegation of the Congress was a political or a religious body', to which the president answered that it was political. The final delegation included two Christians (Shammas and Saᶜd) and four Muslims, plus two secretaries, one of whom was Shibley Jamal. Once again, Christians had requested substantial representation, but received relatively limited roles.

These intercommunal tensions are telling. In public pronouncements the MCA insisted that Christians and Muslims were united, but unity against Zionism did not mean that the two religious communities had fully negotiated their places in the emerging political field. According to the above account, an individual's religion was sometimes deemed more important, for instance, than equitable geographic representation or even political utility.

Palestinian Arab notables created the MCA to maintain their authority and to alter the course of Britain's pro-Zionist policies. The organisation allowed Arabs to identify both by ethnicity and religion, a prospect that suited most Muslims and Christians. Many Muslims were accustomed from Ottoman days to a position of privilege over minority communities and were not willing to let go of their superior status. Some Christians, on the other hand, were willing to use religious differentiation to their advantage when possible, and wanted to hedge their bets and be prepared for either an Arab-controlled or a British-controlled political future. Furthermore, many believed that the British would respond well to a strong Christian presence in Arab political bodies.

Despite the creative blend of ethnic and communal identification and the MCA's initial ability to garner support from many segments of society, the organisation failed to maintain its strength past the ratification of the Mandate. As a result, most historians, such as Khalidi and Segev, downplay the importance of the organisation in their accounts of the Mandate period. But the MCA was the leading Arab organisation prior to the 1923 implementation of the Mandate, as well as an important voice in the debate about religious versus national identification. Yet, due to a combination of internal and external forces, the MCA collapsed, and the nationalist movement splintered. A few reasons for this collapse are clear. Some participants believed that cooperation with the British was a better way to achieve national independence, others were simply frustrated by the MCA's failure to gain any concessions, and still others sought personal gain by undermining those in control. While overt inter-religious cooperation was certainly a casualty of the MCA's collapse, it is not clear if communalist tensions were among the causes of its dissolution.

The MCA's ideology of ethno-religious cooperation appears in later documents as a weakness. In the 1940s, ᶜArif al-ᶜArif, the noted Palestinian nationalist who eventually became mayor of Jerusalem in the 1950s, told a Jewish friend that in the MCA era 'he would write in favour of [intercommunal] unity, but it was mostly a trick. The Arab Nationalists wanted to get weapons out of Europe and Europe's intention was to create a problem of a Christian minority.'[148] If this source is to be trusted, evidence suggests that al-ᶜArif supported religious unity in the 1920s for strictly political reasons. Al-Sakakini, however, truly desired such unity, but was well aware of the societal tensions. In 1919, *al-Nadi al-ᶜArabi* invited him to speak about the Prophet Muhammad. The audience was large, as he had hoped, but there were only three Christians among them: most attendees were village men and students from Islamic schools. His

47

journal entry reveals his concern over lecturing on Islamic history to a non-elite, mostly Muslim crowd, fearing that this group would not trust him, as a Christian, to discuss Muhammad in a respectful manner.[149] While the lecture apparently proceeded without further complication, the story suggests that al-Sakakini's desires for interreligious harmony were tainted by fears of conflict.

Christian–Muslim relations were also influenced by a conflict involving another former Ottoman region: Turkey. In 1922, Samuel suggested that Arab Christians had come to fear pan-Islam and Muslims more than they feared Zionism,[150] an idea he reasserted in 1924 when local Muslim's interest in pan-Islam increased as a result of the Turkish victory in their war with Greece.[151] Arab Muslims collected funds for Turkish victims, only to be countered with a Christian collection for Greek victims.[152] And when the AE delegation travelled to London via Turkey in the autumn of 1922, Christian members joined up with the group in London since they were unwilling to visit the country that had so recently abused its Christian population.[153]

The rise of organised opposition to the MCA was a much clearer contributor to its demise. Rifts among nationalists were used by the Zionists and the British to weaken the movement as a whole. Arabs who openly supported the British, Zionist immigration or the building of strong Jewish–Arab relations were suspected of receiving secret Zionist funding, and the suspicions were usually justified.[154] Some Zionists encouraged Arabs to confront the standard anti-Zionist nationalism of the MCA and AE. Usually Zionist 'encouragement' took the form of bribes or even being put on the Zionist Executive's monthly payroll.

The most important figure involved in so-called 'Arab–Jewish rapprochement' was Chaim Margaliyot Kalvaryski. Kalvaryski was a controversial character on every front: Zionists worried that he spent too much time and money working with Arabs, and Arab nationalists condemned as traitors all who took his money in exchange for more Zionist-friendly politics.[155] He assisted the disgruntled Nashashibi family in founding and funding 'Farmers' Parties' that catered to rural Arabs and focused on advancing the economic needs of Arab farmers.[156] He also established (and paid for) an Arab–Jewish club in Tiberias.[157] One of his most notorious projects was funding the National Muslim Society (NMS) as a Nashashibi-run alternative to the MCA in an effort to split the Arab national leadership.[158] In addition to challenging the role of the MCA as the centre of the national movement and suggesting that closer relations with the British might be more useful, the NMS also publicly challenged the role of Christians in the national movement and society in general.

Those Arabs willing to participate in such a movement were often members of elite families who fell outside the circles of MCA power. In the early 1920s the Nashashibi family openly established the National Party in official opposition to the Husayni-driven MCA.

Even the name 'National Muslim Society', which highlighted the Muslim aspect of Arab identity instead of following the lead of the MCA, was troublesome to some Christians. Porath suggests that the party harnessed Muslim resentment of Christians to form organisations in many northern Palestinian towns.[159] In addition, while the NMS used the newspaper *Lisan al-Arab* as its major propaganda mouthpiece, at a 1922 meeting one member recommended finding a different newspaper since *Lisan al-Arab* was edited by a Christian.[160] Perhaps to compensate for Zionist support of the organisation, the NMS accused the MCA of being an instrument of Christian control. Some Christians responded by trying to form a National Christian Society in 1922, although the movement went nowhere since the majority of Christian notables still focused their efforts on intercommunal cooperation.[161]

Because the NMS was overtly pro-Zionist, it gained only a small following. Still, it provided a basis for a stronger and more legitimate opposition in subsequent years that was careful to avoid the appearance of Zionist leanings. More importantly, the NMS was never taken seriously by the government. Kalvaryski's inability to create a serious Arab following is apparent in the collapse of the NMS when Zionist funds dried up. The president of the Kalvaryski-funded Palestine Club in Tiberias also threatened to return to the MCA, but he waited when 'he heard that Kalvaryski [was] returning and that he was going to receive his monthly payment'.[162] The NMS, it seems, attracted those whose interest in personal financial gain was more important than ideology.

Christian names are noticeably absent from Zionist-funded organisations and anti-MCA petitions at this time, and perhaps the failure of Zionist agents to co-opt Christian leaders contributed to Zionist disdain for that community. The Zionist Executive was convinced that the MCA existed solely for the purpose of destroying the Zionist dream, and that 'the Christian element is the life and soul of the Christian–Moslem Society'.[163] Mordechai Ben-Hillel Hacohen, a Zionist historian who helped settle Tel Aviv in 1907, was sceptical of European-educated Arab Christians, pointing specifically to al-Sakakini when he wrote, 'They adopted the "well-preserved appearance" of European culture, but "their souls are still full of the filth of savagery".'[164] What is clear is that the MCA was the only place for elite Arab Christians to participate in national politics.

Blaming Christians for the MCA's strength and voicing frustrations over its unbending anti-Zionism pales in comparison with Zionist official David Miller's efforts to incite Muslim–Christian violence in Nablus. While some Zionist officials argued that 'we intended to be on peaceful relations with both Moslems and Christians, [and] we did not come here to stir up any antagonism between them',[165] Miller was willing to utilise any technique to further Zionist aims. In a letter to Dr Eder, he described an incident in which a young Muslim woman fled to Bethlehem to convert to Christianity. Miller believed the potential for local communal violence was high and viewed it as 'an opportunity . . . to increase the split between our enemies. I wished very much for [an assault upon Christians] to take place, but I wanted some money for that and I had none . . . Such an assault could have been of great benefit to us.'[166] While Miller's method of fomenting Christian–Muslim enmity was not widely accepted in Zionist circles, it provides evidence of Zionists' fear of Palestinian Arab unity and of their efforts to undermine it. Even Kalvaryski's efforts, despite his seemingly honest faith in Jewish–Arab relations, exacerbated damaging rifts in the fragile fabric of Arab politics.

More important than Zionist efforts to sabotage Arab cooperation was Britain's pro-Zionist policy. The British government developed a policy of 'non-negotiation' on the Balfour Declaration and refused to work with any Arabs who challenged Britain's goal of building a Jewish national home. When the MCA appointed a delegation to travel to Europe in 1921, the Colonial Secretary wrote to Samuel that he should let them know his intentions about creating a 'scheme of popular representation', and that if they still insisted on travelling to London they should be aware that:

> administrative reform can only proceed on [the] basis of acceptance of the policy of creation of a National Home for the Jews, which remains a cardinal article of British policy . . . No representative bodies that may be established will be permitted to interfere with measures (i.e., immigration, etc.) designed to give effect to principle of a National Home or to challenge this principle.[167]

Even while other facets of British rule varied, Mandate officials generally stood by this policy, refusing to recognise any Palestinian organisation that threatened the essence of the Balfour Declaration.

Due to this policy the British treated Arab delegations poorly, and in Palestine they dismissed the MCA as unimportant despite its standing among the Arab population. In 1922, the government held the MCA delegation in London until the completion of the *Nebi Musa*/Easter season in order to prevent incitement. A government official explained that after the festival, 'we shall have nothing to do with them in all probability and may send them away'.[168] Samuel wrote in 1920 that 'the Muslim–Christian Associations were few and not to be taken seriously, although undoubtedly they stand for a considerable body of opinion latent in the country, which might at any time be stirred into activity by an aggressive or unsympathetic policy on the part of the Government.'[169] The high commissioner himself recognised that the MCA was, in fact, representative of much of the population's opinion, but he refused to give it traction as a political force.

Even though communalist arguments emerged along with the opposition, intercommunal unity was mainly a casualty of the growing split between the mainstream and opposition national movements, not its cause. But the debate about the role of Christians in the national movement and society was reopened as new voices sought to define the meaning of belonging in Mandate Palestine.

Conclusion

In the first years of the Mandate, the MCA opposed British, Zionist and Christian hierarchies as they presented a carefully managed image of national and religious unity. The Association's leadership was made up entirely of the elite strata, Muslims and Christians who had prospered in Ottoman times, and they established the MCA and AE to fight against Zionism and to make demands of the British government. They firmly believed that espousing a strong vision of intercommunal support for an independent Arab nation provided the strongest possibility that the Mandate authorities would listen.

While interreligious unity had been an important political tool, some among the political elite were willing to set such ideas aside if doing so would benefit them personally. Increased political opposition broke the MCA's authority over the nationalist vision, particularly as the Association failed to achieve any of its aims and Zionist immigration continued. The MCA's vision of intercommunal unity allowed Christians to be largely accepted by, and as part of, the Arab political leadership. In fact, they not only participated, but were (as some Zionists and Muslims complained) in partial control of the movement. Muslim and Christian Arabs were accepted as equal members in the Association and, by extension, in society. The MCA's failure to achieve its aims in the early 1920s caused problems for Christians who relied on this message, and the organisation's failures opened the door for criticism by Muslims who felt threatened by Christian leaders. As factionalism widened rifts between Muslim elites,

Arab Christians had to renegotiate their position in society, leading to increased disagreement about how best to fit into a fractured political field.

Notes

1. ISA M 7/7, F. Berout of the MCA, open letter to the President of the League of Nations, 25 October 1919.
2. PRO 733/1, Keith-Roach to Churchill, 14 February 1921.
3. *Suriyah al-Janubiyah*, 7 March 1920.
4. Contrary to the views of Daphne Tsimhoni, who argues that 'the Palestinian Arab movement [was] marked by the attempt to give Christians an equal position, and to disregard their religious affiliation', Tsimhoni, 'The Arab Christians', p. 73.
5. Halil Inalcik, 'The Meaning of Legitimacy: The Ottoman Case', in Carl Brown (ed.), *Imperial Legacy: The Ottoman Imprint on the Balkans and the Middle East* (New York: Columbia University Press, 1996), p. 24.
6. Kemal H. Karpat, *Studies on Ottoman Social and Political History* (Boston, MA: Brill, 2002), p. 615.
7. Elie Kedourie, *The Chatham House Version and Other Middle-Eastern Studies* (London: Weidenfeld & Nicolson, 1970), pp. 315–16.
8. Karpat, *Studies on Ottoman Social and Political History*, p. 611.
9. Robert Haddad, 'The Ottoman Empire in the Contemporary Middle East', in *Aftermath of Empire: In Honor of Professor Max Salvadori* (Northampton, MA: Smith College, 1975), p. 43.
10. Karpat, *Studies on Ottoman Social and Political History*, p. 626; Ariel Salzmann, 'An Ancien Regime Revisited: "Privatization" and Political Economy in the Eighteenth-Century Ottoman Empire', *Politics and Society*, 21(4) (1993), pp. 393–423.
11. Karpat, *Studies on Ottoman Social and Political History*, p. 628.
12. Maghak°ia Ormanean *et al.*, *The Church of Armenia: Her History, Doctrine, Discipline, Liturgy, Literature, and Existing Condition*, 2nd edn (London: Mowbray, 1955), p. 61; Karpat, *Studies on Ottoman Social and Political History*, p. 612.
13. Inalcik, 'The Meaning of Legitimacy', p. 24. See also, Karpat, *Studies on Ottoman Social and Political History*, p. 611.
14. John James Moscrop, *Measuring Jerusalem: The Palestine Exploration Fund and British Interests in the Holy Land* (New York: Continuum, 2000), p. 8. See also, Derek Hopwood, *The Russian Presence in Syria and Palestine, 1843–1914: Church and Politics in the Near East* (Oxford: Clarendon Press, 1969).
15. Makdisi, *Culture of Sectarianism*, p. 11.
16. Caroline Finkel, *Osman's Dream: The Story of the Ottoman Empire, 1300–1923* (New York: Basic Books, 2006), p. 475.
17. Kemal H. Karpat, *The Politicization of Islam: Reconstructing Identity,*

State, Faith, and Community in the Late Ottoman State (Oxford: Oxford University Press, 2001), p. 177. See also, Selim Deringil, *The Well-Protected Domains: Ideology and the Legitimation of Power in the Ottoman Empire, 1876–1909* (New York: I. B. Tauris, 1999).

18. Hasan Kayali, *Arabs and Young Turks: Ottomanism, Arabism, and Islamism in the Ottoman Empire, 1908–1918* (Berkeley, CA: University of California Press, 1997), p. 50.
19. Kayali, *Arabs and Young Turks*, p. 11.
20. See R. Khalidi, *Palestinian Identity*, p. 6, and Muhammad Muslih, *Origins*.
21. R. Khalidi, *Palestinian Identity*, p. 125.
22. R. Khalidi, *Palestinian Identity*, p. 126.
23. William Ochsenwald, 'Islam and the Ottoman Legacy in the Modern Middle East', in Carl Brown (ed.), *Imperial Legacy*, p. 271.
24. Benjamin Braude and Bernard Lewis (eds), *Christians and Jews in the Ottoman Empire: The Functioning of a Plural Society* (New York: Holmes & Meier, 1982), p. 5.
25. Antonio Cassese, *Self-Determination of Peoples: A Legal Reappraisal* (Cambridge: Cambridge University Press, 1995), pp. 20–1.
26. H. G. Wells, *The Idea of a League of Nations* (Boston, MA: Atlantic Monthly Press, 1919).
27. Rashid Khalidi, *The Iron Cage: The Story of the Palestinian Struggle for Statehood* (Boston, MA: Beacon Press, 2006), p. 44.
28. Campos, *Ottoman Brothers*, p. 225.
29. See Mazza, *Jerusalem*, and Jacobson, *From Empire to Empire*.
30. PRO 733–4; Shuckburgh to the Duke of Sutherland, 12 July 1921.
31. Keith-Roach, *Pasha of Jerusalem*, p. 78.
32. Fleischmann, *The Nation and its 'New' Women*, pp. 192–3; HC to Colonial Office (CO), 3 August 1921, in Jarman, *Political Diaries*, vol. 1, p. 68.
33. PRO 733/1, Keith-Roach to Churchill, 14 February 1921.
34. Pittman, 'Missionaries and Emissaries', p. 118.
35. Tsimhoni, 'The British Mandate', p. 134.
36. Tsimhoni, 'The British Mandate', p. 206 ff. n. 4.
37. PRO FO 609/99, gloss from Ormsby-Gore on Petition from Inhabitants of Nablus against Zionist Domination in Palestine, 20 February 1919.
38. ISA P656/11, December 1924 Political Report from District Officer, Ramallah subdistrict, 2 January 1925.
39. CZA S25/4377, Palestine Zionist Executive to Dr Eder, ZO London, 16 August 1922.
40. CZA S25/665/4, unknown to Kisch, 2 February 1923.
41. CZA S25/518/1, Miller to Kisch, 25 April 1923.
42. ISA M6/1, Kisch to Samuel, 30 November 1923.
43. CZA S25/665/4, following a letter dated 30 January 1925, although it is not clear if they were attached.
44. Tsimhoni, 'Arab Christians', p. 75.

45. Mazza, *Jerusalem*, p. 47.
46. This story begins in the Introduction, pp. 11–12. See Robson, *Colonialism and Christianity*, ch. 3, for another look at the Arab Orthodox controversy.
47. Bertram and Luke, *Report of the Commission . . . into the Affairs of the Orthodox Patriarchate of Jerusalem*, pp. 3–7.
48. For the full text, see *Filastin*, 7 August 1923. For a detailed account of the Congress and the financial and political woes of the patriarchate, see Tsimhoni, 'The British Mandate', pp. 80–107.
49. Sir Anton Bertram and J. W. A. Young, *Report of the Commission appointed by the Government of Palestine to inquire into the affairs of the Orthodox Patriarchate of Jerusalem* (New York: Oxford University Press, 1926), pp. 9–14.
50. Bertram and Young, *Report of the Commission . . . into the affairs of the Orthodox Patriarchate of Jerusalem*, pp. 12–13.
51. The first historians of Arab nationalism, such as George Antonius and Albert Hourani, argued that Christians played a disproportionate role in the birth of the movement during its formative years. See Antonius, *The Arab Awakening: The Story of the Arab National Movement* (London: Arab Centre, 1939), and Hourani, *Arabic Thought in the Liberal Age, 1798–1939* (Cambridge: Cambridge University Press, 1983).
52. Bertram and Young, *Report of the Commission . . . into the affairs of the Orthodox Patriarchate of Jerusalem*, pp. 273–8.
53. Bertram and Young, *Report of the Commission . . . into the affairs of the Orthodox Patriarchate of Jerusalem*, pp. 103–5, 279. See also, Shahadeh Khoury and Nicola Khoury, *A Survey of the History of the Orthodox Church of Jerusalem* (Amman: Feras, 2002), p. 246.
54. Khoury and Khoury, *Survey*, pp. 246–9.
55. See, for example, Musallam, *Yawmiyat Khalil al-Sakakini*, vol. 2, pp. 49–50 and 156–8. Entries for 1 January 1914 and 21 March 1915. Al-Sakakini wrote of his frustrations with the church and contemplated converting to Protestantism, but decided 'I am not Christian, nor Buddhist, nor Muslim, nor Jewish. I am not Arab, or English, or French, or German, or Russian, or Turkish, but I am one of the human race.'
56. For instance, see ISA M30/24, citation from *Filastin*, in 'Extract from Review of the Palestine Press', 23 September 1943.
57. Barlassina was not well-liked by the Vatican, and the Pope bypassed Barlassina by appointing a Permanent Apostolic Visitor to handle political matters, leaving Barlassina to deal with the more mundane duties of his patriarchal position. See ISA M7/1 and M7/2 for extensive documentation of Barlassina's conflicts with the British and Vatican.
58. Tsimhoni, 'Arab Christians', pp. 84–6.
59. Latin Patriarchate Archive, Pastoral Letter 2, 11 April 1920.
60. Latin Patriarchate Archive, Pastoral Letter 2; and Pastoral Letter 30, 21 August 1932.

61. ISA M3/43, Roger Thyme to Lord Curzon, September 1920.
62. ISA M7/2, Barlassina to Samuel, 16 July 1920
63. ISA M7/2, Barlassina to Samuel, 30 March 1921
64. PRO FO 141/667, H. C. Luke to Chief Secretary, 16 June 1923.
65. Musallam, *Yawmiyat Khalil al-Sakakini*, vol. 3, p. 142. Entry for 3 September 1919.
66. See more about the al-Bahri murder in Chapter 3.
67. ISA M4/21, Kisch to ZO Political Secretary, Report on the 6th Palestinian Conference, 25 June 1923.
68. See Tsimhoni, 'Arab Christians', p. 84.
69. ISA M4/1, Report to Jerusalem CID, 29 June 1922.
70. Tom Segev, for instance, uses al-Sakakini as his main Arab source, allowing al-Sakakini to speak for the whole of Palestinian Arab society: *One Palestine, Complete: Jews and Arabs Under the British Mandate* (New York: Macmillan, 2001).
71. Qustandi Shomali, 'Palestinian Christians: Politics, Press and Religious Identity, 1900–1948', in Anthony O'Mahony (ed.), *The Christian Heritage*, p. 229; Segev, *One Palestine*, p. 28.
72. Segev, *One Palestine*, p. 27. Levin and al-Sakakini both ended up in an Ottoman prison and were transferred to Damascus during the war.
73. Musallam, *Yawmiyat Khalil al-Sakakini*, vol. 1, pp. 264–6. Entry from 17 July 1908.
74. Musallam, *Yawmiyat Khalil al-Sakakini*, vol. 2, p. 57. Entry for 5 February 1914.
75. Musallam, *Yawmiyat Khalil al-Sakakini*, vol. 2, pp. 49–50. Entry for 1 January 1914.
76. See Musallam, *Yawmiyat Khalil al-Sakakini*, vol 1, p. 29, Salim Tamari's introduction; and Salim Tamari, 'A Miserable Year in Brooklyn: Khalil Sakakini in America, 1907–1908', *Jerusalem Quarterly*, 17 (2003), 19–40.
77. Al-Sakakini's diaries give detailed accounts of his daily activities, his visits to Waters-Taylor, General Storrs, Herbert Samuel and members of the Khalidi, Husayni and Nashashibi families.
78. Musallam, *Yawmiyat Khalil al-Sakakini*, vol. 3, p. 191. See also, pp. 193–4. Entries for 11 and 15 July 1919.
79. Musallam, *Yawmiyat Khalil al-Sakakini*, vol. 3, pp. 56–8. Entry for 25 January 1919.
80. Shomali, 'Politics, Press', p. 228.
81. Shomali, 'Politics, Press', pp. 228–9. Tsimhoni suggests (without a citation) that Nassar converted to the United Free Church of Scotland 'before the First World War, but retain[ed] his affiliations with the Orthodox community': 'The British Mandate', p. 202 ff. n. 4.
82. Najar Aida Ali, 'The Arabic Press and Nationalism in Palestine', Doctoral dissertation, Syracuse University, New York, 1975, p. 34.

83. Najib al-Khuri Nassar, *Al-Sihyuniyya: Tarikhuha, gharaduha, ahamiyy-atuha* (Zionism: Its History, Objective and Importance) (Haifa: Al-Karmil Press, 1911).

84. Neville Mandel, *The Arabs and Zionism before World War I* (Berkeley, CA: University of California Press, 1976), p. 87.

85. Ali, 'Arabic Press', p. 62.

86. Ali, 'Arabic Press', p. 35.

87. ISA M1/2, Jewish Committee at Haifa to Governor of Haifa, 9 March 1920.

88. ISA M1/2, Muslim and Christian Committees to Governor of Haifa, 8 March 1920. Nassar signed this document along with many other Christian leaders from Haifa, including Fuᶜad Saᶜd.

89. CZA S25/518/2, 'Open Letter to the Pope', extracts from an unknown Zionist source, 18 November 1924.

90. 'Open Letter to the Pope'.

91. In 1922, Christians comprised less than 10 per cent of the population of Palestine as a whole. In Bethlehem, nearly 90 per cent of the population was Christian (McCarthy, *Population of Palestine*, p. 35, Table 2.14 and p. 158, Table A8.5).

92. ᶜAdnan Musallam, *Folded Pages from Local Palestinian History: Developments in Politics, Society, Press and Thought in Bethlehem in the British Era, 1917–1948* (Bethlehem: Wiꜣam Centre, 2002), pp. 78–9.

93. ᶜAdnan Ayyub Musallam's Collection on Bethlehem, The Holy Land (documents collected for writing *Folded Pages*), University of Michigan, BBC8; Bandak to Musallam, 15 July 1971.

94. Musallam, *Folded Pages*, p. 78.

95. Musallam, *Folded Pages*, p. 79.

96. Tsimhoni, 'The British Mandate', pp. 205–6. Porath provides a more nuanced understanding of Muslim–Christian relations with regard to the MCA (Porath, *Emergence*, p. 294).

97. ISA M7/7, MCA Draft memo, 1918; M7/12, Societies and their Membership Numbers, n.d.

98. ISA M7/12, CID Memo from Quigley; 23 December 1920.

99. PRO, FO 608–99, 'Arab Movement and Zionism', Camp (Assistant Political Officer, Jerusalem) to the Chief Political Officer, Cairo, 12 August 1919.

100. Tsimhoni, 'The British Mandate', p. 207. Tsimhoni's history of the MCA is excellent, with much detail concerning the dates of organisation, types of protests and relations to other societies, such as *al-Nadi al-ᶜArabi* and *al-Muntada al-Adabi*; 'The British Mandate', p. 205. Tsimhoni does not list Tiberias as an MCA city, but it is found in a list in ISA M4/1, List of Registered MCA Clubs as of 22 October 1922.

101. CZA S25/3008, Zionist Intelligence Report; Autobiographies of major Arab personalities; n.d., post-1930.

102. May Seikaly, *Haifa: Transformation of an Arab Society, 1918–1939* (London: I. B. Tauris, 2002), p. 168.

103. CZA S25517/9, Zionist Intelligence Report, includes lists of members from various societies, dated only 1927; ISA M1/2, Translation of the Programme of Demonstration by MCA of Haifa, 6 March 1920; the dual organisations are also included in a 'List of Registered MCA Clubs as of 22 October 1922', ISA M4/1. In 1921, the president of the MCA, Musa Kazim al-Husayni, travelled to Haifa to hold a meeting of the 'Moslem Christian Society' in order to raise funds for an MCA delegation to travel to Europe. Presumably, the meeting included both the Muslim and Christian committees (PRO 733-3, Political report for April 1921).

104. Ann Mosely Lesch, *Arab Politics in Palestine, 1917–1939: The Frustration of a Nationalist Movement* (Ithaca, NY: Cornell University Press, 1979), p. 91.

105. Lesch, *Arab Politics*, pp. 94–5.

106. For full text of the Fourteen Points speech of 8 January 1918, see A. S. Link (ed.), *The Papers of Woodrow Wilson, vol. 45: 1917–1918* (Princeton, NJ: Princeton University Press, 1984), pp. 536–9.

107. ISA M1/2, Jerusalem MCA to Chief Administrator, Jerusalem, 14 April 1920; ISA M4/2, Jamal al-Husayni to HC, 2 February 1923. Samuel complimented them for such action during a tense period in 1921, PRO 733-3, 8 May 1921.

108. At the Forth Arab Congress (June 1922) they voted to send a delegation to the Vatican (ISA M4/1, Report to Jerusalem CID, 29 June 1922).

109. Doreen Ingrams, *Palestine Papers, 1917–1922: Seeds of Conflict* (New York: George Braziller, 1973), p. 138; Tsimhoni, 'Arab Christians', p. 88. Francis Newton was the daughter of a former Consul General of Beirut, and worked as a CMS missionary in Palestine until 1914, resigning over disagreements about her rights and responsibilities as a woman. She returned to Palestine in 1919, a private British citizen living in Haifa (see Newton's autobiography, *Fifty Years in Palestine* (London: Britons Publishing Society, 1948).

110. PRO FO 608-99, J. N. Camp to Chief Political Officer, Cairo, 12 August 1919.

111. Newton, *Fifty Years*, p. 127.

112. Tsimhoni, 'The British Mandate', p. 206; Musallam, *Yawmiyat Khalil al-Sakakini*, vol. 3, p. 57. Entry for 25 January 1919.

113. Segev, *One Palestine*, p. 106; CZA J1/8777, Minutes of the fifth assembly of the temporary commission, 9 June 1919.

114. ISA M7/12, MCA Basic Law, 1919.

115. ISA M7/15, Musa Kazim to High Commissioner, 18 December 1920.

116. Segev, *One Palestine*, p. 106.

117. ISA M7/12, Statues of the MCA in Jerusalem, 1919. The document contains a mathematical error; it says the society is composed of forty members, but only accounts for thirty. I have assumed that it should read thirty, leaving Christians with one-third of the seats.

118. McCarthy, *Population of Palestine*, p. 35.

119. In al-Sakakini's account of an MCA meeting held in May 1919, he advocates for a national holiday recognising Arab Independence in conjunction
with the start of the Great Arab Revolt. Muslims and Orthodox Christians
agree readily, but the Latin representatives insist on speaking among themselves prior to agreeing (Musallam, *Yawmiyat Khalil al-Sakakini*, vol. 3,
p. 142. Entry for 3 May 1919).

120. ISA M4/21, Kisch's report on the Sixth Palestinian Arab Congress, 25 June
1923.

121. ISA M1/2, Galilee Military Governor to Headquarters, 24 March 1920;
CZA S25/4380; Miller to Eder, n.d., file from 1922.

122. ISA M1/2, Nazareth Notables to British Deputy Military Governor,
Nazareth, 20 March 1920.

123. ISA M1/2, British Military Governor's Report from Nazareth, 22 March
1920.

124. ISA M1/2, Muslim and Christian Ladies to Chief Administrator, 23 March
1920.

125. Fleishmann explains that the women's movement officially began in
1929 with the first Palestinian Arab Women's Congress, but unofficially
the movement began before that in the organisations founded and run by
Palestinian Arab women, particularly in cities with larger Christian populations. Charitable Orthodox Women's groups were the most important
among these: *Nation and its New Women*, pp. 95–114.

126. For details, see Porath, *Emergence*, pp. 97–8 and Lesch, *Arab Politics*,
pp. 201–4.

127. Segev, *One Palestine*, pp. 128–9; also Musallam, *Yawmiyat Khalil al-
Sakakini*, vol. 3, p. 213. Entry for 4 April 1920.

128. PRO 733-3; April Political Report, 8 May 1921.

129. Segev, *One Palestine*, p. 140.

130. PRO 733-3, Samuel to Churchill, 3 May 1921.

131. PRO 733-3, Samuel to Churchill, 15 May 1921.

132. PRO 733-3, Residents of Tulkarm to Minister of Foreign Affairs, May
1921.

133. PRO 733-3, Samuel to Churchill, 15 May 1921. The Christian, Elias
Mushabek, was an Orthodox member of the Jerusalem MCA (Musallam,
Yawmiyat Khalil al-Sakakini, vol. 2, p. 142. Entry from 25 December 1914).

134. Samih K Farsoun and Naseer Hasan Aruri, *Palestine and the Palestinians:
A Social and Political History* (Boulder, CO: Westview Press, 2006),
pp. 85–6.

135. Lesch, *Arab Politics*, p. 179.

136. See Lesch, *Arab Politics*, pp. 179–97, for details on Legislative Council
proposals and the politics surrounding it.

137. PRO 733/54, Shuckburgh to Secretary of State and others, 11 January 1923.

138. PRO 733/42, Samuel to the Duke of Devonshire, 11 February 1923. The

conditions set forth in Nasif's conversation with Samuel ranged from the acceptable, such as yearly caps on Jewish immigration, to the absolutely unacceptable, such as an Arab emir overseeing Palestine alongside the British high commissioner. Still, the British were very encouraged by the emergence of a moderate elite. In the wake of the Legislative Council's failure, Samuel created a new advisory council. Nasif was invited to participate.

139. *Mirat al-Sharq*, 4 September 1922; English summary in ISA M6/18.
140. PRO M6/20, HC Report on Elections, 11 May 1923. The MCA was suspected of widespread intimidation against those willing to participate; in fact, the Government arrested two MCA members on charges of threatening violence against nominees (Attorney-General to HC, 1 June 1923).
141. PRO M6/20, ʿAbd al-Qadir al-Muzaffar to The Nation, 1923.
142. PRO 733/13, 'Report on the Fourth Arab Congress', 21 June 1921.
143. PRO 733/13, 'Report on the Fourth Arab Congress', 21 June 1921.
144. PRO 733/13, 'Report on the Fourth Arab Congress', 21 June 1921.
145. McCarthy, *Population of Palestine*, p. 37. The percentage of Christians at the congress could have been could have been as high as 18 per cent; see n. 147, below.
146. Christian members were 22 per cent (two of nine) of the Third Congress' executive committee; 17 per cent (four of twenty-three) at the Fifth Congress; and 16 per cent (five of thirty-one) at the Sixth Congress (Tsimhoni, 'The British Mandate', Appendix X, p. 355).
147. While the list of participants found in the report only notes eight Christians, I am able to conclusively add four more, and I have suspicions about the religious affiliation of several others. Regardless, at least twelve Christians were present, and only fourteen of seventy-six voted for Saʿd.
148. CZA S25/6608, 'Several Days with Aref al-ʿAref', by Menacham Kapeliuk, 30 April 1941.
149. Musallam, *Yawmiyat Khalil al-Sakakini*, vol. 3, pp. 158–9. Entry for 25 May 1919.
150. PRO 733/28, Samuel to the Duke of Devonshire, 8 December 1922.
151. Samuel to J. H. Thomas, Secretary of State for the Colonies, 25 February 1924 (Jane Priestland (ed.), *Records of Jerusalem 1917–1971*, vol. 2 (Oxford: Archive Editions, 2002), p. 353).
152. Porath, *Emergence*, pp. 299–300.
153. Tsimhoni, 'The British Mandate', p. 241.
154. See ISA M1/2 for examples of this; the Mayor of Haifa, Hassan Shukhri, was one such figure, as was the entire Abu Gosh clan.
155. See Abigail Jacobson, 'Alternative Voices in Late Ottoman Palestine: A Historical Note', *Jerusalem Quarterly*, 21 (2004), pp. 41–8; and Cohen, *Army of Shadows*, Pt 1, for more about Kalvaryski.
156. Farsoun and Aruri, *Palestine and the Palestinians*, pp. 86–7.
157. The Palestine Club, as it was called, was a controversial use of precious

Zionist funds. See CZA S25/4380, Achuse of Tiberias to Dr Thon, 12 May 1922.

158. PRO 733-7; Political Report, 18 November 1921. The National Muslim Society is also referred to at times as the National Muslim Association.
159. Porath, *Emergence*, p. 217.
160. CZA S25/4380, notes of a NMS meeting at the home of Dr Eder, 3 April 1922.
161. Porath, *Emergence*, p. 216. See also HC to Churchill, 9 August 1921 (Jarman, *Political Diaries*, vol. 1, p. 95) and HC to Churchill, 2 February 1922 (Jarman, *Political Diaries*, vol. 1, pp. 216–17).
162. CZA S25/4380, Political Secretary, ZO London to Dr Thon, Jerusalem, 5 December 1922.
163. CZA S25/665/4, 'On Behalf of the ZE' to Deeds, 30 January 1925.
164. Mordechai Ben-Hillel Hacohen, *The Wars of the Nations* (Jerusalem: Yad Ben-Zvi, 1985) (in Hebrew). As quoted in Segev, *One Palestine*, p. 152 ff. n. 25.
165. CZA S25/PZE to ZO, London, 17 July 1922.
166. S25/4380, Miller to Eder, n.d., probably 1922.
167. PRO 733/13, 'Moslem–Christian Delegation', July 1921.
168. ISA M4/1, to Sir Wyndham Deeds, 30 March 1922.
169. Porath, *Emergence*, p. 126.

2

1923–1929: Christians and a Divided
National Movement

Arab Christians should be the first to recognise the rights of their Moslem Brethren over public positions and support them with the Government [even] though some Christian officials might suffer from the grant[ing] of Moslem demands.[1]

ʿIsa Bandak, 14 January 1928

Many Christians would prefer the protection of a Western power to a Muslim rule headed by Hajj Amin al-Husseini . . . Throughout the British Mandate, Christians tended to rally for the Nashashibi family, who formed the opposition to the Husseini family, [which] based its political support largely on the urban middle class and was less affiliated with Islam.[2]

Daphne Tsimhoni, 'Palestinian Christians and the Peace Process', 1998

In 1931, a group of leaders from the Nashashibi-led National Party demanded that the Husayni-run Supreme Muslim Council stop renting mosques to Christians, complaining that Armenians were storing wine in the *mihrab* of one mosque and someone was keeping pigs in another.[3] Another sign of emerging factionalism occurred in the 1930s when a Nashashibi leader wrote to followers in the Nablus, Jenin and Tulkarm subdistricts alerting them to a large number of Christians in a Husayni delegation to London. Fakhri al-Nashashibi assured regional organisers that raising this issue among the rural population would increase support for the National Party 'in view of the religious susceptibilities of the Moslem fellaheen'.[4] These anecdotes highlight the rising importance of religious differentiation in factional politics as Palestinian Arab nationalist unity devolved into factional fighting.

If the first five years of British rule were marked by the MCA's show of nationalist unity across political and religious lines, the second half of the 1920s was a time of political and religious disunity. The Muslim Christian Association's disintegration in the mid-1920s was triggered by a variety of factors, though no factor was more important than the rise of factionalism between the Husayni and Nashashibi families.[5] On one side was the Husayni clan that had held the office of Mufti of Jerusalem since the seventeenth century; opposing them were the Nashashibis, a notable Jerusalem family since the late 1400s who had been representatives from Jerusalem in the Ottoman legislative body. Their power struggle was enhanced by British policies that exacerbated pre-existing tensions which had been temporarily obscured by the aura of national unity. Rather than espousing a consistent line of Muslim–Christian unity along Arab nationalist lines, the rift between powerful Muslim families opened the door for the emergence of additional social fault lines. Intercommunal tensions had always existed behind the MCA's united front, but those tensions did not cause the MCA to collapse. Rather, the experiment in intercommunal unity was undermined by factionalism which weakened the MCA's goal of a shared Arab identification and led to intercommunal hostilities.

The British appointment of Hajj Amin al-Husayni to two important religious posts, Grand Mufti of Jerusalem and President of the Supreme Muslim Council, provided Palestinian Arabs with a central figure around whom to build the national movement. The British appointment of Raghib al-Nashashibi, replacing Musa Kazim al-Husayni, as mayor of Jerusalem, contributed to the power struggle between the families. The Nashashibis established the National Party to provide an ideological and factional alternative to Husayni-dominated politics. Historians often argue that Christians moved towards the Nashashibi camp for fear that al-Husayni was too religious and that his leadership would alter their position among the nationalist elite. In fact, it was more common for the National Party to encourage anti-Christian sentiments among its Muslim supporters. The simple division between a Muslim/Husayni leadership and a secular Nashashibi-led opposition fails to withstand scrutiny. Rather, Christians based their support for the factional leaders on a number of factors, only one of which was their individual interpretation of the meaning and importance of religion and its relationship to nationalism.

British policies exacerbated communal politics as well. By bolstering al-Husayni in the religious realm, the British inadvertently added religious meaning to the national movement, combining religious and political identification in a way not conceived of by early Arab nationalists in Palestine. As a result, religion became a common point of legitimation and differentiation for the leading factions. The politicisation of religious identification was visible in debates surrounding the foundation of the Young Men's Muslim Association (YMMA), Arab responses to an international missionary conference in Jerusalem, and the debate over the number of Arab Christians working for the British government. With the MCA's non-religious nationalist formula undermined, Christians developed a variety of ways to reaffirm and reformulate their relationship to the movement. Some demanded equality regardless of religion, others accepted Muslim dominance within a nationalist framework, and still others sought enhanced Christian minority rights along the lines of the Ottoman *millet* system.

Factionalism and religious politicisation had profound implications for the Palestinian nationalist movement. Instead of one organisation speaking publicly on behalf of the entire population, two major factions fought (mostly through words, though increasingly with violence) for political power and British attention. For Christians, the divide created particularly pressing problems. Whereas religious unity had been a nationalist tool, factional politics turned religious differentiation into a weapon.

The Impact of British Policy on Arab Society

British policy decisions in the first years of the Mandate upset the balance of power between the prominent Husayni and Nashashibi families. The task of creating free-standing Palestinian governmental institutions was difficult. Local politics could not remain unchanged following the collapse of the Ottoman Empire. A solution to one problem, however, often led to unintended consequences and new difficulties.

Hajj Amin al-Husayni's rise to a position of national and religious importance, due largely to British policies, triggered increased factionalism. One of the most significant problems the British faced was organising the Muslim community which had, during Ottoman times, been subordinate to an imperial Islamic hierarchy based in Istanbul. As Jerusalem's importance grew in the nineteenth century, the Mufti of Jerusalem emerged as a prominent religious figure. When Palestine was severed from Ottoman authority, the British granted the Mufti the additional responsibility of control over the Shariᶜa Court of Appeals in Jerusalem and renamed the position *al-Mufti al-Akbar*, the Grand Mufti. At the time, in the immediate aftermath of the British occupation, this decision made sense: Kamil al-Husayni was Mufti of Jerusalem like his father and grandfather before him, and he agreed to cooperate with the British in exchange for enhanced power. The position became more important upon Kamil's death in 1921 when the British had to appoint a new Grand Mufti.[6]

While not officially a hereditary position, a Husayni had been Mufti of Jerusalem since the seventeenth century. Once powerful throughout the region, the family had been weakened by a number of events in the early twentieth century and needed to retain the position of Mufti in order to retain its traditional importance. Amin al-Husayni, Kamil's younger brother, was chosen as the family candidate. Al-Husayni's role in the Nebi Musa violence of April 1920 tainted his reputation among British officials. He fled to Jordan after the Palin Commission, which had been appointed to investigate the situation, found him guilty of instigating violence. Less than six months later, in August 1920, High Commissioner Herbert Samuel pardoned him, and al-Husayni returned to Jerusalem shortly before his brother's death. Despite the pardon, many in the British and Jewish communities were wary of al-Husayni's ability to serve as Mufti under British rule. He was young and without the proper religious training, but he was bright and well-educated, and the British believed him to understand the position well. More importantly, the British believed he was indebted to the government because of the pardon, and thought he would be amenable to their influence.[7]

The British also appointed Raghib al-Nashashibi as mayor of Jerusalem in 1920, replacing a Husayni, and the new mayor hoped for eventual factional control of Palestinian religious institutions as well.[8] With these hopes in mind, the Nashashibis opposed al-Husayni's appointment and nominated one of their supporters, Husam al-Din Jarallah, a political moderate who was also more religiously qualified.

Historians disagree as to why High Commissioner Samuel fixed the elections in order to have al-Husayni elected as Mufti. Some Zionist scholars suggest it was evidence of Britain's pro-Arab stance, but that seems unlikely.[9] The process was complicated, particularly because al-Husayni did not get enough votes from a council of Muslim clerics to even qualify for consideration. Still, Kamil al-Husayni had served the British well, and Samuel thought that Amin al-Husayni would as well. The Husaynis had broad support throughout Palestine and were able to rally the populace behind them in Amin's favour. The Jaffa violence in 1921 caused Samuel to believe that Arab demands had to be met, and he thought that most Palestinians supported al-Husayni.[10] The hope was that, by siding with the Husaynis, Hajj Amin would return the favour and lead in a moderate fashion. The British also wanted to avoid ordaining a single family with all powerful positions in their newly mandated territory.

Al-Husayni's appointment was met with approval from Arabs around the country, particularly from Muslim leaders, but from outside Islamic circles as well. The Qadi of Jerusalem claimed to speak 'on behalf of the three divine religions, the Moslem, Christian and Jewish and their believers',[11] while head clergy of the Syrian Orthodox, Coptic, Armenian and Greek Orthodox churches wrote personally in support of al-Husayni's nomination. Sulaiman Nasif, a moderate Christian, met with the assistant chief secretary, E. T. Richmond, to voice his support as well.[12]

Despite the presence of the Grand Mufti, severing the connection with Istanbul still left religious institutions under British, and therefore ostensibly Christian, control, creating a situation unacceptable to some Muslims. In response, the British created the Supreme Muslim Council in 1921 to return the religious establishment to Muslim control. The new body controlled religious schools, orphanages, mosques, courts and *awqaf* funds (religious endowments),[13] and in January 1922 Hajj Amin al-Husayni was chosen as the first president of the Council.[14] Once again Raghib al-Nashashibi and the opposition mounted a campaign against him, but this time al-Husayni was elected without controversy.[15] Porath contends that the British, and High Commissioner Samuel in particular, believed that establishing a centralised Muslim leadership parallel to the government-recognised Palestine Zionist Executive which controlled Jewish affairs in Mandate Palestine (established in 1921 and reformulated as the Jewish Agency in 1929) would satisfy Arab demands and reduce political tensions.[16] As with al-Husayni's appointment as Grand Mufti, many Palestinian Arabs viewed the establishment of the SMC as a victory. The AE and various MCA branches wrote to the government expressing their support.[17]

Early indications suggested that Samuel's trust in al-Husayni's calming presence was misplaced. Storrs expressed concern in 1924 that 'the Council is at least as active in political as in religious affairs and surprise is from time to time expressed that the Government should tolerate this almost overt intervention in politics on the part of persons in receipt of official emoluments.'[18] The SMC also failed to unify the Muslim community, instead filling official posts with Husayni supporters who adhered to al-Husayni's political ideology. British officials noted that sheikhs, qadis and other religious officials who did not toe the party line were dismissed, and minor officials appointed by the SMC knew that 'their tenure of office would become insecure unless they displayed enthusiasm for the "National Cause"'.[19] Al-Husayni used the powers granted to him by the British to bring other Palestinians into line with his goals or to dismiss them as traitors. In essence, al-Husayni took advantage of the vast powers of the SMC to become the most powerful Palestinian Arab nationalist leader and to create a 'state within a state', undermining Britain's effectiveness.[20]

While al-Husayni became a nationalist icon, it is important not to overstate his personal role in the day-to-day political affairs of the national movement in the mid-1920s, though other members of his extended family were also highly influential. As Grand Mufti and SMC President, al-Husayni provided moral support to the nationalist movement, but the AE remained at the centre of Arab diplomatic efforts.[21] Even though Hajj

Amin was not in direct control of the AE, it was closely allied to the SMC and received funding and political legitimacy through that relationship. It was, in fact, controlled by Musa Kazim al-Husayni, the former mayor of Jerusalem, while Jamal al-Husayni served as secretary. Despite the alliance and close familial connections between al-Husayni and the AE, the Executive did not use Islamic language in its petitions to the government, nor did it employ MCA rhetoric of Muslim–Christian unity, even though the AE was created at the behest of that organisation.[22] Instead, the AE generally left aside religious references of all sorts in favour of non-religious categorisation of the Arab community.

The AE's most important task throughout the 1920s was to continue presenting the Palestinian Arab perspective to the Mandate government, and it also maintained contacts with the League of Nations.[23] The process of negotiating with the British was arduous and frustrating, and the AE brought about very little change in British policy. Al-Husayni's personal role was quite different. While he occasionally and cautiously challenged Zionism and even British policies, the British had given him religious power in exchange for political moderation. Instead of serving as an overt political body, the SMC served to strengthen Muslim institutions, national identity and religious legitimacy for its supporters, including those in more overtly political positions.[24] Thus, while the SMC was not explicitly political, in the sense that it did not, for instance, actively petition the government to abandon the Balfour Declaration, it was clear that al-Husayni was the leader of all segments of the faction. Even this distinction was undermined when, in 1927, the AE faltered due to financial reasons and AE secretary and leading nationalist Jamal al-Husayni accepted a post as secretary of the SMC.[25]

The relationship between political organisation and religious identification was not always clear. That al-Husayni, as Grand Mufti and head of the Supreme Muslim Council, was recognised by most Palestinians as the head of the nationalist movement says much about the ideological basis of Palestinian nationalism. One biographer argues that al-Husayni's initiatives 'during the 1920s stimulated an Islamic revival throughout Palestine',[26] and Ann Lesch argues that al-Husayni's role as a religious leader prevented him from becoming a truly national political leader.[27] This contention is predicated on the assumption that 'true' nationalism is essentially secular. Yet many among the British believed that Palestinian Arab nationalism was closely connected with Islam,[28] and their policies empowered a leader who further blurred that distinction. Al-Husayni's political leadership, joined closely with his religious leadership, certainly affected the way Palestinians understood the relationship between religion and politics. Palestinian Christians were certainly aware of the potential conflict: a 1925 article in *al-Karmil*, a newspaper edited by Najib Nassar, described the Council as 'the vanguard of the Nationalist movement, despite its being a religious body'.[29]

When the British granted Hajj Amin al-Husayni religious authority, al-Husayni transformed that power into political authority as well, merging religious and political ideologies. The tendency to blur religious and political authority was not new in the 1920s, but it is notable that al-Husayni was the only nationalist leader in Palestine, and indeed in the whole of the twentieth-century Middle East, 'whose base of power was a "traditional" religious institution, albeit a newly invented one'.[30] After the initial dream of a pan-Arab state evaporated, the nationalist leadership sought alternative means of political organisation. The British refused to grant the Arab elite political legitimacy within the Mandate system, so the Arab leadership utilised the cultural resource most immediately available: Islam.

Islam not only served as a rallying point for most of Palestine's local population, but also provided a way to involve neighbouring countries. According to Nels Johnson:

> no other single ideological idiom could speak to the outside world's vast Muslim population, for whom the prospect of Jerusalem under non-Muslim control was anathema. No other single idiom held so much potential threat for the British, who feared a backlash among their Muslim masses, among whom the concept of a secular nationalism was foreign. And none other was so totally and legitimately monopolized by the *aʾyan* [notables].[31]

The same elite Arabs who controlled nationalist organisations also controlled religious ones and used them towards the same end. In the inter-Arab struggle for power that marked the second half of the 1920s and beyond, various elite elements struggled for control of Islamic institutions and rhetoric because religion in various forms was among the most important tools of political control.

The National Party and its Christian Supporters

The Nashashibi-affiliated National Party (*al-Hizb al-Watani*) was founded in 1923, serving to formalise the Nashashibi opposition following the new Husayni monopoly on official religious leadership. While the initial point of conflict between the Husaynis and Nashashibis was based on relatively long-standing inter-family politics, the opposition quickly developed an alternative political approach to the Mandate as a way to differentiate itself from the Husayni faction.

Like the MCA, the National Party stated in its platform that 'Palestine should remain Arab for its inhabitants, clean from all European and Zionist influence', and it insisted on non-recognition of the Balfour Declaration or Palestine as a homeland for the Jews.[32] In fact, in order to compensate for its opposition status and early financial support from the Zionists, the National Party sought to appear even more anti-Zionist than the AE.[33] Both the Husayni and Nashashibi factions avoided using religion as a political tool in official correspondence with the British. In fact, they continued (to a somewhat lesser extent than in previous years) to promulgate the concept of interreligious unity. Beyond these publicly espoused ideologies, differences prevailed. According to Mattar, Raghib al-Nashashibi 'once told a friend that he would oppose any position that the Mufti took', which helps to explain his divergence from some standard nationalist policies.[34] Some joined the opposition because they, like al-Nashashibi, were dissatisfied with al-Husayni himself.[35]

For most supporters of the opposition, the MCA's failure to meet any of its main goals led them to reconsider the movement's main premise of opposition to British rule. Thus, the chief difference between the parties was that the National Party was willing to work openly with the British in exchange for British support for their party. Some wealthy Palestinians, fearful that non-cooperation with the British could lead to financial injury, joined the Nashashibis out of self-interest.[36] Others truly believed that the best way to defeat Zionism was to work with the British and encourage the abandonment of the Balfour Declaration through cooperation instead of protest. Collaborating with the British remained a contentious issue, however, because most nationalists continued to view support for the British as tantamount to cooperating with the Zionists, something the National Party tried to publicly avoid. In later years, when the Husayni–Nashashibi rift turned violent, the National Party took its support for the British to an extreme, establishing 'peace bands' to fight against Arab rebels during the 1936–9 revolt.

Hajj Amin al-Husayni's authority over Islamic religious institutions highlights a second difference between the two Arab factions. Husayni supporters were willing to use religious differentiation as a critical division between Arabs and Jews. The National Party, due to its lack of religious credentials, sought to abandon religious rhetoric altogether and made a conscious decision to refrain from attacking Jews on religious grounds. The MCA had commonly blamed the conflict on all Jewish immigrants,[37] accused Jews of adhering to Bolshevism,[38] protested the opening of Hebrew University,[39] and, in an article in ʿIsa Bandak's *Sawt al-Shaʿb*, accused 'Christian Europe' of handing over the 'Christian Kaaba' to the

Jews while the Islamic world defended Palestine.[40] Instead of pursuing religious labelling or slander, or even blaming Arab problems on the Jews, the National Party sought to focus on political arguments. In May 1924, the editor of *Mirat al-Sharq*, Bulus Shihada (a Protestant Christian), condemned assaults on Judaism and insisted on distinguishing between Judaism as a religion and Zionism as a political movement.[41] In addition, Tsimhoni suggests that the National Party as a whole 'endeavoured to make a distinction between religion and politics and its affiliation with Islam . . . less pronounced' than that of the AE and SMC.[42] The National Party's funding from Zionist sources may have depended on this approach.

While such a distinction may have been true at times, the National Party utilised religious argumentation when advantageous. When writing to the Imam of Yemen in June 1924, National Party president Sheikh Sulaiman al-Taji al-Farouki painted the party leadership as a Muslim answer to a Muslim problem. The new party was, he argued, the solution to the 'greed of certain Moslems, coupled with tricks of foreign colonization' that have led to conflict among Muslims.[43] In reality, the National Party's insistence on a separation of politics and religion was an anti-SMC ploy, since splitting the religious and political leadership would weaken al-Husayni's power.

Throughout the 1920s, the opposition grew in strength, and later in the decade the opposition nearly overpowered the Husayni faction.[44] In 1927, its candidates defeated SMC-supported candidates in the Jerusalem municipal elections.[45] A year later the opposition even emerged from the Seventh Palestinian Congress as the more powerful party in a revitalised AE.[46] National Party advances were stemmed only when the 1929 Wailing Wall crisis provided al-Husayni with the opportunity to re-establish his position as the country's most powerful Arab leader.[47]

Christian responses to the rise in factional politics varied, though some of the most prominent members of that community certainly supported the National Party. The British (and many later historians) interpreted this as evidence of widespread Christian support for the opposition and inferred that religious and political affiliations were connected. Newspaper editors were some of the most visible Christians of the day, and some were early participants in the National Party. Bulus Shihada of *Mirat al-Sharq* was among its founders and, over the next five years, many other high-profile Christians joined as well. Historians often explain this tendency by arguing that al-Husayni's leadership was too religiously charged for many Christians.[48] While it is true that al-Husayni integrated religion and politics, this explanation fails to explain why some important Christians remained firmly in the Husayni camp or why many Muslims also joined the opposition. The actions of Christian newspaper editors are not indicative of the views of all Christians. Their decision to join the opposition was based on a number of factors, of which communal identification was only one. In fact, Christians, like Muslims, were divided, with some supporting the Husaynis and others the Nashashibis. Examining the nature of disagreement among Christians can provide an explanation of the varied meanings of religious identification, a far more helpful pursuit than relying on religious stereotyping.

One common explanation for Christian support of the National Party is that Christians were, for personal or financial reasons, more inclined to work more closely with the government.[49] British officials assumed their shared religious affiliation with Arab Christians would lead to closer relations with the government. In reality, those Christians who supported the British did so for a variety of reasons. A few Christians, such as Sulaiman Nasif, had been advocates of strong Arab–British relations from the beginning of British rule, and confirmed British hopes.[50] Najib Nassar advocated acceptance of British rule explicitly because he believed British support was essential for defeating Zionism. While Nashashibi resistance to the SMC may have been based in anti-Husayni sentiments, it is important to note that Christian participation, at least according to this explanation, had little to do with religion. The common theme for these Christians was pragmatism, and they supported the opposition because they believed that it provided the best path to a solution to Zionism. Yet while some high profile Christians advocated working with the colonial government, they were the minority within their religious community. Most Christians remained staunch opponents of the British.

The other common explanation for Christian support of the opposition was, as Tsimhoni argues, Christians' 'growing fears of Muslim extremism'.[51] Yet this is an equally inadequate explanation despite its popularity among scholars of the period. The blurred distinction between the national movement and the Muslim religious establishment was indeed a concern for some Christians, but neither they nor their Muslim counterparts were in agreement on how to respond. Some Christians and Muslims alike criticised the SMC, while other Christians and Muslims maintained their support for al-Husayni. Even the YMMA, known for its emphasis on challenging missionary activity and encouraging stronger religiosity among Muslims, wrote to the government in 1925 to complain about al-Husayni's personal power over Islamic institutions and to request government oversight of the SMC elections.[52] Some Christians, though, regarded Raghib al-Nashashibi, the shadow president of the National Party and mayor of Jerusalem, as a friend of their community. He was European-educated, married to a Christian woman and, according to al-Sakakini, 'there [was] not, among the important Muslims, another who mingle[d] with Christians more than Ragheb Bey'.[53] Al-Nashashibi would not, some believed, abandon the Christian community. But for Sakakini, at least, al-Nashashibi's good relations with Christians were not enough; he remained committed to the Husayni faction.

Christian Politics in an Unsettled Environment: Defining Communal Identification

The differing political perspectives espoused by Arab Christians reflected their varying assessments of the relationship between national and communal identification. Many factors played into Christians' decision-making and understanding of political opportunity, but religion in its various meanings was an essential element of Christian self-identification and identification by others. Religious identification became more prominent during the 1920s as a result of the increased Islamic rhetoric used by some Palestinian Muslims, particularly the YMMA, in defining their national goals. In response, within a divided national movement that developed throughout the decade, Christian leaders developed a variety of nuanced interpretations of their status and role in society.

Analysts of 'minority-group aspirations' have divided minority demands into two basic categories: one demanding 'recognition, access, participation', with the other seeking 'separation, autonomy, independence'.[54] With few exceptions in this period, Christians considered separation to be neither desirable nor viable. The Christian population was too small, on the one hand, and was too bound up with the Palestinian Arab nationalist movement, on the other. Islam and nationalism may have been increasingly connected, but that did not trump Christian dedication to the national project.

Assessing the political views of the non-elite class is extremely difficult during this period due to the absence of documentation. Still, even the more accessible elite voices provide enough variation and contrast to suggest some of the ways in which Christians understood their shifting place in Palestinian society. Bulus Shihada, ᶜIsa al-ᶜIsa and ᶜIsa Bandak represent different attitudes and approaches to the nationalist divide: Shihada was among the founders of the National Party; al-ᶜIsa switched his allegiance to the National Party in 1927; and Bandak maintained his support for the Husaynis into the next decade.[55] These three figures provide examples of the influence that generation, geography and denomination have on individual political perspectives.

There is little biographical information available about Bulus Shihada, a Protestant, from the Ottoman period. He began publishing *Mirat al-Sharq* in Jerusalem in 1918, for the first few years in both Arabic and English.[56] Although he was active in the MCA, Shihada also sought to maintain good relations with the British. His initial inclination towards cooperation with the British remained, and he became a founding member of the National Party in 1923.

Immediately after the formation of the National Party, Shihada published the new party's critique of the SMC in *Mirat al-Sharq*, the party's official organ. His critique of the SMC created a firestorm of protest by organisations allied with the SMC, including the AE and the MCA. A group of Muslim notables from the Hebron district supported Shihada, arguing that 'the attacks of Miraat Al Shark against the Supreme Moslem Council contain nothing that affects the Moslem Religion and are merely political differences'.[57] Other National Party supporters simply voiced their approval of the new party. In addition, some Muslims also voiced dissatisfaction with al-Husayni and the SMC, but counter-attacks on Shihada often cited his religious affiliation as a major concern. The Moslem Society at Haifa declared that it would 'confirm the Moslem Council with all its power and regard every insult directed to the Supreme Muslim Council as directed to the whole Moslem Nation'.[58] The 'Youngmen of Tulkarem' offered general criticism of Shihada and 'his party',[59] while Gaza notables were more direct in their counter-attack on *Mirat al-Sharq*'s editor:

> Your Excellency is no doubt aware of the affronts put by Bulos Shehadeh, who is a Christian, upon the Supreme Moslem Council, which is the highest Moslem religious authority ... Such transgression on morale, humanity, liberty of Islam and public order, naturally stirs up the religious spirit of the Moslem Nation.[60]

A protest from Jaffa declared that 'had such affronts been offered by a Moslem to a Christian or Jewish religious authority, a great trouble would have resulted therefrom'.[61] Both groups called on the government to punish Shihada. Immediately, then, the emergence of the National Party led to intercommunal finger-pointing.

Husayni supporters also accused Shihada of supporting Zionism, a claim based in truth. Shihada and other members of the National Party may not have openly supported Zionism, but they were secretly on the payroll of the Zionist Executive. A 1924 letter from Kisch to Kalvaryski discussing payoffs to another Arab informer has a handwritten addendum: 'Merat El Shark. L20 for 3 months. Dec. Jan. Feb.'[62] In exchange for Zionist support, Shihada tempered his critiques of Zionism and instead challenged the SMC and other Husayni-affiliated groups such as the MCA, which he argued was 'a small party of extremists who make a lot of noise but there is a larger party, the cautious National Party, who in sorrow and distress see the abyss to which these extremists are leading the nation'.[63] Suspicions about his secret connections to Zionists led to sharp reactions from SMC supporters, and in 1925, Husayni-affiliated youths burned the newspaper's offices during a protest against the opposition.[64]

Shihada also incorporated support of the British in his critique of the SMC. The title of an ongoing series in 1924 read, 'This is Not What We Wanted to Allow the SMC [to do]', later shortened to 'This is Not What We Wanted'.[65] The articles suggested that the British had made a goodwill gesture by turning over control of the *awqaf* to the SMC, but that al-Husayni had squandered the opportunity and failed to manage the funds properly. Shihada's newspaper also published the opinions of various anti-Husayni Muslims, such as the director of Gaza's *awqaf*, Amin Mitwalli, who demanded that Hajj Amin manage *awqaf* income more transparently.[66] The National Party backed Shihada by sending letters directly to the government outlining the SMC's alleged abuses of power.[67] While at least three other Christian-edited newspapers, *al-Karmil*, *Lisan al-Arab* and *al-Nafir*, also supported the opposition and British policies, only Shihada was targeted in reprisals. This suggests that Shihada's religion was not the real issue, but rather his active role in founding the opposition and collusion with the Zionists.[68]

Not surprisingly, SMC supporters accused Shihada and the National Party of sabotaging nationalist goals by dividing the movement. Shihada most clearly fitted the predicted Christian mould in his open criticism of what he saw as the Islamicisation of the Husayni power structure. Lesch, Tsimhoni and Porath all agree that this was the primary basis for National Party support among Christians. Shihada answered the shift towards Islamic rhetoric by downplaying the Christian element of his identity, while also arguing that Islam should not be the primary identifier for Palestine's Muslims. In a front-page letter rebuking Hassan al-Dajani, a politician and AE supporter from a well-respected family, Shihada declared, 'your right in this country is not greater than my right because you are a Muslim and I am a Christian . . . we are, all of us, citizens of Palestine'. He continued, 'You are trying to make Palestine a country of Muslims and Christians and I am trying to make Palestine an Arabic country, since there is no liberation for us except if Muslims and Christians are Arab before all things.'[69] Even when not focusing explicitly on the SMC, Shihada hoped that 'perhaps [Palestine] will change its policies in connection with the leaders who have no other interests besides that of the country and all its inhabitants without distinction of creed and religion'.[70] The concern for Christians was whether Shihada's religious arguments would serve to exacerbate mild sectarian tendencies instead of encouraging non-religious Palestinian national identification.

Shihada's support for Britain and the support received from Zionists served to undermine his nationalist credentials, making it all the more difficult to know how seriously others took his call for secular Arabism. The Arab public knew, or assumed anyway, that Shihada and the whole of the National Party were in collaboration with the Zionists, and many of them were. Hillel Cohen summarises Shihada's situation clearly: 'Shihada seems to have thought of himself as a politician searching for a solution to the crisis. For the Zionists, he was a source of information, while in the eyes of the Palestinian mainstream, he was a collaborator.'[71]

ᶜIsa al-ᶜIsa came to support the National Party through a different path. His home town of Jaffa was one of the cities most affected by Zionist immigration because of the new Jewish city of Tel Aviv sprouting up nearby. The town's local newspaper, *Filastin*, was among the most radical of the Arab newspapers in the early 1920s. In 1921, publication of the paper was suspended, and its editor al-ᶜIsa was tried for incitement. When publication resumed, the newspaper printed an article boasting that 'within two months, the newspaper had been suppressed twice and taken to court once for "its nationalist mood"'.[72]

When *Mirat al-Sharq* levelled its attacks against the SMC, *Filastin* was the first to criticise the opposition for fracturing the national movement.[73] Al-ᶜIsa wrote hopefully of efforts to ease tensions among the Arab elite, expressing a desire to end the factional dispute which might undermine the opposition's very existence.[74] He explicitly blamed Shihada for fostering dissention within Palestinian society,[75] and discounted the National Party as a fringe minority.[76]

Al-ᶜIsa blamed inter-family politics for the political rift, and pushed hard for the opposition to fall back in line behind al-Husayni's leadership. He was cautious, trying not to exacerbate tensions even more. Even while criticising the new party, al-ᶜIsa suggested that the mainstream nationalist movement should be willing to accept National Party supporters if they could prove that they were interested in healing the nationalist rift and could demonstrate their dedication to the Palestinian cause.[77] Rather than rebuke the opposition, he tried to gently encourage them back into the fold. In 1924, he organised a Palestinian Arab Journalists' Conference attended by ten journalists from around the country, including Shihada, Bandak and al-ᶜIsa. The purpose of the conference was to advocate for 'national reconciliation'.[78]

Figure 2.1 Khalil al-Sakakini (bottom left): politician, educator and Arab nationalist.
Courtesy of the Sakakini Center and Institute of Jerusalem Studies

Al-ʿIsa represents a very different perspective to that of Shihada on the Christian role in Arab society. Rather than assume Arabness as divorced from religion, early in the 1920s al-ʿIsa argued that Islam was a foundational element of Arab society, for Christians and Muslims alike. As the Husayni–Nashashibi rift began to widen late in 1923, *Filastin* published an article declaring that the Prophet Muhammad was 'the greatest Arab man, and it is appropriate for every Arab to be proud of him and share in his glory, not in the name of religion [but] in the name of nationalism', and he argued that gatherings in honour of the Prophet's birthday were more nationalist than religious.[79] That is, he accepted Islam as a foundational element of Arabness by acknowledging the prophet's central role in Arabs' historical memory, a tactic that played well to the Muslim majority.

Al-ʿIsa, for years a stalwart supporter of the Husaynis, left the faction in 1927. He did not immediately join the National Party, instead founding a party of his own, *al-Hizb al-Hurr al-Filastini* (Free Party of Palestine), although ultimately he and his paper became fully associated with the

Nashashibis.[80] The timing of his shift in allegiance merits some attention, since the reason was not obvious, unlike Najib Nassar of *al-Karmil*, who immediately supported the British following the First World War, or Shihada, who helped initiate the National Party. On the contrary, Zionist immigration had decreased dramatically in the mid-1920s, with more Jews leaving Palestine than arriving in 1927, with immigration numbers remaining below 5,000 a year for the rest of the decade. Efforts were underway to reunify the Arab national movement, with various factions weighing in on the structure of the Seventh Arab Congress to be held in June 1928.[81] Two events may have contributed to his decision: first, the Husayni family continued to solidify control of the party by founding its own newspaper in 1927, *al-Jamiʿa al-ʿArabiyya*. Until that point al-ʿIsa's paper had been one of the party's most important mouthpieces, and the creation of a family-run paper marginalised his efforts. Secondly, the National Party performed well in the Jerusalem municipal elections in 1927, finally emerging as a credible alternative to the Husayni-dominated faction. Al-ʿIsa's marginalisation in the Husayni camp, coupled with the growing strength of the opposition, may have triggered his decision to change sides.

Al-ʿIsa's view of minority relations in Palestinian politics shifted along with his political allegiance. In articles following his departure from the Husayni camp, he no longer highlighted Islam's importance as a foundational element of Arab identity. Al-ʿIsa did not address this issue openly in *Filastin*, but he appeared to seek an alternative foundation for Arabness, one shared by Christians and Muslims. In the late 1920s, he simply stopped talking about the importance of Islam as he had earlier in the decade. Furthermore, contrary to most Christian notables, he justified the international Christian presence in Palestine, using an historical argument to describe the importance of the Holy Land to Christians.[82] Finally, *Filastin* published a poem in 1930 that located the origins of Arab identity prior to Islam: 'Before Jesus and Muhammad we were already Arab', the poet claims. 'What is [my country's] religion, but that Christians are brothers to Muslims?'[83] Rather than nationalise Muhammad, as he had done when supporting the SMC, this poem reflects al-ʿIsa's desire to move towards ethnic, instead of religious, nationalism.

Not surprisingly, al-ʿIsa's abandonment of the Husaynis brought about retaliation in the pages of the Husayni press. Yet the editor of *al-Jamiʿa al-ʿArabiyya* was careful not to turn his attacks on al-ʿIsa into an opportunity for communalist tension, as had occurred five years earlier when Husayni supporters attacked Shihada for his criticism of the SMC. The *al-Jamiʿa al-ʿArabiyya* editorial questioning al-ʿIsa's criticism of the

Supreme Muslim Council distinguished carefully between those who were undermining the national cause (like al-ᶜIsa) and the Christian community at large. Rather than labelling all Christians as anti-Muslim, the journalist called on 'our reasonable Orthodox Christian brothers for whom al-ᶜIsa claims his paper speaks' to speak for themselves.[84] Still, someone must have protested because the paper published a follow-up article clarifying that it disapproved only of al-ᶜIsa and was not anti-Christian.[85] Christian fears of being communally identified, despite their best efforts to remain outside such categorisation, are confirmed here. Al-ᶜIsa never claimed to speak in the name of Orthodox Christians, although some observers made the connection anyway.

ᶜIsa Bandak's newspaper, *Sawt al-Shaᶜb* (Voice of the People), provided an intensely different picture of Palestinian politics to that of his colleagues at *Mirat al-Sharq* and *Filastin*. In fact, Bandak's arguments more closely paralleled those of *al-Jamiᶜa al-ᶜArabiyya*, the mouthpiece of the SMC/AE, than those in other Christian-owned papers. Yet as an active Christian himself, with a long history of supporting Christian causes in Palestine and the Palestinian diaspora, Bandak's critiques of other Christians did not raise communalist tensions.

Unlike the newspapers discussed above, Bandak paid very close attention to local religious issues, such as the Orthodox problem and a conflict between Bethlehem Latins and Patriarch Barlassina. In nearly every issue of *Sawt al-Shaᶜb*, he published articles such as 'The Arab Catholic Awakening',[86] 'The Franciscan School in Bethlehem'[87] and 'The Vatican and Church Unity'.[88] Despite his focus on Christian politics and issues at the local level, on the national level Bandak was very supportive of al-Husayni's nationalist leadership. He praised Muslims for protecting Arab Christian rights,[89] and when ᶜIsa al-ᶜIsa published an article in support of the opposition, Bandak was quick to accuse the editor of *Filastin* of using communalist politics to drive a wedge between segments of society.[90] He accused al-ᶜIsa of being in the service of the colonialists who employed 'the wicked and vile members of the nation to break the bonds of unity between the Muslims and Arab Christians!'[91] In subsequent articles, he directly accused al-ᶜIsa of spreading false accusations and slander against Muslim nationalist leaders and of 'trying to serve the imperialists through the revival of religious pride'.[92]

Bandak replaced Shihada's secular nationalism and al-ᶜIsa's acknowledgement of Islam's historical importance with full acceptance of Islamic nationalism. As the SMC became more prominent and Islamic rhetoric was increasingly coupled with Palestinian Arab political goals, the non-communal nationalism advocated by many Christians became increasingly compromised. Rather than fight the rise of Islamic nationalism with either secularism or a parallel form of Christian nationalism, Bandak's commentaries took on a decidedly anti-Western Christian, pro-Islamic tone. In his criticism of al-ᶜIsa, Bandak justified Muslim resentment of Christians by blaming a small group of Christian sectarians.[93] And when national debates erupted over the dearth of Muslim government employees, Bandak published an editorial titled 'Injustice to Muslim Rights' in which he agreed with Muslim concerns about their lack of representation in the workforce.[94]

The Mandate government was the primary focus of Bandak's criticisms. As described above, he argued that the government was behind al-ᶜIsa's actions and those of the National Party as a whole. Bandak argued that while the First World War was originally a display of interreligious and international solidarity against both Muslim and Christian enemies, the British turned it into a Protestant crusade against Islamic Palestine.[95] Britain's pro-Christian bias was also evident, he claimed, when in 1929 the mandatory government offered emergency assistance to Christians before helping Muslims after an earthquake damaged both the Orthodox Club and a mosque in Jaffa.[96]

Unlike Shihada and al-ᶜIsa, Bandak supported al-Husayni throughout the 1920s. Other Christian leaders, like al-Sakakini, also backed al-Husayni, but Bandak remained active in Orthodox denominational issues, whereas Sakakini sought to distance himself from his religious grouping. For Bandak, there was no contradiction in fighting for both communal and national goals.

What was it that caused Bandak to take this approach? A few unique factors stand out in Bandak's biographical background that shed light on his divergence from other members of the Christian elite. Once again, coming from the Christian town of Bethlehem was highly significant. While not elected mayor of the town until 1934, Bandak knew that the top local office was monopolised by Christians. In a sense all local issues in Bethlehem were Christian issues, and he neither wanted nor tried to remove the Christian element from his local activities. When organising local citizens in efforts to increase literacy and spread nationalism in the region, the 'secular educational' Young Men's Club was comprised largely, if not solely, of Christians.[97]

Bandak was the local spokesman for his home town in national affairs, representing Bethlehem and the surrounding subdistrict on the AE from 1920 until 1934.[98] Bethlehem became an important city during the Mandate because of its status as a subdistrict centre, but it was still a small city and, compared with Jaffa, Jerusalem and Haifa, experienced much less direct impact from Zionist immigration. Although there were many Muslims in the surrounding villages, interreligious relations were not as politically charged as those in the larger, religiously mixed cities, and even Bandak's seat on the AE was geographically, not communally, determined.

As described in Chapter 1, Bandak's educational and international experiences were quite different to those of the traditional Christian elite class. Bandak never did attend college, and his plans to travel abroad were dashed by the onset of the First World War. Instead, he visited only nearby Arab regions while working for the Ottomans.[99] Moreover, the high levels of Arab emigration from the Middle East during the nineteenth and early twentieth centuries, particularly among Christians, shaped his approach to religious identification and also influenced his view of British and Zionist influence in Palestine.[100] Christian flight from Palestine to the West was seriously endangering the religion in the place where it originated.[101] The result of these experiences was that Bandak's first interaction with Europe or Europeans (with the exception of religious and medical religious missions in Bethlehem) was the Mandate and the Balfour Declaration. Rather than being enamoured with the education and social practices of Europeans, as some Palestinians were, Bandak saw Europe as a threat to the regional Christian community, not a solution.

Finally, and perhaps most importantly, there was a generational difference between Bandak and the other newspaper editors. While generation generally refers to age or age groupings, it can also involve, according to John Collins, a 'more discursive notion of "generation" as describing processes through which social identities and political projects are symbolically produced, reproduced, and transformed'.[102] While Shihada and al-ʿIsa were part of a generation who had achieved its elite status based on wealth, family and political connections, Bandak began both his professional and political careers during the period of transition from Ottoman to British rule. Moreover, Nassar and al-ʿIsa started publishing their newspapers in 1908 and 1916, respectively, with Shihada founding *Mirat al-Sharq* following the First World War. Most importantly, Bandak's Arabness was among the first solid labels he adopted as a young man. This difference, in combination with the geographical one, helps to explain his different approach to the British, the SMC and the changing face of Palestinian nationalism.

Divisive Issues of Communal Importance

Internal conflict and continued (albeit uneven) Zionist expansion were the driving forces of Palestinian self-examination, but the divergent and nuanced perspectives of Arab Christians are illuminated by their varied responses to three major issues that emerged during the 1920s which highlighted communal identification. First, the merger of nationalist and Islamic rhetoric, particularly as used by the YMMA, was emblematic of religious tensions that threatened the MCA's discourse of intercommunal unity. Secondly, the YMMA and other Muslim organisations protested an international missions conference held in Jerusalem in 1928. Thirdly, the high percentage of Christians in government service, a perennial topic of debate, emerged in 1925 as a major catalyst of intercommunal tension.

The Husayni–Nashashibi rift broke the monopoly on nationalist rhetoric enjoyed by the MCA in the early 1920s and opened the political field to additional voices. Some Muslims believed that Mandate institutions discriminated against them, a sentiment that encouraged greater communal organisation. In 1924, a British official suggested that Muslims resented their diminishing 'supremacy over Christians and Jews' and sought to 'quicken the religious (Islamic) sentiment which is the principal motive force in Moslem political action',[103] an assertion that seems valid in describing the sentiments of at least Palestinian Muslims. Zionist Executive leader Kisch cited opposition to missionary activity and 'the increasing predominance of the Christians among the Arab officials employed by Government' as causes of Muslim organisation.[104] He also refers to the group as a 'youth movement', signifying the beginning of elite loss of control over Arab political discourse.

Among the new organisations resulting from these sentiments was the YMMA, a group dedicated to preserving Muslim rights. The broader organisation, which was a direct response to the British-associated YMCA, was founded in Egypt in the mid-1920s to 'preserve Islamic values and learning among young Muslim men'.[105] In 1928, Palestinian Muslims formed their own branch to challenge what they believed to be Britain's preferential treatment of Christians, both internationally and locally. ʿIzz al-Din al-Qassam, a Muslim cleric who fled Syria for Palestine following his resistance to French rule and who became a driving force in the militarisation of the Palestinian resistance in the early 1930s, was among the founders of the Haifa branch.[106] It comes as no surprise that an active Muslim organisation developed in Palestine at this point, since similar developments were taking place across the Arab world in the wake of the Islamic reform movement founded by figures such as Jamal al-Din al-Afghani, Rashid Rida and Muhammad ᶜAbduh.[107] The most famous and long-lasting organisation to emerge during that time period was the Egyptian Muslim Brotherhood, founded by Hasan al-Banna in 1928. The Brotherhood itself became directly involved in Palestine in the 1930s.[108]

The YMMA was ostensibly a social organisation and its branches were, according to Lesch, 'relatively independent' of the SMC and other Islamic institutions.[109] Its charter explicitly stated: 'This society does not engage in politics . . . The society does not involve itself in factional disputes and no member is permitted to use it for that.'[110] Yet while formally a non-political organisation, many members of the YMMA took an active role in politics. In 1932, the government shut down the organisation's Acre branch 'owing to the Association's complete departure from its avowed social, non-political objects'.[111] And despite officially standing outside the nationalist rift, Lesch asserts that 'their pan-Islamic and anti-Christian tendencies were supported by such conservative (and anti-SMC) leaders as Sulaiman al-Taji al-Faruqi, former head of the National Party and editor of the newspaper *al-Jamiᶜa al-Islamiyya*'.[112] In fact, the YMMA could not escape the Husayni–Nashashibi conflict: both the Acre and Jaffa branches eventually split along pro-SMC/anti-SMC lines.[113]

Despite the specifically Muslim origins and purpose of the YMMA, historian Weldon Matthews argues that the organisation is better understood as a predecessor to the Arab *Istiqlal* (Independence) Party, a nationalist party founded in the early 1930s. Indeed, he argues, many of the party's founders had previously been involved in YMMA activities.[114] Such a relationship between the YMMA, an organisation founded to protect Muslim interests, and Istiqlal, an explicitly pan-Arab political party, suggests that for some YMMA members, the issues at stake were more political than religious. Islamic solidarity was simply the best way to achieve their goals in the 1920s, while in the 1930s many of the same activists opted for pan-Arabism.

Regardless of the reasons for adopting a communally-based organisation, the Islamic nature of the group politicised religious identification, and some Christians, such as Shihada, viewed them with apprehension. While not often addressing the YMMA directly, Shihada did challenge the rising tendency towards communal identification, continually insisting that Christians and Muslims had a shared culture, political situation and historical narrative.[115] Al-ᶜIsa challenged the religiously charged environment by ignoring it. Religion only rarely appeared in *Filastin* headlines, and usually as a functional descriptor instead of as an opportunity for discussing communalist trends or conflicts.

Bandak took a different approach. Despite differences between the YMMA and the SMC, Bandak used similar arguments in defence of both Islamic institutions. As explained above, in his support of the SMC, Bandak accepted Islamic nationalism as a driving ideology for Palestinian Arabs of all religions. Bandak condemned what he called *Filastin*'s 'disgusting attacks against the most important Islamic personalities in the country',[116] and he supported YMMA communal organisation, arguing that the group was defending Islam rather than attacking Christianity.[117] He argued, in effect, that the SMC should participate in leading the nationalist movement *because* of its religious standing. He also insisted that Christians must remain secular nationalists rather than turning towards communal organisation as well.

Despite their different sources and functions, the SMC and the YMMA incidentally collaborated in one important area: the transformation of the political discourse. Rather than focusing on issues of national concern from a position of intercommunal unity, as the MCA had done, these groups focused more attention on the religious impact of British rule and the Zionist threat. The AE was still in operation throughout the 1920s and continued to utilise non-religious nationalist language, but that approach was no longer the strongest Arab voice. When the YMMA claimed to protect Islamic interests, the SMC was forced to prove its own Islamic credentials by joining in defence of the faith, further raising the importance of religious legitimacy among nationalist leaders.

Contentious Issues: The Missionary Conference and Government Employment

A 1928 missionary conference serves as a good example of the increasingly politicised meaning of religion and religious identification. Muslim leaders had long complained about missionary activity in the Levant and throughout the Muslim world. In 1925, a correspondent from the Vatican newspaper *Osservatore Romano* reported that at the Beirut Congress of Muslim Students of Palestine 'the defiance of the intellectual class of the new Islamic generation is against Christian missionary activity in the domain of public education', which he attributed to their Islamic response to evangelical activity.[118] In March 1928, *al-Jami'a al-'Arabiyya* broke the story of a missionary conference to be held in Jerusalem that month. The conference, lasting for two weeks, was organised by the International Missionary Council and was attended by missionaries from around the world.

Newspaper coverage in the Palestinian press was extensive and nearly universally negative throughout the conference. Many objected to the fact that the British government had allowed such a conference to take place in Palestine, which proved, they contended, Britain's lack of respect for Islam. A missionary conference in Jerusalem was an attack on Islam and a clear attempt to convert Muslims.[119] In contrast, many articles argued, Muslims respected other nations' religious choices, which is why they did not send Muslim missionaries to London.[120]

In addition to concerns about perceived government support for Christian missionary activity, the pro-Husayni *al-Jamiᶜa al-ᶜArabiyya* attacked missionary activity directly. Missionaries 'stroll about the streets of the Muslim world carrying the epistle of Jesus, yelling loudly, "God of Love", and "thank God on high and on Earth"', although the paper claimed that such nonsense had not converted a single Muslim. Christian missions were also called the newest crusade.[121] Attacking missionaries and proselytisation was one thing, but some newspaper articles went further by equating local Christians with foreign missionaries.[122] This conflation of Arab and foreign Christians highlights the ways in which national and religious identification were contested in this new social climate.

Vocal Arab Christians, particularly the Arab Orthodox, wanted no part of the missionary meeting. Missionaries had often tried to convert Orthodox Christians to Protestantism in the late nineteenth and early twentieth centuries, and much tension remained between these two major branches of Christianity, particularly concerning proselytisation. As a result, not a single member of the 'ancient Orthodox church of the Near East' attended.[123] Instead, members of the Young Orthodox Club of Jaffa submitted a statement to *al-Jamiᶜa al-ᶜArabiyya* in which they declared, in very strong language, their disgust at such a conference being held in their country. The newspaper headline read 'Our Christian Brothers are Angry', and the statement itself claimed that the majority of Orthodox Christians believed that the conference was 'an attack on Islam'. The statement called on the government to limit this type of activity in the future, and was published in *al-Jamiᶜa al-ᶜArabiyya* alongside a similar statement that emerged from a meeting of Arab Christians in Bethlehem. The resolutions from that meeting took the form of an open letter to the high commissioner reminding him of the political unity between Palestinian Christians and Muslims and accusing the government of exacerbating intercommunal strife.[124] The essence of both statements was that if Arab Muslims were offended, so too were Arab Christians.

Confronted with a situation in which anti-missionary sentiments were sometimes blurred with anti-Christian sentiments, Bandak offered a critique of 'religious fanaticism' in general, with the clear implication that both Christian missionaries and Islamic zealots could cause problems. Bandak appealed for 'true nationalism', suggesting that the nation had two choices: 'either religious fanaticism, which would result in divisiveness, deadlock, death and extinction . . . or religious toleration, which would result in unity, life and rejuvenation'.[125] Bandak did not call for ethnic nationalism, but instead stressed the importance of Muslims tolerating Christians as well as Christians tolerating, and indeed respecting, the country's Muslim majority.

In contrast to attacks by Bandak and the Husayni camp on the British for permitting such a conference, Shihada took the opportunity to praise the British for ending what he argued was as a long period of communal strife under Ottoman rule. Shihada did blame Europe for some of the horrors of the past, reviving memories of the Crusades and European intervention in the Ottoman Empire, and criticising the European use of missionary hospitals and schools to gain a foothold in the East. But he then turned the blame towards the Arabs themselves for accepting the communal labels imposed by the Ottoman *millet* system. It was religious identification that had damaged the fabric of the community 'and [caused] ruptures of separation between the sons of this one country that expanded from day to day until the Great World War stopped it in 1918'.[126] Shihada argued that, thankfully, the British had ushered in 'an era of nationalism' and that Arabs needed to unite as they had immediately following the war in a show of secular nationalism.

Al-ᶜIsa offered a very nuanced view of missionary activity in general and an even more hair-splitting assessment of the missionary conference. It is no wonder that *al-Jamiᶜa al-ᶜArabiyya* attacked al-ᶜIsa as a supporter of the conference.[127] In 1927, a year before the missionary conference emerged as a major controversy in the press and shortly after his departure from the Husayni camp, al-ᶜIsa published a front-page article with a heavily nuanced challenge to missionaries in the East. The article was in direct response to Ahmed al-Hanidi of Lydda who questioned his nationalist credentials. Al-Hanidi accused al-ᶜIsa of not speaking out forcefully against foreign missionaries, whom al-Hanidi blamed for sowing dissention between Muslims and Christians.[128] Al-ᶜIsa responded defensively, assuring his readers that Arab Christians were not happy with missionary efforts, not only 'because this work strains national relations between the Muslim and Christian residents . . . [but] because it created difficulties among Christians from different denominations also'.[129] In fact, his critique of missionary activity focused almost completely on its alleged role in the creation of tensions among Arab Christian denominations, offering only a superficial confirmation of its impact on Muslim–

Christian tensions. He concluded by suggesting that since almost all Palestinian Arabs believed in God missionaries should turn their attention elsewhere. Such a conclusion was unlikely to have satisfied al-Hanidi, who opposed all Christian missionary activity in a predominantly Muslim country.

Muslim critics also deemed al-ʿIsa's response to the 1928 missionary conference to be unsatisfactory. Rather than publish an unequivocal repudiation of the meeting in the style of Bandak, al-ʿIsa offered a history lesson on the expansion of the church and the importance of Palestine in Christian history.[130] He justified the gathering in Jerusalem on the grounds of Jerusalem's centrality to Christianity, as well as Palestine's convenient geographic location for attendees from both European churches and nationalised church communities in India, China, Japan and elsewhere. The reason for holding the conference in Jerusalem, in his assessment, was not related at all to any missionary designs on the Holy Land itself or the conversion of its Muslims. While al-ʿIsa's argument may in fact have been valid, it served only to anger his political opponents and deepen the division between Husayni and Nashashibi supporters.

Neither the missionary conference nor any other single event caused a total deterioration of Muslim–Christian relations. Uri Kupferschmidt, for example, highlights the tensions caused by the conference, but concludes that 'the relationship between Muslims and Christians in Palestine, which had been an early characteristic of the Palestinian-Arab movement, [never] completely broke down. The common political fate and destiny of local Palestinian Muslims and Christians were occasionally reemphasised. However, the relationship became more ambiguous.'[131] It was an ambiguity born of a set of historical circumstances that led various participants to identify themselves in different ways.

Intercommunal relations were further strained by some Muslims' belief that Arab Christians were offered employment in government service at the expense of Muslims. Indeed, despite only comprising approximately 10 per cent of the population, there were more Christians employed by the government than Muslims. A tally from July 1929 counted 1,176 Christians, 1,111 Muslims and 714 Jews in civil service posts.[132] Christians had long enjoyed better educational opportunities (another source of communal tension) and were thus better prepared to secure civil service jobs at the beginning of the Mandate period.[133] By the end of the 1920s, British efforts had greatly increased the education level in the country. Substantial numbers of Muslims had become fluent in English, an important prerequisite for government employment, but government employment remained disproportionate.

The large proportion of Christians particularly troubled the new generation of educated Muslims who desired work in government service,
leading a group of young Muslims to organise 'the Preparatory Committee
of Young Educated Muslims' to advocate for their cause in the early
1930s.[134] The YMMA also rallied around this issue, and Porath suggests
that 'in less public meetings, the heads of the organization did not hesi-
tate to state explicitly that "the Christians are robbing the Muslims of
their rights to Government offices"'.[135] Even more than the missionary
conference, the employment issue challenged Muslim–Christian unity.
Attacking Christian employment in government service without blaming
Christians themselves proved to be difficult, and some Muslims were open
about their disgust with Arab Christians.

Porath suggests that the 'radical pan-Islamic' newspaper *al-Jami^c a
al-Islamiyya* addressed this issue 'with a ferocity bordering on open
incitement against the Christians'.[136] In addition, a Zionist businessman
reported in 1928 that the Mufti of Safad and his family believed 'it had
been a very great mistake on the part of the Moslems to go together with
the Christian Arabs . . . that gross injustice was being done particularly to
the Moslems, inasmuch as nearly all Government posts were being held
by Christians'. His report notes that at least one member of the Mufti's
family had been removed from government service and 'replaced by a
Christian'.[137] Tensions only increased over the years that followed. The
British failed to reduce the employment gap, and the government's annual
report to the League of Nations in 1932 noted that 'a bitter campaign was
conducted in the Moslem Press against the alleged favouritism enjoyed by
the Christian community in obtaining Government appointments'.[138]

Porath contends that the issue of Christians in the civil service, like that
of missionary activity, 'gradually became a public issue of primary importance, arousing anger and affecting relations between the two communities'.[139] While he cites some Muslim groups which did specifically blame
Arab Christians for British hiring practices, many other Arabs responded
to the threat of communalism by re-dedicating themselves to intercommunal unity and strongly expressing their support for one another. In the
same way *al-Jami^c a al-^c Arabiyya* published articles insisting that attacking al-^c Isa was different to attacking the Christian community as a whole,
the mainstream Arab press insisted that the British, not Arab Christians,
were to blame for the employment gap.

Christian newspaper editors unanimously agreed with this distinction,
but variations concerning minority–majority relations emerged in their
articles on the topic. Bandak, Shihada, and al-^c Isa responded to Muslim
anger at the employment gap in ways that reflected their basic understand-

ing of the status of Christians in society. Much to the surprise of a Zionist observer, an article in *Sawt al-Shaᶜb* mirrored those found in Muslim-owned papers. Bandak argued that 'Arab Christians should be the first to recognise the rights of their Moslem Brethren over public positions and support them with the Government [even] though some Christian officials might suffer from the grant[ing] of Moslem demands.'[140] This is among Bandak's most clearly stated argument that unity could and should be gained through recognition of the power and benevolence of the Muslim majority, even if such recognition temporarily harmed some Christians.

Shihada acknowledged that there was inequality in government employment, but he argued that Christians were not to blame and could do nothing about it.[141] Religion, he insisted, should not be the basis for hiring or not hiring a prospective employee. Christians were inherently no more capable than Muslims, nor should they receive special treatment. It would also be wrong to require them to step aside for Muslims, since 'the rights of Muslims and Christians in this country are the same, [they are] natural rights . . . of Arab nationalism, not communalism (*taᶜifiyya*)'.[142] His argument concerning employment is an extension of his insistence that Christians should not be considered a minority in Palestine because they were simply part of the Arab majority.[143]

Writing about this issue after joining the National Party, al-ᶜIsa shared Shihada's conclusion but, in a nod to his past advocacy for the SMC, explicitly criticised the government. Like *Mirat al-Sharq*, *Filastin* blamed those Muslims who were demanding better treatment based on religious identity for the rising communal tensions. Al-ᶜIsa argued that the Muslim demand for greater representation in government jobs was

> regrettable because it constitutes the proof that after having unsuccessfully fought against the foreign usurper the Arabs have started quarrelling with one another and that in spite of all their efforts for the so-called unity and nationalism they seize the first opportunity to return to old communal disputes.[144]

In an effort to remove religion from the equation, he proposed an ethnic distinction, protesting the government's practice of hiring British and Jewish workers.

Al-Jamiᶜa al-ᶜArabiyya cautioned Muslims, encouraging them to 'not confuse Muslim employment rights with the unity of Muslims and Christians in Palestine'.[145] Another article in that paper argued that demanding Muslim majority rights was not at odds with continued cooperation and unity with Arab Christians on political matters.[146] That is, placing some blame on the Christian community was legitimate, but only as long as tensions did not extend beyond that issue. The perspective set forth in *al-Jamiᶜa al-ᶜArabiyya* paralleled Bandak's view, agreeing that national unity was important, but that it had to be based on acceptance of the superior status of the country's Muslim majority.

Conclusion

Tsimhoni concludes that by 1924 Christians recognised the failure of Arab nationalism, since it was 'overwhelmed by Muslims' religious feelings, a movement in which Arab Christians would have little or no part; in the new reality they would be accepted as equals no longer'.[147] In response, she continues, Christians flocked to the National Party, the only viable alternative. This conclusion, one repeated by many historians, is not completely wrong; many elite Christians did join the Nashashibi faction in the 1920s. But she ignores the great diversity within the Arab Christian community. A careful look at Christian arguments about some of the important challenges of the decade shows a range of views among Christians and demands a more complex explanation.

Tsimhoni simplifies both the Christian and Muslim communities in her assessment of Palestinian communalism in the 1920s. By suggesting that Palestinian nationalism was 'overwhelmed by Muslims' religious feelings', she ignores significant portions of Arab society that did not advocate enhanced religious identification. Hajj Amin al-Husayni, in his roles as head of the SMC and Grand Mufti, was indeed a religious figure, and he and other Palestinian leaders 'use[d] Islamic belief and institutions to further their own brand of Palestinian nationalism . . . one in which they would remain the leaders of the Palestinian Arabs to the same extent, and with the same social parameters, as they had in the preceding years'.[148] For al-Husayni, retaining religious power was no more important than retaining class power. Still, the leadership roles granted to him by the British were religious in nature, providing al-Husayni with control of a specifically religious institution. The YMMA also based its social and political platform on advocating for religious issues. In both cases, a combination of British policies and political expedience led to the politicisation of religion. The SMC was the only major Arab entity recognised by the British, and al-Husayni adapted the committee's religious functions to serve political ends. Missionaries were viewed as colonial entities with close connections to the Mandate government, so the YMMA developed religious arguments to fight religious battles.

Religion had influenced individual identification throughout the Ottoman years as well, but whereas Arab leaders following the First World War sought to subsume religion within a broader nationalist identification, the social and political climate of the 1920s triggered a resurgence in communal identification. Ethnicity, the foundational element on which MCA-era Palestinian unity had been based, did not disappear, but was subjugated to religious identification for some. As a result, Christian–Muslim tensions did arise, but many Arabs also actively advocated intercommunal unity. The SMC aggressively sought to strengthen ties to the Arab Christian population, particularly the Orthodox community.[149] Christian leaders, too, tried to stop Palestinian communalisation. Some, like Bandak, argued for a redefinition of the place of Arab Christians in Palestinian society as a religiously different but ethnically similar minority that would retain full rights. Others, such as Shihada and later al-ʿIsa, instead defined Christians as part of the Arab majority in an effort to reduce the importance of religion in national identification.

The Husayni–Nashashibi divide irreparably damaged the MCA's call for national unity in all its forms. While the MCA had focused public attention on religious unity, it is even more remarkable that, in the earliest years, the organisation succeeded in overcoming family rivalries in its bid for recognition as the mouthpiece of the Arab population. MCA leaders hoped that intercommunal cooperation would help their chances of achieving political independence, but when inter-Arab factionalism destroyed that unity, religious identification emerged as a divisive issue, albeit in multiple and often contradictory ways. Al-Husayni both utilised his position in the SMC to bolster the religious legitimacy of his faction and to maintain the secular AE: for al-Husayni, 'Pan-Arab and Pan-Islamic ideas coexisted with Palestinian nationalism without contradiction throughout his career.'[150]

While many Christians did join the opposition, some likely fearing the Islamicisation of Palestinian nationalism, Christian support for the National Party was not universal. It is difficult to accurately tally the percentage of Christians who supported the Nashashibis, particularly when it comes to the non-elite. At times many Christians did appear to support the National Party. The phenomenal success of the opposition in the Jerusalem municipal elections of 1927 is one such example. In Christian opposition to the 1928 missionary conference, however, some portion of the Orthodox community, at least, continued following al-Husayni's lead. A number of Christians also remained in leadership positions in the AE and MCA throughout the decade, although their importance was understandably limited in the SMC.

The Husyani–Nashashibi divide, Britain's establishment of the SMC and the growth of the YMMA did indeed lead to a situation in which Arab religious identification increased in importance and religious tensions coloured political problems. When the YMMA and other Muslim groups attacked the missionary conference and Christian employment in government service, Muslim rights and societal primacy were foundational arguments. More accurately, the issues were political, while the mode of resistance was religious.

Resistance using religious terminology did not lead directly to inter-communal strife or violence, but it was a significant shift for Arab Christians. The three newspaper editors described above responded in different ways: Shihada expressed discomfort with accepting Islam as a shared national tradition despite one's religious affiliation and focused on ethnic nationalism; Bandak accepted Islam as the shared cultural basis of Palestinian Arab society, even though he was not a secularist, like Shihada, but an active member of the Orthodox Church; Al-ʿIsa changed his opinion, first agreeing with Bandak that Islam was foundational to Arab culture, while later suggesting that Arabness came before religion.

At the outset of the Mandate, the British implemented new policies that changed the way religious communities were structured. New Arab voices joined the national dialogue concerning the Mandate, Zionism and the meaning of national identification. Some of these voices challenged the basic premises of the MCA era, with some advocating a greater role for religion in politics and others turning towards communalism as they challenged the British and Zionism. Porath argues that in the same way that the Husayni–Nashashibi rift 'cracked the plaster of the united Muslim community, so it uncovered the split between Christians and Muslims'.[151] Yet more than uncovering a communal split, the Husayni–Nashashibi conflict helped to create one. Despite this shift, many Christians still advocated for non-religious nationalism, and many Muslims and Christians alike continued to advocate interreligious unity.

Notes

1. S25/3004, summary of *Sawt al-Shaʿb*, 14 January 1928.
2. Daphne Tsimhoni, 'Palestinian Christians and the Peace Process', in Ilan Peleg (ed), *The Middle East Peace Process: Interdisciplinary Perspectives* (Albany, NY: SUNY Press, 1998), p. 142.
3. Kupferschmidt, *Supreme Muslim Council*, p. 160.
4. CZA S25/22714, CID Intelligence Summary 5/39, 21 January 1939.
5. Various MCA branches did remain sporadically active throughout the 1930s, but as an influential national conglomerate, the Association was defunct by the end of the 1920s.
6. Mattar, *Mufti of Jerusalem*, p. 22.

7. Mattar, *Mufti of Jerusalem*, p. 23.
8. Mattar, *Mufti of Jerusalem*, p. 24.
9. Joan Peters, *From Time Immemorial: The Origins of the Arab–Jewish Conflict Over Palestine* (New York: Harper & Row, 1984), pp. 274–5.
10. Mattar, *Mufti of Jerusalem*, p. 27.
11. M10/12; Cadi of Jerusalem to Samuel, 24 March 1921.
12. Richmond to Samuel, 6 July 1921; cited in Tsimhoni, 'The British Mandate', p. 262 ff. n. 1. Besides Nasif, other Christian leaders who expressed support were all foreigners, and Tsimhoni suggests that they may have been asked to do so by the government in order to justify the appointment.
13. See Kupferschmidt, *The Supreme Muslim Council*, for the most detailed account of the SMC.
14. Porath, *Emergence*, pp. 184–207.
15. Mattar, *Mufti of Jerusalem*, p. 29.
16. Porath, *Emergence*, p. 199.
17. Porath, *Emergence*, p. 200.
18. ISA M4/2, Storrs to Samuel, 4 January 1924.
19. ISA M4/2, Symes to Samuel, 6 December 1923.
20. Kenneth Stein, review of Kupferschmidt, *The Supreme Muslim Council*, and Mattar, *The Mufti of Jerusalem*, *International Journal of Middle Eastern Studies*, 23(4) (1991)); Porath, *Emergence*, p. 197.
21. Matter, *Mufti of Jerusalem*, p. 30.
22. See, for instance, ISA M4/24, Jamal Husayni, Secretary of AE to Samuel, 28 November 1924.
23. See ISA M4/26 for the AE's 1925 petition to the Permanent Mandate Commission.
24. Mattar, *Mufti of Jerusalem*, p. 30.
25. Porath, *Emergence*, p. 243.
26. Mattar, *Mufti of Jerusalem*, p. 29.
27. Lesch, *Arab Politics*, p. 80.
28. Keith-Roach, p. 78, for instance.
29. *Al-Karmil*, 22 August 1925.
30. Rashid Khalidi, 'The Palestinians and 1948: The Underlying Causes of Failure', in Eugene L. Rogan and Avi Shlaim (eds), *The War for Palestine: Rewriting the History of 1948* (Cambridge: Cambridge University Press, 2007), pp. 22–3.
31. Johnson, *Islam and the Politics of Meaning*, p. 16.
32. PRO 733-52, Samuel to Secretary of State for the Colonies, November Political Report, 14 December 1923.
33. Lesch, *Arab Politics*, p. 97.
34. Mattar, *Mufti of Jerusalem*, p. 31.
35. ISA M4/2, Symes to Samuel, 6 December 1923.
36. Lesch, *Arab Politics*, pp. 95–7.
37. ISA M4/1, Jamal al-Husayni to High Commissioner, 2 April 1922.

38. PRO 733/14, Shuckburgh, Account of Conversation with Palestine Delegation, 11 August 1921.
39. PRO 733/92, Political Reports, April 1925.
40. *Sawt al-Sha'b*, 8 March 1922.
41. *Mirat al-Sharq*, 14 May 1924; see also CZA S25/4378, Zionist (unknown author) 'Arab Press Report', September 1923.
42. Tsimhoni, 'The British Mandate', p. 289.
43. ISA M4/22; Sulaiman al-Faruki, National Party, to Hamid al-Din, Imam of Yemen, 13 June 1924.
44. Porath, *Emergence*, p. 6.
45. Porath, *Emergence*, p. 239.
46. Porath, *Emergence*, pp. 253–4.
47. Porath, *Emergence*, p. 271.
48. Lesch, *Arab Politics*, p. 80.
49. In private, NP leaders supported positive relations with the British. See, for example, Faruqi (Leader of the NP) to Lord Plumer, welcoming the new high commissioner to Palestine (ISA M4/22, 28 August 1925). The office party platform called for elections and an independent Arab state (PRO 733-52, Samuel to Secretary of State for the Colonies, November Political Report, 14 December 1923).
50. Tsimhoni, 'The British Mandate', p. 288; PRO 733/42, Samuel to the Duke of Devonshire, 11 February 1923.
51. Tsimhoni, 'The British Mandate', p. 286.
52. ISA M5/1, YMMA to High Commissioner, 2 August 1925, 27 August 1925.
53. Musallam, *Yawmiyat Khalil al-Sakakini*, vol. 3, p. 138. Entry for 27 April 1919.
54. Marvin W. Mikesell and Alexander B Murphy, 'A Framework for Comparative Study of Minority-Group Aspirations', *Annals of the Association of American Geographers*, 81(4) (1991), p. 582.
55. Eventually, Bandak also left the Husayni faction, although it is unclear when, or why, that occurred.
56. Shomali, 'Palestinian Christians', p. 230.
57. ISA M4/22, Mohammed Jamil al Khalib al Tamimi and thirty-two others to High Commissioner, 20 December 1923.
58. ISA M4/22, Sulaiman Salah, President Muslim Society to Samuel, 29 November 1923.
59. ISA M4/22, Sa'id al-Khalil and seven others to High Commissioner, 9 November 1923.
60. ISA M4/22, Sa'id al-Husayni and eighteen others to High Commissioner, 31 December 1923.
61. ISA M4/22, Yusef al-Dajani and sixteen others to High Commissioner, 2 December 1923.
62. S25/518/2, Kisch to Kalvaryski, 14 November 1924.
63. *Mirat al-Sharq*, 27 September 1923.

64. Emil al-Ghuri, *Palestine in Sixty Years* (Beirut: Dar al-Nahar, 1974), p. 7.
65. *Mirat al-Sharq*, 24 September 1924 and 18 October 1924; no author is listed, but it is likely that it was written by the editor. At the very least he certainly approved it.
66. 'An Open Letter to the President of the Supreme Muslim Council from Ahmen Mitouli', *Mirat al-Sharq*, 19 November 1924.
67. See, for example, ISA M4/2, Abdullah Mukhless, Secretary, National Party, to High Commissioner, 21 November 1923.
68. Aida Ali Najjar, 'The Arabic Press', p. 70. *Lisan al-Arab* was the mouthpiece of the Muslim National Party, a more openly pro-Zionist predecessor of the National Party; despite the paper's willingness to support their cause, the party sought to establish a new paper with a Muslim owner (CZA S25/4380; Meeting of the Arabs at the House of Dr Eder, 4 March 1922).
69. *Mirat al-Sharq*, 1 October 1925.
70. *Mirat al-Sharq*, 27 September 1923.
71. Michael J. Cohen, *Palestine to Israel: From Mandate to Independence* (London: Frank Cass, 1988), p. 117.
72. Najjar, 'The Arabic Press', p. 66, citing article from 8 June 1921.
73. Najjar, 'The Arabic Press', p. 71.
74. CZA S25/4378, the citation is quoted in the Zionist (unknown author) 'Arab Press Report', September 1923, from *Mirat al-Sharq*, 27 September 1923, challenging the *Filastin* article, date unknown.
75. *Filastin*, 2 October 1923.
76. *Filastin*, 27 November 1923.
77. *Filastin*, 20 November 1923.
78. Najjar, 'The Arabic Press', p. 72.
79. *Filastin*, 23 October 1923.
80. Najjar, 'The Arabic Press', p. 77.
81. Lesch, *Arab Politics*, pp. 100–1.
82. *Filastin*, 2 March 1928.
83. *Filastin*, 11 October 1930
84. *Al-Jamiᶜa al-ᶜArabiyya*, 18 July 1929.
85. *Al-Jamiᶜa al-ᶜArabiyya*, 1 August 1929.
86. *Sawt al-Shaᶜb*, 18 March 1927.
87. *Sawt al-Shaᶜb*, 17 July 1927.
88. *Sawt al-Shaᶜb*, 25 January 1928.
89. *Sawt al-Shaᶜb*, 3 August 1922.
90. *Sawt al-Shaᶜb*, 30 July 1927.
91. *Sawt al-Shaᶜb*, 30 July 1927.
92. *Sawt al-Shaᶜb*, 8 October 1927.
93. *Sawt al-Shaᶜb*, 8 October 1927.
94. *Sawt al-Shaᶜb*, 14 January 1928.
95. *Sawt al-Shaᶜb*, 15 December 1928.
96. *Sawt al-Shaᶜb*, 27 March 1929.

97. See member list in Musallam, *Folded Pages*, p. 93.
98. Bandak's Christian support came from the villages of Bethlehem, Beit Jala and Beit Sahour, which were over 90 per cent Christian; the rural area of the subdistrict was over 90 per cent Muslim; a Muslim majority was found in the subdistrict as a whole (McCarthy, *Population of Palestine*, pp. 156–7).
99. Musallam, *Folded Pages*, pp. 78–9.
100. See, for instance, Akhram Fouad Khater, *Inventing Home: Emigration, Gender, and the Middle Class in Lebanon, 1870–1920* (Berkeley, CA: University of California Press, 2001).
101. Musallam, *Folded Pages*, pp. 80 and 87. When Patriarch Barlassina sued Dakart over anti-Catholic sentiments in a novel, Dakart returned to Argentina. Upon his departure, Bandak and Dakart's literary journal folded, and the Literary Club closed as well.
102. John Collins, *Occupied by Memory: The Intifada Generation and the Palestinian State of Emergency* (New York: New York University Press, 2004), p. 13.
103. Symes to Chief Secretary, 29 May 1924, in Jarman, *Political Diaries*, vol. 1, p. 46.
104. CZA S25/3004, Kisch, 'Note on Recent Developments in the Internal Arab Political Situation', February 1928.
105. Matthews, *Confronting an Empire*, p. 56.
106. Matthews, *Confronting an Empire*, p. 57.
107. Eric Davis, 'The Concept of Revival and the Study of Islam and Politics', in Barbara Freyer Stowasser (ed.), *The Islamic Impulse* (Washington, DC: Taylor & Francis, 1987), p. 46.
108. Ziyad Abu ʿAmr, *Islamic Fundamentalism in the West Bank and Gaza: Muslim Brotherhood and Islamic Jihad* (Bloomington, IN: Indiana University Press, 1994), pp. 1–2. See also, Richard Paul Mitchell, *The Society of the Muslim Brothers* (Oxford: Oxford University Press, 1969), p. 55.
109. Lesch, *Arab Politics*, p. 107.
110. As cited in Matthews, *Confronting an Empire*, p. 56.
111. ISA M5000/16, 26 June 1928.
112. Lesch, *Arab Politics*, p. 107.
113. ISA M5000/16, 26 June 1928; see ISA M5/2 for complaints from various YMMA organisations against the SMC; Matthews, *Confronting an Empire*, p. 61.
114. For more on the YMMA, see Matthews, *Confronting an Empire*, pp. 56–68.
115. *Mirat al-Sharq*, 9 December 1925.
116. *Sawt al-Shaʿb*, 24 July 1929.
117. *Sawt al-Shaʿb*, 10 April 1929.
118. CZA Z4/41030; Dante Lattes to ZO London, 13 November 1925, citing an article from the *Osservatore Romano*, 4 November 1925.
119. *Al-Jamiʿa al-ʿArabiyya*, 19 March 1928.

120. *Al-Jamiᶜa al-ᶜArabiyya*, 24 March 1928.
121. *Al-Jamiᶜa al-ᶜArabiyya*, 24 March 1928.
122. Porath, *Emergence*, p. 300.
123. Samuel McCrea Cavert, 'Beginning at Jerusalem', *Christian Century*, 10 May 1928.
124. *Al-Jamiᶜa al-ᶜArabiyya*, 16 March 1928.
125. Musallam, *Folded Pages*, p. 92; *Sawt al-Shab*, 19 May 1928.
126. *Mirat al-Sharq*, 12 April 1928.
127. Najjar, 'The Arabic Press', p. 77; *Al-Jamiᶜa al-ᶜArabiyya*, 14 April 1928.
128. *Filastin*, 4 October 1927.
129. *Filastin*, 4 October 1927.
130. *Filastin*, 2 March 1928.
131. Kupferschmidt, *Supreme Muslim Council*, p. 248.
132. Paul Hanna, *British Policy in Palestine* (Washington, DC: American Council on Public Affairs, 1942), ff. 1, p. 185, citing statistics found in the *Palestine Commission of the Disturbances of August, 1929: Evidence*.
133. *Mirat al-Sharq*, 8 December 1923.
134. Porath, *Emergence*, p. 301.
135. Porath, *Emergence*, p. 301.
136. Porath, *Emergence*, p. 301. Jordanian Muslims made similar claims as early as 1928 (see 'Situation Report on Trans-Jordan by British Resident for the Period 1/1/28–31/3/28', in Jarman, *Political Diaries*, vol. 2, p. 239).
137. CZA S25/3004, General Manager of Anglo-Palestine Company Ltd to Mr S. A. Van Vreisland, Jerusalem, 6 June 1928.
138. 'Report by His Majesty's Government in the United Kingdom of Great Britain and Northern Ireland to the Council of the League of Nations on the Administration of Palestine and Trans-Jordan For the Year 1932,' UNISPAL.
139. Porath, *Emergence*, p. 301.
140. S25/3004, Zionist memo to Palestine Zionist Executive, London, summarising articles in *Sawt al-Shaᶜb*, 14 January 1928, and *Filastin*, 10 January 1928.
141. *Mirat al-Sharq*, 28 September 1932.
142. *Mirat al-Sharq*, 10 October 1925. The Arabic word *taᶜifiyya* is the adjectival form of *taᶜifa*, which can mean denomination, confession (as in a religious community) or congregation.
143. *Mirat al-Sharq*, 8 October 1932.
144. S25/3004, Zionist memo to Palestine Zionist Executive, London, summarising articles in *Sawt al-Shaᶜb*, 14 January 1928, and *Filastin*, 10 January 1928.
145. *Al-Jamiᶜa al-ᶜArabiyya*, 29 September 1932.
146. *Al-Jamiᶜa al-ᶜArabiyya*, 29 September 1932.
147. Tsimhoni, 'The British Mandate', p. 268.
148. Johnson, *Islam and the Politics of Meaning*, p. 29.

149. Kuperschmidt, *Supreme Muslim Council*, p. 219.
150. Mattar, *Mufti of Jerusalem*, p. 18.
151. Yehoshua Porath, 'The Political Organization of the Palestinian Arabs under the British', in Moshe Ma'oz (ed.), *Palestinian Arab Politics* (Jerusalem: Jerusalem Academic Press, 1975), pp. 14–15.

3

1929–1936: Towards Communalism

We call upon the Muslim world, since the Christian-European world is asleep and does not care for its Holy Places, to act before it is too late if they are really concerned about the fate of the Muslim holy places in Palestine and all other Arab countries.[1]

Emil al-Ghuri (Orthodox Christian), 29 August 1929

The Buraq (Western Wall) is a purely Moslem Place and is a part of the Holy Masjid al-Aksa. The rights of the Moslems in the Buraq are indisputable. [And] in the cause of the Buraq the Moslems and Christians are one and the same racially, nationally, and politically.[2]

Yaᶜcoub Farraj (Orthodox Christian), 27 October 1929

It was Tuesday, 27 August 1929, just four days after a dispute over *al-Buraq* (the Western Wall) triggered violent Arab riots and Jewish counter-attacks. Yusef Marroum and his wife (unnamed in police records) of Qalunya, a village of roughly 500 citizens about four miles from Jerusalem, heard a car pull up in front of their house. Marroum slowly opened the shutters to see who had arrived in the otherwise quiet town. He was greeted with a bullet to the face. As he lay bleeding on the floor, he heard boot steps come around to the door and enter. The British soldier fired two more shots before he saw Marroum's wife. As he paused, Yusef shouted out, 'I'm a Christian!' The soldier fired once more for good measure, but then left Marroum lying on the floor. It was an hour before Marroum's wife was able to flag down another military vehicle, which arranged to have her injured husband transferred to the hospital.[3]

This anecdote, gleaned from police logs of those injured during the 1929 violence, is emblematic of Arab Christians' complex position in Palestine from 1929 until the mid-1930s. While most Christians were openly supportive of the nationalist movement, at least in its opposition to the Balfour Declaration and Zionist settlement, the increased use of Islam as tool of nationalist rhetoric placed them in an uncertain position. Musa Buderi argues that during the Mandate:

Islam served to shape an ideology of resistance to an other, who not only belonged to a different faith but was also an outsider and openly proclaimed that the realization of his aims involved emptying the country of its original inhabitants. The tools for this campaign were the *Imams* and *Khatibs* of village and town mosques who used the Friday sermon to convey the necessity of resistance as a religious duty. Islamic concepts and historical parallels were utilized to mobilize the people en masse to social action. Religion was the medium not the message. The language and the symbols were cultural categories familiar to a society that through the long years of Ottoman rule had grown accustomed to viewing itself in religious terms.[4]

While this assessment may have been true for the nationalist elite, the language and symbols of Islam were more than simple campaign tools to many who heard and employed them.

Three major themes affected the relationship between national and religious identification. First, elite factionalism of the 1920s opened the political arena for many voices to participate in nationalist debates. The Husaynis and Nashashibis no longer controlled the range of political and social debate. Secondly, both elite nationalists and the new, non-elite actors continued to increase the connection between Islam and the Palestinian situation, risking alienation of Arab Christians. Finally, as Christians debated their role in this new context, rifts emerged within the Christian community, often along denominational lines, but occasionally between members of the same community.

A series of events, beginning with the 1929 riots and ending just before the outbreak of the 'Great Revolt' of 1936–1939, highlights these themes. While there was no watershed moment in the relationship between Palestine's Christians and Muslims, when read together these events represent a changing pattern of intercommunal interaction. As Weldon Matthews argues, 'concepts of identity, whether expressed through kinship relations, citizenship, or religious and national identity, are generated, chosen, and manipulated in specific historical circumstances'.[5] Continued failure to stop British colonialism and Zionist expansion led to a change of strategy. Insisting on interreligious unity became a tactic of the past. Factionalism in political circles and the increasing merger of Islamic and nationalist demands continued to push Palestinian Arabs closer to 'religious factionalism', that is, communalism.

1929 Western Wall Violence

Conflict over the use of the Western Wall in August 1929 triggered the most deadly confrontation up to that point. The details have been analysed extensively from many angles, because it was a major turning point in the Zionist–Arab conflict as well as in the Palestinian nationalist movement.[6] Lesch argues that the riots 'demonstrate[ed] not only the volatility of the Arab public but also their potential for mobilization'.[7] The violence triggered widespread participation in the national movement as a broad segment of the Palestinian population joined the resistance, engaging in acts of sabotage throughout the countryside and organising anti-British and anti-Zionist demonstrations in urban areas. For the purposes of understanding the shift towards communalism, two features of the 1929 violence are essential. Most importantly, Hajj Amin al-Husayni used the conflict as a way to draw the international Muslim community into the Palestinian situation. Secondly, the conflict drew many into the resistance who had not been active in the past, including non-elite Palestinians from rural areas, changing the socio-economic make-up of nationalist leadership. While Christians maintained vocal and practical support for the nationalist programme, the changing interreligious dynamics altered their self-identification.

Both Zionist and Muslims leaders used the Western Wall as a focal point of political agitation. The wall holds religious significance for Muslims and Jews alike. For Arabs the wall is named for the miraculous steed (*al-buraq*) that carried Muhammad to Jerusalem on his mystical night journey and which Muhammad tied to the wall when he ascended into heaven. The area behind the wall holds the al-Aqsa Mosque and the Dome of the Rock, an important Muslim shrine. For Jews, the wall is celebrated as the only remaining remnant of the Second Temple, destroyed by the Romans in 70 CE. It is a place of prayer and lament, and the mournful Jewish prayers voiced there have led to the name 'Wailing Wall'. Jews had maintained access to the narrow alley in front of the wall since at least the nineteenth century, and perhaps much earlier. Such access was secured both by Ottoman permission and local Arab acceptance during times of minimal religious tension. These 'arrangements' were logical at times of relative peace, though could become obstacles when the circumstances changed.[8] However, in the early twentieth century Zionists used the religious site to pursue political ambitions. In 1911, Arab complaints about Jewish efforts to increase their influence at the wall led the Ottomans to forbid Jewish worshipers from bringing chairs and screens for worship. Throughout the 1920s, the Zionists challenged this ruling, though Muslims interpreted such activities as a threat and a sign of the Zionists' growing strength in Jerusalem and Palestine in general.[9]

On 24 September 1928, Jewish worshippers brought a screen to the small worship space to provide separate areas for men and women. Prior to the Zionist movement such actions would have been benign, but as Zionist ambitions were well-known, Arabs protested this change in Jewish usage of the holy site. The protests triggered British intervention, and the screen was forcibly removed the following day. Zionist leaders responded quickly, accused the British of police brutality and lodged protests with London and the League of Nations. Al-Husayni responded by calling on Muslims to protect their rights at the wall and formed a committee to carry out that goal.[10]

By the summer of 1929 tensions had reached dangerous levels. Triggered by further Jewish efforts to bring a screen to the wall, Arab Muslims responded with violence. On 23 August, Muslim worshipers attacked Jewish residents following Friday prayers at the al-Aqsa Mosque. Rumours spread quickly throughout the country, and more violence followed. The most deadly attack occurred the following day, when Arabs attacked Jews in Hebron, killing sixty. Violence continued throughout the month and into September. The decade had been a quiet one, and the British were slow to respond since they had not expected such a violent response. The Jewish community answered with protests and counter-attacks, enhancing its community defence force, the *Haganah*, which had been formed in 1920. By the time violence ended, 133 Jews and 116 Arabs had been killed.[11]

The impact of the events of 1929 on the Christian minority and its relationship to the nationalist movement was indirect. The violence was largely Muslim–Jewish, causing a religious turn in the Arab–Zionist conflict. Defence of a specific Muslim holy site became the primary focus of Palestinian resistance. In the mid- to late 1920s al-Husayni's power was solidified by his religious positions, but there was no specifically religious goal driving Muslim involvement in the national movement. Christian participation in Palestinian politics was unhindered by any form of strict religious categorisation. That changed in 1929. Islam was, some insisted, under attack, an argument that helped to mobilise widespread popular resistance among Palestinian Arabs and throughout the Islamic world. While historians argue about whether or not Husayni encouraged violence, there is no question that he utilised religious sentiments to broaden support among Muslims. Both the urban and rural Muslim masses became engaged in the struggle against Zionism because that struggle was framed in terms of religious rights. Nels Johnson suggests that for Palestinian nationalism 'the politics of ideology – of social meaning – [took] its vocabulary from many modes of discourse, including Islam'.[12] The Western Wall crisis pushed a specific mode of Islamic discourse to the centre of the political arena, a mode of discourse that filled political goals with religious meaning, turning a national issue into a fully-fledged pan-Islamic concern.[13]

Christians responded to the violence and to the shift towards an Islamic mode of discourse in various ways. Some reacted to the 1929 violence by protesting verbally or in writing, while steering clear of violence. In a letter to the AE, Muslim, Christian and Druze representatives from Shefaᶜamr (where there was a Christian majority) gave the issue a nationalist tint by confirming their support for *Arab* claims to *al-Buraq* and blamed British inaction for allowing the violence to erupt.[14] The 'Christians and Muslims of Birzeit' (another largely Christian village) sent a telegram to the high commissioner protesting the government's position.[15] Those branches of the MCA still in operation also filed protests in support of Arab claims.[16] Such petitions to the government are perhaps more reflective of the elite status of village religious leaders and MCA participants than of a communal political perspective, although Christians certainly wanted to make it clear to the wider Palestinian population that they stood behind Muslim concerns about Zionist designs for the Western Wall and temple area.

High-profile Christian politicians spoke out, reaffirming nationalist unity and trying to infuse a very Muslim issue with cross-communal meaning. A statement from a gathering of elite Arab leaders, signed by Yaᶜcoub Farraj as president of the meeting, merged Muslim religious rights with Arab national and political rights:

> The Buraq is a purely Moslem Place and is a part of the Holy Masjid El-Aksa. The rights of the Moslems in the Buraq are indisputable . . . In the cause of the Buraq the Moslems and Christians are one and the same racially, nationally and politically.[17]

ᶜIsa al-ᶜIsa signed and published a similar statement declaring that 'Moslems and Christians alike are concerned [about *al-Buraq*] from a national, patriotic and political point of view',[18] while Emil al-Ghuri encouraged Muslim nations to intervene on behalf of *al-Buraq*.[19] Many Arab leaders protested against High Commissioner John Chancellor's declaration that Arabs had proved themselves unfit for self-rule because of the violence. Episcopal lawyer Mughannam Mughannam was among the signatories of an AE telegram to the high commissioner declaring the innocence of all Arabs in the August violence.[20] Husayni supporter and AE member Alfred Rok (a Latin Christian), headed the Christian Committee for the Relief of Moslem Sufferers at Jaffa, and also organised a meeting of Muslims and Christians in Jaffa to send formal protests to the Colonial Office.[21] Despite support from some Christians, others distanced themselves from the violence, exhibiting frustration at being lumped together with the Muslim population as, in the words of the high commissioner, a

Figure 3.1 Crosses on Christian houses to prevent looting during 1929 violence.
Library of Congress

people 'unworthy of self-government'. Some British reports suggested that Arab Christians were indignant; they had not participated in the violent events and therefore should not have been held accountable.[22]

British reports confirm that Christians were under-represented in the casualty count from 1929. Only four Christians were killed and sixteen wounded, compared with eighty-three Muslims killed and 164 wounded. Thus only 5 per cent of Arab casualties were Christian, and at least one of those killed was a victim of random violence, as opposed to being a participant in the protests. In Haifa, all Christian casualties resulted from Jewish attacks on Arab pedestrians, not from injuries sustained while participating in violent protests.[23]

Lesch suggests that the primary result of the 1929 ordeal was a turn towards militancy as expressed through the activities of 'youth groups, the pan-Arab Hizb al-Istiqlal, pan-Islamic societies, and clandestine revolutionary cells'.[24] Christians participated in some of these organisations more than others, but within the context of a much more definitive nationalisation of Muslim political concerns. That is, the Zionist–Arab conflict became a Jewish–Muslim conflict in the eyes of many Palestinians, particularly those who became active in response to Western Wall tensions. Christians were still able to participate as Arabs, but for many months the national movement focused on a specifically Islamic issue. Christian identification with the national movement required a greater willingness to accept Islam, rather than Arabism, as a central focus of the movement.

1930: The al-Bahri Murder

An incident the following year threatened Christian–Muslim unity more directly and also sparked interdenominational tensions. In September 1930, a confrontation over proprietorship of a Haifa cemetery ended with the murder of a prominent Haifa Melkite Christian, Jamil al-Bahri, editor of the local newspaper *al-Zuhour* and president of the Haifa YMCA. The conflict stemmed from Muslim claims of ownership of the whole of Mazar Cemetery. Local Melkite leaders insisted that only a few wooden huts in the cemetery belonged to the Muslims, with the rest of the land being Christian property.[25] What began as a disagreement over property rights was transformed by inflammatory speeches by local Muslim leaders, some of whom incited violence against any Christian who entered the cemetery.[26] One of the antagonists was Rashid al-Hajj Ibrahim, a trustee of the Muslim *waqf* in Haifa whose newspaper, *al-Yarmuk*, later served as the Muslim community's mouthpiece in post-murder debates.[27] The conflict had been simmering for some time when, in early September 1930, a group of Melkites tried to build a hut in the cemetery to solidify their claim. A group of Muslims attacked the Christians, stoning and stabbing al-Bahri.[28] Six other Christians were also injured in the mêlée. The British police arrested seventeen men in connection with the murder, although seven of them, including chief suspects Hajj Ibrahim and Ramzi Omar, were soon released.[29]

The 1930 British report to the League of Nations summarised the story with little fanfare: 'relations between Moslem and Christian Arabs were, however, temporarily estranged as a result of a dispute over the ownership of a cemetery at Haifa, ending in a fracas in which a Christian sustained fatal injuries'.[30] The British focused on the legal aspect of the episode, and long after al-Bahri's murder were still engaged in the dispute, sending inspectors to determine who was buried in the cemetery, closely examining land deeds and *waqf* papers, and debating whether laws concerning land use or religious sites should apply to the case.[31] Perhaps the British did not fully understand the impact of such intercommunal violence, or maybe they had reason to downplay its importance to the Permanent Mandatory Commission. Whatever the case, they were wrong about both the short- and long-term impact of al-Bahri's murder.

Some Christians, particularly those in Haifa, appear to have been truly shaken by the intercommunal violence, particularly by the Muslim community's defensive posturing following the murder. Christians were incensed when Muslim notables attended al-Bahri's funeral, and only Bishop Hajjar's direct intervention prevented further confrontation.[32] That a religious property dispute should end in murder was frightening for Christians, and *al-Zuhour*'s tone reflected this sense of fear. In the first edition of *al-Zuhour* published after Jamil al-Bahri's death, his brother, Hanna al-Bahri, eulogised the deceased as 'a mediator of the brittle Arab unity and solidarity between Muslims and Christians'.[33] He blamed the pro-SMC paper *al-Yarmuk* for fanning the fires of sectarianism, although an article in *al-Yarmuk* accused *al-Zuhour* of the same.[34] Hanna al-Bahri's main concern was that *al-Yarmuk* demonstrated no compassion for the victim, instead offering only a 'defence of the Muslims and the people who want to blot out this crime'.[35] In a nod towards moderate elements, he tried to paint *al-Yarmuk*'s stance as communally divisive and suggested that 'the infractions and violations that happened in Haifa were against the calm Christian residents and the Muslim believers for whom their religion is one of peace and their work is for unity'.[36]

Two weeks later, *al-Zuhour* expanded its criticism to include the entire Muslim community. The writer (presumably Hanna al-Bahri again) stated that he had been inclined to consider the event a solitary case of anti-Christian violence, an exception to otherwise good interreligious relations in Haifa, but the evidence now suggested a more concerning trend. Not only did *al-Yarmuk* publish articles specifically defending the suspects, but demonstrations in the city included 'fiery speeches [suggesting that]

Figure 3.2 Cover of *al-Zuhour* from 27 October 1930, a special issue in remembrance of Jamil al-Bahri. *Courtesy of the National Library of Israel*

Christians are a corrupt race'.[37] Rather than trying to rebuild communal ties, the Muslims, Hanna al-Bahri suggested, had responded as if they were the victims rather than the aggressors.

In addition to offering a harsh critique of Haifa's Muslims, *al-Zuhour* attacked the AE and the SMC for their inaction. Al-Bahri was a devoted nationalist, the article claimed, who raised 'the flag of the national jihad', but he had been 'murdered by some of [the movement's] treacherous members' for trying to uphold communal rights.[38] Eventually, national leaders become involved and sought to calm tempers by assuring Christians that the murder resulted from a personal conflict that had nothing to do with religion.[39] That argument, combined with the leadership's initial silence, frustrated Haifa Melkites. For them, al-Bahri's murder was only the most violent case of intercommunal tension. Muslim complaints about Christians employed by the government continued, the YMMA's anti-missionary campaign had occasionally blurred the line between foreign and local Christians, and the national movement remained focused on the religious rights of Muslims in Jerusalem. Christians believed that their place in the nationalist movement was shrinking.

In addition to the general feeling of tension, the al-Bahri murder led to further intercommunal violence. A week after al-Bahri's murder a Catholic Arab (presumably Melkite, although the source does not clarify) attacked a Muslim newspaper editor in Jaffa, apparently in retaliation for the Haifa murder. Later, an argument about that attack erupted in a Jaffa café. A Muslim and a Christian exchanged angry words before the latter fled, but by the time police arrived Muslims had seriously beaten two Christians.[40] The spread of communal violence must have frightened Christians who knew of the horrors of sectarian violence, particularly in nineteenth-century Lebanon.

The Catholic community (both Latin and Melkite) demanded Christian solidarity across denominational lines. Instead, Catholics' defensive communalism led to a widening rift between Catholic and Orthodox Arabs. Particularly in Haifa, relations between the Christian communities soured. Al-Bahri was Melkite, and Latin and Greek Catholics invited other denominations to join in protest against Muslim treatment of Arab Christians. Bishop Hajjar held a meeting at his home designed to unify Christian ranks, but it turned into a political battle.[41] The Orthodox representatives left the meeting in anger and published their own declaration reaffirming their refusal to take part in any Christian attack on Islam. Greek Catholics subsequently withdrew their support from the AE, and the Society of Christian Youth in Haifa (a multi-denominational group of which al-Bahri was member) delivered the following message to the undersecretary for the colonies:

> We, the undersigned, who represent a majority of the Christian Arabs of Haifa, call your attention to the fact that the Palestine Arab Executive, having presented to you their demands in the name of all Christian Arabs in Palestine, we protest and declare they have no right to talk in the name of Christians who do not support that Executive, and whose spiritual leaders are all against them, we therefore ask the British Government not to take notice of the declarations and to remember that, being a minority in this land, we want to have our rights protected by the mandatory power to whom we swear allegiance.[42]

While British and Zionist observers had often noted denominational differences on political issues, Christians themselves were usually careful to try to present a united Christian front. They were simply too small a minority to subdivide themselves further. Furthermore, the ensuing debates crossed national party lines, with pro-Husayni and pro-Nashashibi Orthodox taking sides against Melkites, who also put national politics aside for the sake of denominational unity.

As clear as the division between Orthodox and Catholic voices on this issue appeared, there were some Christians who went against their denominational leanings. The AE received letters of concern from Orthodox groups in Bethlehem and Jaffa,[43] but a third telegram stands out. Khalil Sabbagh of Tulkarm wrote to the AE in October 1930 declaring: 'All Christians of Tulkarem disapprove of the work of the group of men in Haifa and their absurd demands. [The Christians] declare publicly their support for the path of unity of Muslims and Christians under the Arab Executive of Jerusalem.'[44] It is unclear if Sabbagh was Latin or Melkite, but sources agree that he was Catholic and a strong advocate of Muslim–Christian cooperation. He was a signatory of a joint Muslim–Christian letter protesting the Balfour Declaration and Zionism in 1921, and when the Indian Muslim leader Shawkat Ali went to Tulkarm in 1931, Sabbagh was one of three local leaders who made speeches at the mosque during his visit.[45] His reasons for remaining supportive of intercommunal Arab unity, despite the unpopularity of such a stance among Catholics, are unclear. Still, such a reaction reinforces the idea that personal political opinions are based on a wide variety of reasons, including, but not limited to, religious identification.

ʿIsa Bandak clearly articulated his perspective of the Haifa incident on the front pages of *Sawt al-Shaʿb*. He lamented the 'distressing events in Haifa', but focused on the importance of national, rather than religious, identification. He insisted that 'Christian Arabs don't support any group of Christians who try to view the Haifa event as a purely communalist (*taʿifi*) occurrence, because the Muslims Arabs do not support any group of Muslims that is trying to injure the cause of Arab nationalism'.[46] Bandak was at least partially wrong about both Christians and Muslims; some on both sides did turn more towards their religious identification, even at the expense of national identification. Still, he persisted in rejecting communalism, decrying the notion that the Arab leadership should be either Christian or Muslim and insisting that Christians would not let 'their importance . . . and honour [be] tarnished by a group of those wronged by a crime of vileness and indignity'.[47] Claims that Christians needed protection from the Muslims were embarrassing for Bandak, and he declared that Christians would 'remain a great power in the battleground of jihad' following the path of 'Arab nationalism and holy solidarity'.[48]

His next article attacked 'young Catholics in Haifa' specifically and even suggested that Bishop Hajjar had exploited the incident for personal ends. Hajjar 'aspired to bring unity to the Christian front', Bandak accused, 'and to become its leader and to speak in its name in political and national matters'.[49] Bandak urged caution, however, in putting political responsibility into the hands of 'a man of the church', particularly because 'the Latin denomination is a minuscule minority'.[50] His response to the rise of communalism was to blame a small group despite their status as victims of intercommunal violence.

Al-ʿIsa opted for the middle ground and sought to blame someone besides the Muslim suspects or the Catholic sectarians. He published an article in *Filastin* blaming the Zionists for 'paying large sums of money to both Christians and Moslems for the express purpose of bringing about enmity and quarrels between them'.[51] Zionist involvement was unproven, although the leadership had been paying close attention to developments. Zionist Executive Chairman Kisch wrote in his diary:

> Aziz Doment, the [pro-Zionist] Christian–Arab author, called to see me. He was much excited about the Christian–Moslem split at Haifa, but I made it clear that we would not fish in troubled waters, although if the Christian Arabs now realize that they have been unwise to stimulate Moslem fanaticism, I believe that such a change of attitude is for their own eventual safety.[52]

For Kisch and the Zionists, watching inter-Arab fighting from the sidelines was effective enough, since intercommunal disunity weakened Palestinian abilities to confront British policies.

Because the sources concerning this event provide narrative rather than statistical analysis, it is difficult to determine what portion of the community was involved in this intercommunal conflict that began in the Haifa cemetery and spread to other parts of the country. The fact that two major Haifa papers, *al-Zuhour* and *al-Yarmuk*, devoted so much space to the conflict, that violence did spread, albeit in limited fashion, that the British, Zionists and Arab nationalist notables, and international press all watched the events unfold, hints at its weight. Arabs debated the communal tensions in nationalist terms. Accusations flew in both directions blaming one another for damaging the national cause, and Christians, uncomfortable with Melkite communalism, felt it necessary to reassert their support for the national movement.

1931: The Islamic Congress and Arab Orthodox Congress

Christian fears of the growing connection between nationalist and Islamic themes were enhanced in 1931 when al-Husayni organised an Islamic congress to be held in Jerusalem. The Arab Orthodox laity held a simultaneous congress to consider how best to deal with the death of the long-time patriarch, Damianos. Both meetings were specifically organised along religious lines, but explicitly supported the goals of the greater nationalist programme, an important trend towards communal organisation in support of the nationalist cause.

The Islamic Congress was the culmination of al-Husayni's efforts to garner wider Arab and Muslim support for the Palestinian cause.[53] The invitation to the congress suggested a highly political agenda, such as a promise to 'strengthen Moslem religion against attack of [the] irreligious ... and [to] save Holy Places especially Jerusalem from all foreign ambition and domination'.[54] The official agenda was more limited and consisted of three stated aims: (1) to establish a Muslim university in Jerusalem; (2) to establish a permanent pan-Islamic committee to address political questions; and (3) to discuss the revival of the caliphate.[55] Nearly 150 Muslims from around the world attended.[56] Newspaper coverage was heavy, and the Christian press in particular sought to bring a Christian element into the story. Both *Filastin* and *al-Karmil* often placed headlines for the Islamic Assembly and the Arab Orthodox Congress side by side, and *Filastin* reported on the shared issue of the protection of the holy places and the visit of delegates from each conference to the other.[57]

Al-Husayni used the congress to strengthen bonds between the pan-Islamic movement and his goals for Palestine, and he directed the congress in that direction. He preferred not to address the revival of the caliphate, but included the subject under pressure from Indian Muslims. Leading Indian Muslims supported Palestine politically and had declared a 'Palestine Day' on 16 May 1930, but they were also heavily involved in the caliphate movement and, under the leadership of Shawkat Ali, forced it on to the agenda.[58] The caliphate was not the only contentious issue: the Iranian ex-prime minister Diya° al-Din al-Tabataba°i, argued that the sole purpose of the congress should be 'to combat the Christian Government in Palestine which discriminated in favour of the local Christians and Christian missionaries'.[59] Shawkat Ali refused to criticise the British because of his need to stay on good terms with the government in India, and Hajj Amin did not want to risk alienating the Arab Christians.[60] Such differences in opinion concerning the basic goals of the congress weakened the potential impact of the meeting. Muslim opponents of the congress also challenged al-Husayni's goals, including many newly engaged Palestinian activists who were concerned that applying international political pressure was not enough. Matthews argues that for this group, some of whom eventually helped to establish *Istiqlal*, 'the basis of anti-imperialist activism was not Pan-Islamic but Arab nationalist'.[61] The truth is more likely in between, with pan-Islamists stressing their nationalism due to particular political circumstances.

The British worried a great deal about the congress, but at least from a governmental perspective the meeting went smoothly: a British report declared that 'any apprehensions which might have been entertained that the holding of a Moslem Congress in Jerusalem would lead to disorders proved to be unfounded'.[62] While no violence occurred, the congress stirred up much controversy. Zionists opposed the congress outright and tried to decrease participation. They also hired an Arab journalist to provide negative coverage of the meeting.[63] The Nashashibi faction's National Party opposed the congress on the grounds that al-Husayni's real goal was to strengthen his own authority at the expense of the opposition.[64] One Palestinian scholar reports that the National Party sent operatives to Jaffa to incite Arab Christians against the congress by playing to their fear of pan-Islamism, though they were unsuccessful.[65] Lesch, too, asserts that Christians were concerned that their status in the national movement could be negatively influenced by an Islamic revival.[66] Al-Husayni did his best to assuage those fears, and the final resolutions reflected his goal of retaining Christian support for the nationalist movement. One resolution called on Muslims to fight against Christian missionary activity among Muslims, but also to publicly thank Palestinian and Transjordanian Christians for their support of the Islamic congress, and to congratulate the Arab Orthodox community for its successful congress.[67]

The Orthodox Congress was held in response to the death of Jerusalem Patriarch Damianos on 14 August 1931, a long-standing friend of the British. Despite this legacy, initial coverage of the patriarch's death in

the Arabic press, particularly the Christian-owned papers, was respectful, since Orthodox leaders did not want to damage their credibility prior
to renewing their demands on the patriarchate now that a new leadership
would be installed. *Filastin* featured a front-page picture of Damianos
with detailed coverage of his funeral. Only brief mention of Arab demands
on the patriarch was made in a lengthy second-page biography.[68] *Mirat
al-Sharq* touched briefly on the patriarch's close relations with the British,
while devoting an entire column to listing the numerous attendees.[69]
Hopes for an opportunity to change the patriarchate's relationship with
the Arab laity were well founded. Damianos had been known for his
anti-nationalist stance, perhaps in gratitude to the British for saving him
from being deposed by the Brotherhood of the Holy Sepulchre in 1918.[70]
Zionists counted Damianos as a friend, too: according to Kisch, the patriarch 'took the line that the Greek Christians are, like [the Jews], in the
minority and that we should cooperate, although circumstances [made]
it impossible for him at the moment to speak out openly in this sense'.[71]
Kisch also wrote in his diary that the 'friendship [was] strengthened by the
fact that we have bought land from him for some 200,000 pounds, saving
him and his community from bankruptcy'.[72]

Despite the respect shown for the deceased patriarch, *Mirat al-Sharq*
did encourage the community to utilise the opportunity to seek a major
overhaul of the local Orthodox Church. The Orthodox community had
been passive since its first congress in 1923, claimed the paper, and it
took the death of Damianos to wake it from its sleep.[73] In mid-October
1931, *Filastin* argued, 'It is true that Palestine it is under two mandates,
one the British and the other the Zionist, and it is true that the Orthodox
community is under three mandates: the British, the Zionist, and, thirdly,
the Greek.'[74] Al-ᶜIsa criticised the Greek 'mandatory power' for supporting Zionism and called on all Palestinians, both Christian and Muslim, to
stand together against these three Western occupiers.

Initially, activists within the Arab Orthodox laity responded to
Damianos' death by demanding that the British implement the resolutions of the First Orthodox Congress.[75] The British, claiming that it was
not within their right as a mandatory power to make such changes to a
religious institution, did nothing.[76] The Orthodox community protested
and held the Second Arab Orthodox Congress in Haifa on 28 November
1931 under the leadership of ᶜIsa al-ᶜIsa.[77] Representatives came from
across Palestine and Jordan to reformulate their demands: the election of
an Arab patriarch; British support for the Arab Orthodox cause even in the
face of outside (Greek) pressures; and a boycott of the patriarchal elections 'until the complete rights of the denomination are achieved'.[78] All

attending members came together, *Filastin* reported the following day, to overcome the schisms and suffering of the Arab Orthodox. The demands of the conferences were printed on the front page of that newspaper on 1 December.[79]

Like previous attempts to alter the church leadership, the 1931 congress insisted that Orthodox Christians, like their compatriot Muslims, were Arab. The Muslim–Christian violence in Haifa and Jaffa a year earlier did not affect Orthodox calls for full recognition as part of the Arab majority. Based on the assumption that national and communal identities are inherently contradictory, some scholars, such as Elie Kedourie, have suggested that the Orthodox community joined the national movement knowing it meant 'the abandonment of communal organisation and the defiant assertion that religion was a strictly private affair . . . that [religion] had no political and little social significance'.[80] On the contrary, the Orthodox community insisted that it could be fully nationalist, while also remaining unified as a religious minority community in a shift back towards the *millet* system, an idea that became even more important in the 1940s. It is important to remember here that rather than assuming 'nationalism' to be strong identification with a territorial nation-state, nationalism was a new and unformed notion. The conflict with the patriarchate and the growing importance of Islam in the national movement both contributed to the increased importance of Arab Orthodox self-identification, albeit in different ways. Orthodox Christians saw their demands as Arabs strengthened by their Orthodoxy, and their demands as Orthodox Christians strengthened by their Arabness. The Orthodox community stood out for its efforts to tie those two elements together in an effort to garner political strength; a trend that became even more important in the 1940s and is discussed in detail in Chapter 5. In many ways the application of Orthodox nationalism paralleled efforts by some Muslim leaders to politicise their religious identification.

A later development in the Orthodox controversy illustrates how the Palestinian question influenced Arab Christians. Arab complaints against the patriarchate delayed the election of a new patriarch until June 1935 when another Greek, Timoteus, was elected as the successor to Damianos. Recently founded Orthodox clubs protested the election vigorously, and there were even reports of 'Arab rowdies' attacking Greek monks.[81] Telegrams to the high commissioner arrived from Orthodox Christians in Lydda, Nablus, Jerusalem, Ramallah, Jifna, Beit Jala, Ramle, Nazareth, Haifa, Jaffa and a handful of towns in Transjordan. Among the protests from within Palestine, nearly all rejected Timoteus' election and demanded greater Arab participation. More than half of the telegrams sent by Orthodox Christians from the other side of the Jordan, however, supported the nomination.[82] This discrepancy reflects how the Palestinian Orthodox community's disgust with the patriarchate went deeper than simply the Greek character of the leadership. Damianos' willingness to sell land to the Zionists irritated their nationalist sensibilities as well. Arab Christians in Palestine sought a solution to the Orthodox controversy because of concerns about spiritual as well as political leadership, while their Transjordanian co-religionists were more apt to accept reasonable Greek rule.

One by-product of the Arab–Greek tensions was the galvanisation of the Arab Orthodox community. Internal differences, even those associated with national political rivalries, did not hinder unity on the Orthodox issue. When the Orthodox Executive Committee met in July 1935 to discuss Timoteus' impending election, Ya°coub Farraj, a Nashashibi supporter, led a meeting attended by °Isa Bandak, °Isa al-°Isa and al-Khuri Nicola Khuri, a pro-Husayni Orthodox priest.[83] Even Yusef al-Khuri, a National Party supporter known for his pro-Zionist views, attended.[84]

The Islamic Assembly and the Arab Orthodox Congress held in 1931 and the Arab Orthodox community's overtly nationalist aims illustrate the way in which Muslim and Christian communities were redefining themselves. Arab Orthodox lay leaders tried to enhance the Arab nature of the Orthodox community despite fears that the nationalist movement was becoming defined more by Islam with each passing year. The religiously charged violence of 1929, the al-Bahri murder and its aftermath, and al-Husayni's efforts to rally support from the pan-Islamic movement for the Palestinian cause altered what it meant to be Palestinian, and Christians debated their place within that shifting definition. They became, it appears, more and more comfortable with embracing religious community as an essential piece of their self-identification.

1934: Electoral Politics and Communal Organisation

The communalist tensions of the early 1930s influenced politics as well, with religious affiliation playing an important role in the Arab response to a British proposal for a Palestinian legislative council that abandoned communal representation. The changing political structures also created political alternatives to the Husayni and Nashashibi factions and ultimately led to Arab organisation outside elite circles. Arab Christians responded in a variety of ways: they argued for communal recognition; they sought to position themselves in opposition to other Christian denominations; and they organised denominationally specific social groups.

When the Ottoman Empire embraced constitutional change in 1908, citizens of all religious stripes espoused revolutionary ideas of 'liberty, equality, fraternity and justice'.[85] Arabs in Palestine immediately embraced the new political opportunities and sought representation at the municipal, regional and imperial levels. As discussed in Chapter 1, the British were initially dedicated to maintaining the 'status-quo', which in their assessment meant the pre-*tanzimat*, pre-constitution *millet* system. Thus, any sort of colonial initiative to establish representative councils divided the representatives according to religious community. This was particularly true during Britain's first effort to establish a legislative council in 1923.

In the mid-1930s, the Mandate government once again started planning for a legislative council. In the intervening years, however, the British changed their minds about the most effective way to establish a council. Rather than focus on the tripartite religious division (Muslim, Christian and Jewish), they embraced a racial or ethnic distinction and argued that the council should provide parity for Jews and Arabs. Jerusalem District Commissioner Campbell argued that 'it is highly dangerous, if not impossible, to allow considerations of religion to carry weight in the question of the appointment of Municipal Officers'.[86] This sentiment was in direct opposition to the traditional position of British officials, notably High Commissioner Herbert Samuel, who was concerned with maintaining an acceptable religious balance on every governmental committee, official organisation and elected body. Despite earlier Arab efforts to convince the British that Muslims and Christians all primarily identified themselves as Arabs, Arab Christians were horrified with this change. Robson provides extensive detail on the legislative council debates and concludes that 'Arab Christians across the political spectrum came to support the idea of Christian communal representation'.[87] The reason for 'this unprecedented pan-Christian alignment', she argues, was 'a new sense among Christians that their political existence in the Mandate state was under threat from the increasing Jewish presence in representative institutions of all kinds'.[88] While this is certainly true, increasing tensions between Arab Christians and Muslims further reinforced the importance of specifically Christian representation on the council. They were, it seems, interested in retaining their importance vis-à-vis the Jews, the Muslims and other Christians denominations.

In 1934, the British altered election laws to provide greater representation for the Jerusalem's growing Jewish population. Because of the government's proclivity for preserving the semblance of even-handedness, even while maintaining domination, the division was usually more or less representative of the population, but never reflected the precise proportions of each community. Instead, the British used religious community as a way to bring a pro-Mandate balance to official organisations. For example, the appointed Advisory Council, founded in 1920 under the chairmanship of the high commissioner for the purpose of establishing some element of local representation, included four Muslims, three Arab Christians, three Jews and ten British officials.[89] With this composition, the British appeared to grant Arabs an advisory role, though still retaining a Jewish–British majority. The aborted Legislative Council, which was boycotted by the Arabs, would have comprised twelve elected and ten nominated officials, with at least two Jews and two Christians among those elected. By adding the ten appointed pro-British councillors to the two Jewish councillors, the British guaranteed a reasonably government-friendly council.[90]

There is no single way to manage representative politics, and the British had tried before to alter the meaning of representation in an effort to increase the Jewish presence on the council. The 1926 Municipal Ordinance apportioned seats based on a community's percentage of tax payments rather than on population, while still allotting seats along communal lines.[91] In the 1927 election, Christians lost a seat to the Muslims, although the Jewish–Arab balance remained. The 1934 alteration proved to be much more controversial, since council seats were allotted based on ward rather than religious community. Elections by ward served to bypass the traditional sectarian distribution, resulting in more seats for the growing Jewish majority in Jerusalem. In the end, British efforts were effective in producing a city council that balanced Jewish and Arab interests. Whereas five Muslims, four Jews and three Christians had served on the Jerusalem municipal council elected in 1926, in 1934 the new election law produced a council with only four Muslims and two Christians, but six Jews.[92]

The reduced Christian presence on the council created serious tension between denominations, not surprising given the Latin–Orthodox tensions that emerged following the al-Bahri murder. The Latin leadership protested the new electoral system claiming that, due to the dispersed nature of the Latin population, Latins would receive no seats at all on the local municipal council.[93] Church leaders even suggested that the Latin community might boycott the elections if the system was not changed.[94] Bishop Fellinger met with Max Nurock, the acting chief secretary at the time, and 'said he considered it an injustice to Christians and Catholics to have fixed the number of Christian representatives to the Municipal Council of Jerusalem at 2'. Nurock explained that they had 'definitely not fixed the number', even though it seemed likely that two Christians would be elected, a percentage roughly reflective of their population in the city.[95] To assuage the fears of Latin critics, the high commissioner suggested that

> if after the elections have taken place, the high commissioner is satisfied that any large section of the population of Jerusalem is not represented on the Council and the interests of that section are liable to suffer detriment thereby, then he will doubtless be prepared to consider the position in light of the circumstances.[96]

Arab Orthodox leaders also expressed concerns. An Orthodox lay organisation under the leadership of Nakhleh Kattan protested the participation of the chief clerk of the Orthodox patriarchate on the electoral committee since he was not representative of the Arab Orthodox community, but rather of the Greek leadership.[97] In 1935, Raghib al-Nashashibi argued that in the municipal council religious matters should be voted upon only by representatives of that group, and Judge Francis Khayat and Ya'coub Farraj proposed a Christian subcommittee within the council to deal with such matters.[98]

As Robson clearly displays, Christians were upset at losing seats to the Jews and argued for communal representation as 'a tactic in the continuing struggle against Zionist encroachment'.[99] Mughannam Mughannam, for instance, voiced concerns that many Christian leaders around the country were afraid that the 'Government might submit to Jewish pressure and appoint a Jewish Deputy Mayor' in Jerusalem. Yet Christian concerns were often framed in terms that suggested competition between Arab religious groups, too. Robson recognises such divisions, but focuses instead on the emergence of a 'broadly based Christian communalism'.[100] Christian leaders did hold meetings to discuss 'proper representation for Christians in the country, following the example of what the Mufti's family is for Muslim Arabs',[101] though such efforts were short-lived and were apparently overshadowed by deeper divisions between denominations. The Jewish perspective, while perhaps overstated, was that Arab Christian unity could damage Zionist interests in the short term, but, as Zionist leader Moshe Shertok suggested, might be of long-term benefit to the Jewish movement since the Christians 'will certainly find an axe to grind against their Moslem brethren, and will secretly act about forging weapons of self-protection against the threat of Moslem domination'.[102] Even considering the source of this assessment, it seems correct to conclude that Christians were seeking ways to better organise and unify themselves as a minority population in opposition to Jewish and Muslim movements, something that most prominent Christian leaders had argued against ten years earlier.

While a united Christian front never materialised, Christians did begin organising more seriously along religious lines in the social and cultural field, if not the political. Although this trend tapered off during the 1936–1939 revolt, efforts rebounded in the 1940s. The political elite organised itself in the early years of the Mandate in civil/political organisations such *al-Nadi al-ʿArabi* and *al-Muntada al-Adabi*, but the efforts of the 1930s were markedly different. First, there was a much higher rate of participation in the 1930s. Instead of being centred in Jerusalem, Haifa and Jaffa, and attended only by members of traditional leading families, new organisations emerged in many towns and villages throughout Palestine, with much broader participation. Secondly, while some secular organisations were founded in this period, both Muslim and Christian youth movements began establishing active and well-organised communal organs.

The most important Christian organisations were the various forms of the Orthodox Club, such as the Orthodox Union Club of Jerusalem which was founded in 1931.[103] In addition to the Jerusalem branch, the Orthodox Club and the Orthodox Defence Society, both based in Nazareth, were founded in 1935.[104] In the mid-1930s, Orthodox Christians also formed clubs in Lydda, Jaffa and Acre; by the 1940s, there were at least fifteen branches of the Orthodox Union. Most were eventually brought together under the umbrella of the Union of Arab Orthodox Clubs, which was founded in the early 1940s.[105] Christian social organisation may have been triggered by the rapid expansion of the YMMA movement in the late 1920s, and organisational efforts by Muslims continued throughout the 1930s. The trend also reflects the relative stability of Mandate Palestine in the early 1930s compared with the uncertainty immediately following the British occupation, as well as the growth of a new, better educated generation of Palestinian Arabs.

The growth of social organisations was paralleled by the emergence of a variety of new political parties. The Husayni and Nashashibi factions unified their respective supporters by founding centralised political parties. In December 1934, Raghib al-Nashashibi founded the National Defence Party, of which ʿIsa al-ʿIsa was a founding member.[106] This affront to Husayni authority, in addition to the dissolution of the AE, caused the Husayni faction, under the guidance of Jamal al-Husayni, to found the Palestine Arab Party in April 1935. The highest ranking Christian in that party was vice-president Alfred Rok, and Emil al-Ghuri was elected as general secretary. Al-Ghuri was a journalist who, at the Mufti's request, began publishing the English-language *The Arab Federation* in 1933 and an Arabic weekly newspaper, *al-Shaʿb*, in 1934. Both papers were hostile towards the Nashashibis, and at one point the Nashashibis sued al-Ghuri, who was found guilty of libel.[107] Michel Azar, a Christian from Jaffa, was also added to the party's central leadership soon after its founding.[108]

As the family rivalry continued to evolve into a more structured political form, other elite Palestinian Arabs also founded their own parties. Dr Husayn al-Khalidi, mayor of Jerusalem, organised the Reform Party (*Hizb al-Islah*) in 1935 after his family broke with the Nashashibis during the 1934 Jerusalem municipal elections.[109] The party drew support from former opposition leaders who were unwilling to return to the Husayni camp, but who were, nonetheless, unimpressed with the Nashashibis. The party was run by three secretaries, one of whom was Shibley Jamal, a Protestant. Also involved in the Reform Party were Christians George Salah, ᶜIsa Bandak and Yaᶜcoub Bordqush.[110] The most important policy difference between the Reform Party and the others was Khalidi's willingness to support a British-endorsed legislative council.[111] The last significant mainstream party was the National Bloc Party, formed in 1935 under the direction of ᶜAbd al-Latif Salah, a former member of the SMC who desired to prove to the high commissioner that he could be effective as a relatively moderate leader.[112]

Two other organisations emerged from the political opening of the 1930s, both of which Porath deems 'radical'. The first was the loosely organised Youth Party that emerged from two Arab Youth Conferences held in 1932 and 1936. These gatherings sought to build a political alliance across factional lines and purposefully excluded the most important young leaders from both the Husayni and Nashashibi factions. In addition, the leadership chose Jaffa as its centre of operations in an attempt to avoid close proximity to the most intense factional conflicts. ᶜIsa Bandak, who by this point had left the Husayni faction and joined the Reform Party, was elected vice-president of the movement. Husayni supporter Emil al-Ghuri was also an active participant, suggesting that the youth movement garnered support from across party lines.[113]

Finally, *Hizb al-Istiqlal* (the Independence Party) was a pan-Arab political organisation that emerged from talks begun at the Islamic Congress in 1931 and reached its zenith in 1933. Porath argues that 'to a great extent the emergence of this Party was an outcome of the growth of an educated class of young radicals who saw in Pan-Arabism the panacea for all the illnesses of Arab society'.[114] Despite Christian attempts throughout the earlier Mandate to define themselves, like their Muslim neighbours, as Arabs, the only Christian mentioned among the participants in this pan-Arabist party was Salim Salameh, a doctor from Ramallah.[115]

Despite periodic tensions between segments of the Muslim and Christian population and a more general definition of nationalist goals with Islamic language, Christians continued to spread throughout the leadership of various parties, sitting across factional and policy lines from one another. Christian notables, let alone the non-elite classes, lacked political unity, and even members of the same denomination disagreed. Still, denominations often sought to increase their cohesiveness as a minority community.

1935: Al-Qassam's Martyrdom: Religion and Revolt

A third category of social activists emerged on the fringes of the new political parties and the civil and religious organisations: those preparing for armed rebellion. The 1929 violence had radicalised the population, and many were now willing to fight for their cause. ʿIzz al-Din al-Qassam became the most famous rebel and his efforts spawned a much broader movement by tapping into the frustrations of the lower class.

He was not the only leader of such activity; most of it was conducted by *Istiqlal*, Youth Congresses and the YMMA, as well by as a variety of scout troops and other 'radical supporters of Amin al-Husayni'.[116] There is evidence that a few Christians participated in such clandestine organisations. The underground group *al-Jihad al-Muqaddas* (Sacred Struggle), led by ʿAbd al-Qadir al-Husayni, the son of Musa Kazim al-Husayni, included fourteen Muslims and three Christians. At 15 per cent, those Christians reflected a higher participation rate than their percentage of the population as a whole. With the exception of this group, however, Christians do not explicitly appear in the other clandestine revolutionary groups, such as *al-Kaff al-Khadra* (The Green Palm), *al-Shaʿb al-Thaʾir* (The Rebellious Youth) and *al-Yad al-Sawdaʾ* (The Black Hand), though member lists are far from complete or accurate.[117]

Al-Qassam's death at the hands of the British in 1935, which Palestinians quickly interpreted as political martyrdom, dramatically increased his importance as a symbol of the armed resistance. Before his death, al-Qassam had been relatively unknown in Zionist circles and among government officials. For example, he was not mentioned in either the Zionist-run English daily *The Palestine Post*, or in an extensive collection of CID documents from 1935 until after he was killed during an encounter with British police.[118] The government appears to have been too consumed with Husayni–Nashashibi unification efforts at that time to pay any attention to an itinerant preacher from Haifa. Even after his death, CID documents listed al-Qassam as one of seven leaders involved in organising 'gangs'; the note 'now deceased' next to his name suggests that they believed his threat to be ended.[119] In reality, al-Qassam's influence had just begun.

Al-Qassam's movement was just one of many resistance organisations to emerge in the years following the Western Wall violence. His role in the foundation of the YMMA in Haifa, his official job as imam of al-Istiqlal Mosque (to which he was appointed in 1924) and his work as marriage registrar in the countryside, provided him with an audience.[120] Many Arab peasants lost land and employment during the Mandate due in large part to Zionist land purchases, and they were frustrated by the failure of the Arab elite to address their grievances. While al-Qassam preached a message of reform, seeking to bring Muslims back to a 'more pure' faith,[121] he also supported his militant anti-colonial stance with a radical interpretation of Islamic theology while many nationalists were still advocating a more explicitly political response to Zionism.[122] His importance can best be seen in the response to his death. Al-Qassam's funeral was the largest gathering ever in modern Palestine.[123]

The meaning of al-Qassam's life and his martyrdom immediately provoked much debate.[124] An announcement of his death rang from the minaret of al-Aqsa Mosque in Jerusalem, and his name was included in Friday prayers in mosques around the country on 22 November.[125] As soon as the nationalist leadership realised how important al-Qassam had become in the political imagination of the populace, it tried to co-opt his message for its own uses. Al-ᶜIsa of *Filastin* immediately Arabised the religious leader, denuding him of any Islamic content:

> although al-Qassam was a Syrian by birth, he died for Palestine, thus proving the bond which unites all Arabs. Some years ago, al-Qassam fought against the French in Syria. When the French military got on his heels, he fled to Palestine and resolved to fight the English.[126]

Al-ᶜIsa concluded by arguing that there were no boundaries between Arab nations, and al-Qassam's participation in both Syrian and Palestinian resistance was the best example of Arab unity. Al-ᶜIsa used al-Qassam's pan-Arab resistance to reduce the impact of the martyred leader's religious message.

While there is no specific evidence concerning al-Qassam's perspective on Christianity, his principal intersection with the nationalist movement was through the YMMA, which was created to address Muslim concerns about Christian missionaries. Al-Qassam's vision of a nationalism reinforced by Islam was common among the burgeoning Islamist movement of the 1930s, particularly in Egypt, the homeland of the Muslim Brotherhood.[127] Moreover, al-Qassam's major concern was that Palestine's Muslims were practising their faith improperly, and he sought 'the recovery of Muslim Palestinian identity'.[128] Christians advocating non-religious nationalism must have been wary of this goal and specifically did not want al-Qassam's brand of Islam to gain currency within the mainstream nationalist movement. Islam had always been one form of national legitimation, but not the central one, something Christian leaders wanted to maintain. They feared that al-Qassam's religious activism, which was closely connected to the Salafi movement, could offset that balance. Fortunately for the Christian leadership, traditional elite Muslims were equally threatened by calls for a popular uprising with a strong Islamic component.[129] The religious elements of al-Qassam's movement undermined elite control of Islam, establishing what Johnson calls 'a broadened and heightened popular conception of resistance as a religious, and therefore a moral and ethical, duty'.[130] His populist style of leadership also undermined the elitist, distant attitude of the notable class, creating angst among the ruling class, too.[131]

Not all radical activists were swayed by such Islamic rhetoric. *Istiqlal* and the Youth Congress were not religious organisations, and many of the more radical resistance leaders homed in on al-Qassam's calls for revolt and his adamant anti-British focus rather than on his Islamism. The use of al-Qassam during a 9 December 1935 rally attended by 2,000 people provides an example. A picture of al-Qassam decorated the speakers' platform, and the group agreed on a resolution declaring support for al-Qassam's political views while completely ignoring his religious claims. Christians Michel Mitri and George Matar were among the seven speakers at the rally, although their speeches were not recorded in the British report of the event.[132]

Still, on the outskirts of the political field, al-Qassam's religious message did trigger a rise in Islamic fundamentalist organisations. The British were concerned that peripheral organisations such as the 'Allah Party' (presumably *Hizb Allah*), which they confirmed was the same as The Society to March with the Religious Laws of the Prophet of God and His Messenger, would engage in terrorist acts against them.[133] Other religious groups, such as the Husayni-supported Society to Commend Virtue and Condemn Vice, 'with the exception of exhorting the faithful not to sell their lands to the Jew, appear[ed] to be purely religious in content'.[134] The lesser-known groups were likely more closely affiliated with al-Qassam's immediate followers, who were largely from among the displaced peasants living in Haifa, even if helped organisationally by Hajj Amin and the leaders of *Istiqlal*.[135] During the 1936–9 revolt, such politically active peasants emerged as important players in the national resistance.

Despite these hints of the radical impact of al-Qassam's influence, in the short term his message was successfully co-opted by elite spokesmen.

The Young Men's Congress (*Mu³tamar al-Shabaab*), which was supported by such elite elements, held an *arba°een* (a commemoration event
held forty days after a person's death) in which his message was framed
in moderate terms, ignoring both his call to arms and his call to religious
morality, even though al-Qassam advocated both during his lifetime. The
YMMA and *Istiqlal* held their own *arba°een*, and 'middle-class radicals
delivered speeches which were . . . "strong in their tone"'.[136] Later, when
the traditional leadership lost direct control of Arab rebel activity during
the 1936 revolt, al-Qassam's legacy was evoked in much more controversial ways and often provided the ideological impetus for the most severe
interreligious conflicts of the entire Mandate period.[137]

Conclusions

The increased importance of Islam in the rhetoric of the nationalist movement and a few instances of interreligious tension undermined the unity
Christians once held concerning their role in Palestinian society and politics. One Zionist writer asserted that:

> among the Palestinian Arab Christians were also found [some] who supported
> politically this Moslem-theocratic rule, and when necessary joined in the activ-
> ities of Haj Amin . . . some out of fear, being a minority community dwelling
> among a Moslem majority which also threatened their peace and safety, [and]
> some in the hopes of private gain in one form or another. These Christians
> . . . not only added political weight to the plots of the Mufti and the Supreme
> Muslim Council against the Jews, but first and foremost they sacrificed their
> right as Christians to political equality in Arab affairs in Palestine by their
> support of the Moslem-theocratic rule of Haj Amin.[138]

The writer is correct that Christian support bolstered al-Husayni's position vis-à-vis the Mandate government, since it bolstered his claim to
speak for all Palestinians. Yet this passage provides only two explanations
for Christian support for 'Moslem-theocratic rule' (itself a questionable
formulation): fear and private gain. Certainly, there were Christians who
were hedging their bets. They may have asked themselves, 'What will be
best for us as Christians when we are living under an independent Arab
government?' And there were surely those who sought personal gain, both
among Christians and Muslims, without regard to communal or national
loyalties.

What the writer ignored, however, were the two strands of Christian
thought apparently most prominent among Christian leaders: the secular
Arab nationalist and the communalist. Most Christians fell somewhere

between these two poles, but the intensification of interreligious conflict, such as that which occurred following the murder of al-Bahri and as represented by the Islamic Congress in 1931, deepened the divide between those dedicated to remaining fully within Palestinian nationalist circles and those desiring a return to a *millet*-like system granting special status on a communal basis during Ottoman times.

In the period from 1929 to 1935, the rise of Islamic rhetoric within the national movement, first due to the Western Wall crisis and later in response to al-Qassam's martyrdom and legacy, continued to pressure Christians to examine their place in Palestinian Arab society and the national movement. Plans for an Arab Christian congress, the rise of Christian social organisations and demands for greater Christian representation at the municipal level, suggest an increased awareness among Palestinian Christians of the importance of communal solidarity and the necessity of fighting for the perpetuation of Christians' historically strong role in society. Of course, Christian solidarity was difficult to attain for many reasons. Individual Christians disagreed about the basic political approach that Palestinians should take towards the British, leading some to support the Husaynis and others to support the Nashashibis. There were denominational differences, too. When threatened, Haifa Catholics retreated towards communal isolation, but the Orthodox community refused to join them, criticising them instead for damaging the national movement. Efforts to speak on behalf of 'the Christian community' were thus perpetually undermined by the diversity of Christian views.

While there were other factors in play (such as the growing Zionist threat and an increasingly antagonistic British government), the shift in Christian attitudes towards communalism was a direct response to the growing identification of Palestinian Muslims with their religious community. The importance of Islam in national politics nudged even the most nationalist Christians to rely more on their own communal associations. Among the most important reasons for the rising importance of Islam were the regional increase in Islamic justifications for nationalism, the increasing number of voices shaping debates about Palestinian national and communal identification, and the new implications of those terms. Whereas the traditional elite had once carefully monitored such conversations, the 1930s witnessed the rise of multiple voices claiming to speak on behalf of some segment of the population. The Husayni–Nashashibi rift still drove national politics, and in an effort to increase their bases of support both sides established ties with, and were willing to accept the support of, groups not necessarily dedicated to the publicly declared political and ideological platforms of the elite-centred organisations.[139] In addition, the failure of the elite-centred political movement to make progress with regard to halting Zionist immigration or achieving Arab self-rule left the leadership open to severe criticism.

The 1936–1939 revolt soon altered the political landscape again, forcing Christians to assess their place in society within a radically new framework. Arab Christians never acted as a single, unified whole, but difficult political circumstances did give communalist ideology more credence.

Notes

1. *Al-Jami*ᶜ*a al-*ᶜ*Arabiyya*, 29 August 1929.
2. ISA P-987/22, 'Declaration to the Muslim and Christians World', Yaᶜcoub Farraj, President of General Arab Assembly, 27 October 1929.
3. ISA P3050/16, Casualty Summary, n.d.
4. Musa Buderi, 'The Palestinians: Tensions between Nationalist and Religious Identities', in James P. Jankowski and I. Gershoni (eds), *Rethinking Arab Nationalism* (New York: Columbia University Press, 1997), p. 195.
5. Weldon Matthews, 'Pan-Islam or Arab Nationalism? The Meaning of the 1931 Jerusalem Islamic Congress Reconsidered', *International Journal of Middle Eastern Studies*, 35 (2003), p. 1.
6. For example, see Avraham Sela, 'The "Wailing Wall" Riots (1929) as a Watershed in the Palestine Conflict', *The Muslim World*, 84(1/2) (1994), pp. 60–94; Naomi Cohen, *The Year after the Riots: American Responses to the Palestine Crisis of 1929–1930* (Detroit, MI: Wayne State University Press, 1988); and Mary Ellen Lundsten, 'Wall Politics: Zionist and Palestinian Strategies in Jerusalem, 1928', *Journal of Palestine Studies*, 8(1) (1978), pp. 3–27.
7. Lesch, *Arab Politics*, p. 212.
8. 'Arrangements' and 'obstacles' are terms used by Benjamin Kaplan in *Divided by Faith: Religious Conflict and the Practice of Toleration in Early Modern Europe* (Cambridge, MA: Harvard University Press, 2009) as he describes the ways in which Europeans grew towards toleration of their neighbours and family members who ended up on the opposite side of Reformation-era divides.
9. Simone Ricca, *Reinventing Jerusalem: Israel's Reconstruction of the Jewish Quarter After 1967* (London: I. B. Tauris, 2007), p. 38.
10. Mattar, *Mufti of Jerusalem*, pp. 106–7.
11. Lawrence Summers, *America's Palestine: Popular and Official Perceptions from Balfour to Israeli Statehood* (Gainesville, FL: University Press of Florida, 2001), p. 92.
12. Johnson, *Islam and the Politics of Meaning*, p. 2. Johnson analyses Islam's use by the leadership, revolutionaries in the Great Revolt and by contemporary Palestinian nationalists.

13. Johnson, *Islam and the Politics of Meaning*, p. 35.
14. ISA P986/44, Shefaᶜamr Citizens to AE, 16 October 1929.
15. ISA P986/44, Birzeit Christians to AE, 16 October 1929.
16. ISA P986/44, MCA Safed to AE, 12 October 1929; MCA Nablus to AE, n.d.
17. ISA P987/22, 'A Statement to the Moslem and Christian Worlds', signed by Yaᶜcoub Farraj, president of the Arab General Meeting, 27 October 1929.
18. CZA S25/3004, Sulaiman Faruki, ᶜAbd al-Qadir al-Muzaffar, ᶜIsa al-ᶜIsa, ᶜAbd al-Latif Salah, Omar Salah and Hassan Sudki al-Dajani, 'Resolutions of the Arab Meeting held at Jerusalem on 10/27/29'.
19. *Al-Jamiᶜa al-ᶜArabiyya*, 29 August 1929.
20. ISA P2335/42, AE to HC, 1 September 1929.
21. CZA S25/3008; Autobiographies of Major Arab Personalities. No author or date.
22. Lesch, *Arab Politics*, p. 212, citing Sir Harry Luke.
23. ISA P3050/16, Casualty Summary, n.d. The report suggests that Hanna Karkar was stabbed near Mea Sherim on his way to work. The report does not say if the other Christian casualties were bystanders or participants.
24. Lesch, *Arab Politics*, p. 105.
25. ISA P154/7; Documents of Elias Koussa, lawyer representing Hanna al-Bahri in the Supreme Court of Appeals, 20 February 1931.
26. *New York Times*, 30 September 1930.
27. CZA S25/100006, Ben Zvi to Chief Secretary, 1 September 1933.
28. *New York Times*, 8 September 1930; 14 September 1930.
29. *New York Times*, 9 October 1930.
30. Report by His Majesty's Government in the United Kingdom of Great Britain and Northern Ireland to the Council of the League of Nations on the Administration of Palestine and Transjordan for the Year 1930, 31 December 1930. UNISPAL, available at: unispal.un.org/UNISPAL.NSF/0/ C2FEFF7B90A24815052565E6004E5630, accessed 15 July 2012.
31. See ISA P162/17, 26 November 1934, 8 July 1935 and 25 December 1932; the entire file deals with the disputed ownership of the Haifa cemetery.
32. *New York Times*, 14 September 1930.
33. *Al-Zuhour*, 22 September 1930.
34. *Al-Zuhour*, 22 September 1930. *Al-Yarmuk* is cited as pro-SMC in CZA S25/100006, Ben Zvi to Chief Secretary, 1 September 1933. *Al-Yarmuk*, published twice weekly in Haifa and with a circulation of about 1,000, was founded in 1923 by Rashid al-Hajj Ibrahim and Ahmad Imam, and was published by ᶜAbd al-Ghani Karmi. The Zionist report suggests that in addition to being extremely anti-Zionist, the paper was also anti-British and was 'read mostly by Moslems'.
35. *Al-Zuhour*, 22 September 1930.
36. *Al-Zuhour*, 22 September 1930.
37. *Al-Zuhour*, 6 October 1930.

38. *Al-Zuhour*, 22 September 1930.
39. Porath, *Emergence*, p. 303.
40. *New York Times*, 5 October 1930.
41. See ISA P162/17, Land Appeal Case 2/33, in which Hajjar was defendant and claimed that part of the land in question was a Catholic *waqf*, 3 December 1932.
42. *New York Times*, 21 October 1930. Porath, *Emergence*, p. 303 and Sekaily, *Haifa*, p. 22, acknowledge that some Christians came out in opposition to the nationalist movement as a result of the cemetery incident, but both seem to suggest that the rift was more along Muslim–Christian lines than denominational ones.
43. ISA P986/12, telegrams from Bethlehem, 19 October 1930 and Young Orthodox Club in Jaffa, n.d.
44. ISA P986/12, Sabbagh to AE, 22 October 1930.
45. ISA M7/15, Tulkarm religious leaders to Minister of Foreign Affairs, 11 July 1921 and M5170/4, District Officer, Tulkarm to HC, 16 February 1931.
46. *Sawt al-Sha^cb*, 11 October 1930.
47. *Sawt al-Sha^cb*, 15 October 1930.
48. *Sawt al-Sha^cb*, 15 October 1930.
49. *Sawt al-Sha^cb*, 22 October 1930.
50. *Sawt al-Sha^cb*, 22 October 1930.
51. Cited in *New York Times*, 5 October 1930.
52. Frederick Herman Kisch, *Palestine Diary* (London: Victor Gollancz, 1938), p. 348. Entry for 3 October 1930.
53. Mattar, *Mufti of Jerusalem*, p. 58.
54. As summarised from a letter received by the Turkish government, which turned it over to the British authorities. Document information unclear in Priestland, *Records of Jerusalem*, vol. 3, p. 22.
55. The Marques of Reading to Mr R. I. Campbell (Cairo), 5 November 1931 (Priestland, *Records of Jerusalem*, vol. 3, p. 21). The third aim was hotly debated prior to the congress and did not become a major focus of the Assembly. Al-Husayni claimed that the very idea was ridiculous and was a rumour started by the Zionists to undermine the Assembly ('Memorandum on the Egyptian Press and the Islamic Congress: Oct. 1931', Priestland, *Records of Jerusalem*, vol. 3, p. 20).
56. Weldon Matthews, 'Pan-Islam or Arab Nationalism', p. 1.
57. *Filastin*, 29 November 1931 and 1 December 31.
58. Porath, *Palestinian Arab National Movement*, pp. 9–10.
59. Porath, *Palestinian Arab National Movement*, p. 11.
60. Porath, *Palestinian Arab National Movement*, p. 11.
61. Matthews, 'Pan-Islam or Arab Nationalism', p. 15.
62. Report by His Majesty's Government in the United Kingdom to the Council of the League of Nations on the Administration of Palestine and Trans-Jordan for the Year 1931, p. 11 (in Robert Jarman (ed.), *Palestine*

and *Transjordan Administration Reports, 1918–1948* (Oxford: Archive Editions, 1995), vol. 3, p. 569).

63. Martin Kramer, *Islam Assembled: The Advent of the Muslim Congresses* (New York: Columbia University Press, 1986), p. 126.
64. Kramer, *Islam Assembled*, p. 127.
65. ʿAbd al-Aziz al-Thaʿalibi, *Khalfiyat al-Muʾtamar al-Islam bi-al-Quds, 1350 H, 1931 M.* (*Background of the Islamic Congress in Jerusalem*) (Beirut: Dar al-Arab al-Islaammi, 1988), pp. 116–17. This nationalist narrative claims that the operatives 'returned to Jerusalem in shame', since obviously the Christians had no objection to the Islamic congress.
66. Lesch, *Arab Politics*, p. 140.
67. ʿIsa al-Sifri, *Filastin al-ʿarbiyyah bayna al-intidab wa al-sahyuniyyah* (*Arab Palestine between the Mandate and Zionism*) (Jaffa, 1937), pp. 178–83.
68. *Filastin*, 18 August 1931.
69. *Mirat al-Sharq*, 18 August 1931.
70. Hopwood, *Russian Presence*, pp. 202–3.
71. Kisch, *Diary*, p. 39 (10 March 1923).
72. Kisch, *Diary*, p. 111 (18 March 1924).
73. *Mirat al-Sharq*, 29 August 1931.
74. *Filastin*, 16 October 1931.
75. Khoury and Khoury, *Survey*, p. 250.
76. See *Filastin*, 18–22 October 1931 for the British response and coverage of Orthodox protests in reaction.
77. Khoury and Khoury, *Survey*, p. 250.
78. Khoury and Khoury, *Survey*, p. 251.
79. The official conference statement was also published in *al-Karmil*, 5 December 1931.
80. Kedourie, *Chatham House*, p. 319.
81. ISA M27/29, G. W. Rendel to HC, 14 June 1937.
82. See ISA M27/29 for telegrams from various Orthodox organisations and individuals concerning the election results.
83. *Sawt al-Shaʿb*, 20 July 1935.
84. CZA S25/518/1, Khuri to Zionist Executive, 6 January 1936.
85. Campos, *Ottoman Brothers*, pp. 20–1.
86. ISA M207/40, Campbell to Chief Secretary, 23 June 1934.
87. Robson, *Colonialism and Christianity*, p. 101.
88. Robson, *Colonialism and Christianity*, p. 101.
89. Albert Montefiore Hyamson, *Palestine under the Mandate, 1920–1948* (New York: Taylor & Francis, 1976), p. 96.
90. Hyamson, *Palestine under the Mandate*, p. 98.
91. ISA M207/40, Farraj to HC, 27 February 1934.
92. CZA S25/22724, Ruhi Bey Abdul-Hadi, 'Note on the Question of Parity between Jews and Arabs', 3 July 1935.

93. See ISA M207/40, Keladion to HC, 30 March 1934 and other correspondence in that file.
94. ISA M207/40, Campbell to Chief Secretary, 24 August 1934.
95. ISA M207/40, 'Interview with Bishop Fellinger', 20 August 1934.
96. ISA M207/40, Barlassina to HC, citing previous correspondence received from the HC's office, 21 January 1935; in the end, despite the lack of a Latin councillor, the high commissioner took no such action.
97. ISA M206/9, Kattan to HC, 20 March 1934.
98. CZA S25/22724, Legislative Council Meeting minutes, 29 July 1935.
99. Robson, *Colonialism and Christianity*, p. 113.
100. Robson, *Colonialism and Christianity*, p. 113.
101. CZA S25/5687, M. Shertok to Dr Jacobson, 25 January 1934 and CZA S25/22224, Political Report, 1 June 1934.
102. CZA S25/5687, M. Shertok to Dr Jacobson, 25 January 1934.
103. ISA M4850/1121, By-laws of the Orthodox Young Men's Club, 1931 (the name changed shortly after to the Orthodox Union Club).
104. ISA 5220/11, National Orthodox Club, founded 1933; ISA 5000/26 Orthodox Defence Society, founded 1935.
105. See protest telegrams in ISA M27/29; ISA 5000/21, and Chapter 5, below, for more on the UAOC.
106. CZA S25/9226, Sari al-Sakakini, 'Notes on Palestine Arab Parties', 30 September 1944.
107. CZA S25/9226, Sari al-Sakakini, 'Notes on Palestine Arab Parties'; and CZA S25/3234, Sari al-Sakakini, 'Meeting of the Near and Middle East Association; [notes on the] Address by Mr. Ghory and Miss Newton', n.d.
108. Porath, *Palestinian Arab National Movement*, p. 75.
109. Porath, *Palestinian Arab National Movement*, p. 77.
110. CZA S25/9226, Sari al-Sakakini, 'Notes on Palestine Arab Parties', 30 September 1944.
111. Porath, *Palestinian Arab National Movement*, p. 77.
112. Porath, *Palestinian Arab National Movement*, p. 79.
113. Porath, *Palestinian Arab National Movement*, p. 121.
114. Porath, *Palestinian Arab National Movement*, p. 125.
115. CZA S25/9226, Sari al-Sakakini, 'Notes on Palestine Arab Parties', 30 September 1944. Only a few Christian names appear in connection with Istiqlal, such as the physician Salim Salameh; certainly they did not play an important leadership role in the party (Porath, *Palestinian Arab National Movement*, p. 125). Weldon Matthews lists two Christians among nineteen identifiable members of the party; of twenty-eight members in a 'partial list' of members there are at least three Christians (*Confronting an Empire*, Appendices 2 and 3).
116. Porath, *Palestinian Arab National Movement*, p. 132.
117. Porath, *Palestinian Arab National Movement*, pp. 131–2.
118. CZA S25/22735. Local police were tracking his movements, but it was seen

as a minor issue, not one worthy of national government attention (Monthly Summary of 'Intelligence', Palestine and Transjordan, 30 November 1935).

119. CZA S25/22735, Weekly Summary of 'Intelligence', Palestine and Transjordan, 22 November 1935.
120. Beverly Milton-Edwards, *The Israeli–Palestinian Conflict: A People's War* (London: Taylor & Francis, 2008), p. 42.
121. Basheer M. Nafi, 'Shaykh ʿIzz al-Din al-Qassam: A Reformist and a Rebel Leader', *Journal of Islamic Studies*, 8(2) (1997), 187–215. See also Abdullah Schleiffer, 'The Life and Thought of ʿIzz-id-Din al-Qassam', *Islamic Quarterly*, 23(2) (1979), pp. 61–81.
122. Johnson, *Islam and the Politics of Meaning*, p. 133.
123. Johnson, *Islam and the Politics of Meaning*, p. 45.
124. For the interpretation of al-Qassam from the 1930s to 1980s, see Ted Swedenburg, 'Al-Qassam Remembered', in *Alif: Journal of Comparative Poetics*, No. 7, The Third World: Literature and Consciousness (1987), pp. 7–24.
125. CZA S25/22735, Weekly Summary of 'Intelligence', Palestine and Transjordan, 22 November 1935.
126. *Filastin*, 1 July 1935.
127. Rachel Scott, *Challenge of Political Islam: Non-Muslims and the Egyptian State* (Stanford, CA: Stanford University Press, 2010), p. 41.
128. Milton-Edwards, *Israeli–Palestinian Conflict*, p. 42.
129. Subhi Yasin, *Al-Thawrah al-ʿarabiyah al-kubra fi filasin (The Great Arab Revolt in Palestine)* (Cairo: Dar al-Kitab al-ʿArabi, 1967), p. 32.
130. Johnson, *Islam and the Politics of Meaning*, p. 58.
131. Milton-Edwards, *Israeli–Palestinian Conflict*, p. 43.
132. CZA S25/22735, Weekly Summary of 'Intelligence', Palestine and Transjordan, 13 December 1935.
133. CZA S25/22735, Southern District's Monthly Report, January 1939.
134. CZA S25/22735, 'Security Matters: Armed Gangs, SMC, and Islam', January 1936.
135. Porath, *Palestinian Arab National Movement*, pp. 137–9.
136. Swedenburg, 'Al-Qassam', p. 10.
137. Al-Qassam continues to be invoked by Palestinians fighting against Israeli occupation. Most famous are the al-Qassam Brigades, the militant wing of Hamas, and the Qassam rocket which Hamas often launches from Gaza into southern Israel.
138. CZA S25/4690, author and date unknown, though apparently part of a book written by a Zionist author in the 1930s.
139. Porath, *Palestinian Arab National Movement*, p. 139.

4

1936–1939: Standing Aloof? Arab Christians and the Great Revolt

---

A force from the army went to the village of Rafiydiah . . . The residents of this village are Christians; the Muslim residents are no more than 10%. When the army arrived the residents started to raise the cross sign in front of them, and when the army saw these signs they returned to Nablus without doing anything in the village . . . In the Christian villages now, they have started to do the cross sign on the doors of their homes.[1]

Zionist Intelligence, August 1936

The Muslim and the Christian	their unity is power and immunity
Religion and denomination to God	but the nation is for all
Don't say Christian or Muslim	we are all brothers from the same blood
Whatever you say or do	Adam is our father and Eve our mother!
Everyone understands	that our unity is power and immunity[2]

Nuh Ibrahim, 'The Nation is For All'

In December 1936, the 'Carriers of the Banner of al-Qassam' issued a leaflet calling for a boycott of Arab Christians: 'God is great! God is great! Oh Muslims, boycott the Christians. Boycott them. Boycott them.' The pamphlet contained a list of accusations concerning Arab Christians' lack of dedication to nationalism, specifically calling for communal separatism. Christians, the leaflet explained, 'compromised the nation for their personal benefit': they arrived at protests late because they were unwilling to face risks like Muslims, they held the majority of government jobs, worked as teachers educating Muslim youth 'on the Christian principles that are in contradiction to the text of the Holy Quran', and even worked as spies for the British and French governments. In conclusion, the leaflet claimed, '[Christians] are a stumbling block on the path of independence of the Arab east.'[3]

For decades, now, scholars have accepted this boycott as 'the peak of tensions' between Palestinian Muslims and Christians, a claim first made by Yehoshua Porath who buttresses his conclusion by describing the destruction of Christians' crops, the forced celebration of church ser-

130

vices on Friday (the Muslim holy day), and the rape of Christian girls by (presumably Muslim) rebels. For these reason, Porath argued, Christians remained 'aloof' from the revolt, unwilling to fight on behalf of Palestine while Muslim rebels included attacks on Christians as part of the rebellion.[4] In recent years, revisionist historians have examined the 1936–9 revolt in Palestine from a number of angles, though no definitive account has yet been published.[5] Yet while many facets of older interpretations of Palestinian nationalism at this time have been challenged, assumptions about the role of Christians in the revolt still stand.

Christians, as a singular community, were not 'standing aloof'. Rather, Christian reactions to, and participation in, the revolt fall along a complex spectrum based on their individual responses to cultural, political and communal tensions. The attacks on Christians mentioned above were serious indeed, but it is not at all clear that such hostility was common, accepted by the majority of Muslims or even based on any sense of religious difference. On the contrary, the myth of Christian apathy is founded on examples of interreligious violence that were localised and limited, rather than typical. In fact, beyond the December 1936 leaflet, Porath's source for the other actions listed above is a single Jewish Agency intelligence report that cites two rapes and one instance of rebels 'cutting trees and vineyards' in revenge for non-compliance with Arab efforts.[6] Zionist intelligence also reported that the British believed 'anti-Christian pamphlets distributed under the name of the Flag Carriers of al-Qassam [to be] the doings of Khaman Dajani and Fakhri Nashashibi', two important leaders of the Palestinian opposition party who were specifically trying to create communal tensions as a way of undermining the authority of Hajj Amin al-Husayni.[7] While there is no proof of this claim, it does demand a further look to explain the relationship of Christians to the revolt.

The Great Revolt (*al-thawra al-kubra*), as the resistance against the British from 1936 to 1939 is dubbed in Palestinian historiography and nationalist memory, was the Arabs most aggressive response to the Mandate. The role of Arab Christians in, and relationship to, the revolt ranged from active participation to hesitancy, based in part on the nature of communalist politics. I have no desire to ignore religiously charged conflict when it did occur, but interreligious conflict was only one piece of the Christian story during those years, not its main theme. A full analysis rejects the assumption that Christians acted as a singular community and instead delves into their complex and varied relationship with nationalism, Islam, colonialism, Zionism and their own religious identification.

The Revolt: A Brief Historical Outline

The first week of the revolt clearly illustrated the dramatic shift from a top-down organisation to a spontaneous, or at least bottom-up, movement, perhaps even a 'peasant rebellion'.[8] The traditionally accepted start of the revolt occurred on 15 April 1936, when masked men on a road near Nablus told those they stopped: 'Go and inform the police and the press that we are robbing this money to purchase arms and take vengeance for the murder of the holy Sheikh, Izza Din El Kassam.' Jews were shot and left for dead, while a German Christian who insisted he was not Jewish was released unharmed.[9] Porath argues that, 'in all probability' the attack was carried out by some of al-Qassam's followers who escaped on the day of the religious leader's death.[10] The following day, two Arabs were murdered near a Jewish settlement and a spiral of violence led to assaults, rumours of assaults, demonstrations and police intervention.[11]

By 21 April, newly established 'national committees' in Haifa and Jaffa had issued manifestos confirming their support for a nationwide general strike. Soon after, the traditional leadership formed the Arab Higher Committee (AHC), with members from all major Palestinian political parties, including (for the first time in years) both Husayni and Nashashibi representatives.[12] Most importantly for Hajj Amin al-Husayni, the Nashashibis agreed to allow him to serve as the head of the committee, granting him recognition as the nominal leader of all Palestinian parties and temporarily unifying the national movement.[13] The tensions inherent in a joint organisation were ever present, but the traditional elite did not want to risk losing leadership positions to a band of upstart rebels. The pan-Arab and largely non-elite party *Istiqlal* was a driving force behind the instigation of the widespread strike, as is borne out in its disproportionately large representation on the AHC.[14] The party, which had reached the pinnacle of its influence in 1933, took advantage of the revolt to once again enhance its position within the national movement.

Despite his other, specifically Islamic, leadership roles as Grand Mufti and SMC president, al-Husayni always was, and remained throughout the revolt, an important supporter of Christian participation in the national movement. In addition, he shied away from Islamic rhetoric during the first few months of the revolt to avoid angering the British. Still, non-elite rebel leaders insisted on Islamic justice as the basis for their resistance.[15] Al-Husayni also remained an advocate of Christian participation at the political level and was an important voice in ensuring that Christians were represented on the AHC. Two representatives, both well-known Christian leaders, were specifically chosen as representatives on the new committee:

Figure 4.1 Arab Higher Committee, 1936. Front row (left to right): Raghib al-Nashashibi, Hajj Amin al-Husayni, Ahmed Hilmi Pasha, Abdul Latif al-Salah, Alfred Rok. Back row (left to right): Jamal al-Husayni, Husayn Khalidi, Yaᶜcub al-Ghussein, Fuᶜad Saba. Yaᶜcoub Farraj became a committee member after this photograph was taken. *Library of Congress*

Yaᶜcoub Farraj (Orthodox and a Nashashibi supporter) and Alfred Rok (Latin and a Husayni supporter).[16]

Historians often divide the revolt into three uneven segments. The first, with the general strike and increasing attacks against Jews, Jewish-owned property and the government as its central elements, ran from April to October 1936 when the AHC called off the strike in response to Arab fatigue and the establishment of a royal commission to address Arab grievances. The second stage of the revolt was marked by a lull in the violence while Arabs waited for the publication of the royal commission report. Arab rejection of the commission's recommendations in September 1937 triggered another round of violence, and the third stage began with the high-profile murder of a British official. The British finally quashed the revolt in mid-1939, on the eve of the Second World War.

Short strikes of a day or two had often been used by Palestinians to express their objection to British policies and Zionist immigration, so it is unsurprising that the Arab community called for a strike in response to the growing tensions. Despite the AHC's status as the recognised national leadership, Lesch argues that the committee actually had limited influence over the day-to-day implementation of the strike. Instead, it was carried out by 'local national committees, national guard units, labour societies, the Jaffa boatmen's association, Muslim and Christian sports clubs, Arab boy scouts, and the women's committees'.[17] Striking Palestinians closed down the Jaffa port, prevented peasants from selling fruit and vegetables in city streets, and shut down all Arab road traffic for months. The AHC and women's committees collected and distributed food to the poorest families, but the longevity of the strike still caused hardship for many.[18]

The Palestinian Arabs maintained the general strike for six months, but failed to change British policy or stem Jewish political advances. In fact, the strike damaged the Arab economy and bolstered Zionist calls for an economically independent Jewish community. In addition, anti-Jewish violence, such as setting fire to Jaffa's Jewish quarter, spreading nails on streets, burning Jewish crops and sniping at Jewish passers-by also emboldened Zionist separatism.[19]

Despite these unintended side-effects, the extended revolt, according to the royal commission's report, 'overshadowed all its predecessors. It lasted longer; it extended more completely throughout the whole country; and it was much more efficiently organized.'[20] This assessment dovetailed with that of other observers who argued that the revolt was the culmination of many years of nationalist efforts. The majority of Palestinian Arabs had finally embraced the nationalist movement, a claim supported by the growing importance of rural elements in the revolt. In September 1936, British intelligence reported that villagers delivered speeches at al-Aqsa Mosque in Jerusalem following the Friday service.[21] Not only did peasants comprise the majority of commanders in the rebel groups, but, particularly in the first stage of the revolt, villages throughout Palestine offered extensive support to the rebels.[22] As much as the Arab population may have recognised the importance of the MCA, SMC and other quasi-political bodies in the recent past, the rural peasantry had not participated on a large scale in those elite-led efforts. Now the rebellion brought the national movement quite literally to their front door. AHC delegates contributed to this trend, travelling to villages to garner support.[23] The combination of efforts was successful. According to Mary Wilson, a British teacher at

Birzeit College, 'the nationalist movement swept the country and gripped the imagination of Arab youth as Hitler had gripped Germany's'.[24]

In addition to ratcheting up peasant involvement in the revolt, the AHC sought to involve foreign Arab nations in its struggle for two important reasons. First, Arab fighters from Iraq, Syria and Jordan were encouraged to come to fight Zionists directly. Often these combatants were better trained than their Palestinian counterparts and greatly increased the rebels' fighting ability. Secondly, in the same way that involving Indian Muslims in the early 1930s increased pressure on Britain, al-Husayni wanted to involve the leaders of Jordan, Iraq and Saudi Arabia, all British clients of sorts, in order to provide an added impetus to force the British government to concede to Palestinian demands. Indeed, the efforts of neighbouring Arab leaders led to the end of the revolt's first stage.[25]

The announcement of the commission, commonly referred to as the Peel Commission after its chairman Lord Peel, former Secretary of State for India, made it possible for Palestinians to end the strike without having to accept defeat. The strike had a devastating economic effect on villagers and townspeople alike. In 1933, al-Sakakini marvelled that a strike had lasted for eight days; the 1936 general strike ended on 12 October, after 175 days.[26] The AHC had made exceptions for certain sectors of the economy. Subsistence farmers were encouraged to harvest their crops and to give a portion to the rebels, and many other strikers were paid full or partial wages by the AHC.[27] Still, the length of the strike led to severe hardships that even the well-funded AHC could not overcome. Porath argues that one of the main reasons the strike ended in October was that the citrus crops needed harvesting, a source of revenue that the community desperately needed.[28]

The commission was designed to 'ascertain the underlying causes of the disturbances ... [and] to enquire into the manner in which the Mandate for Palestine is being implemented in relation to the obligations of the Mandatory towards the Arabs and the Jews respectively.'[29] Despite using the commission as a pretence for ending the general strike, the AHC boycotted much of the proceedings, although the Nashashibis supported its work, leading to factional hostilities that would soon divide the AHC. In addition, the AHC supported a complete Arab boycott of all things Jewish to replace the strike and rebellion,[30] and hostilities did not completely stop.[31]

The commission took testimony from numerous Jewish and Arab social, religious and political leaders. Most were from the traditional elite class, preventing the British from gaining a complete understanding of what drove peasant rebels to rise up against the government. Instead of delving into the economic plight and political marginalisation of the *fel-laheen*, the Peel Commission heard only the standard top-down political arguments from elite leaders, concluding that the *fellaheen* were better off than they had been at the start of the Mandate.[32] The royal commission's report was formally published in July 1937, and was the first official suggestion for partition and even forced transfer of some Arabs out of what would become a Jewish state.[33] The recommendation of partition met with resounding Arab opposition and triggered a new round of violent resistance.

This third segment of the revolt was characterised by rebel successes throughout Palestine, but was marred for Palestinians by severe in-fighting between Nashashibi and Husayni supporters. Factional violence weakened the rebellion and, in conjunction with a strong British response, eventually ended the revolt for good. Palestinian rebels resumed their fight with a strong statement against partition: the high-profile murder of the district commissioner of Galilee, L. Y. Andrews, and British Constable McEwan in Nazareth.[34] The British responded by arresting a number of Palestinian activists, particularly in the north, and by banning the national committees and the AHC alike. The high commissioner stripped al-Husayni of the SMC presidency and the Mufti took refuge in the *al-Haram al-Sharif* before fleeing to Lebanon.[35] In an effort not to anger Palestinians unnecessarily, the British had been reluctant to completely destroy and disarm rebel groups in the autumn of 1936, a decision that facilitated a quick resumption of the armed rebellion.[36] Local leaders maintained their roles and were already familiar with successful insurgency tactics. Some rebels who fled Palestine in 1937 settled in Damascus where they established the 'Central Committee of the Jihad', an AHC-supported organisation designed to enhance cooperation among rebel commanders within Palestine, though the group failed to coordinate rebel efforts effectively.[37]

Important differences distinguish this stage of the revolt from the other two stages. The first difference was the British response. In retrospect, leniency towards rebels in the first stage was seen as a terrible mistake. High Commissioner Wauchope, who supported a negotiated end to violence in 1936, was replaced by Howard MacMichael in October 1937. Under MacMichael's guidance the government undertook a series of harsh measures against the rebels and even non-combatants suspected of supporting them. The government executed more than a hundred rebels over the course of the revolt, destroyed homes and placed entire villages under curfew.[38] Despite this approach, British efforts did not end the rebellion as quickly as some officials hoped or anticipated. Wauchope, who returned to Palestine late in 1937 despite having been replaced as high commissioner, sought to put a positive spin on the early efforts to crack down on rebels. Compared with 1936, he argued, rebel bands were smaller and less likely to receive village support.[39]

Such optimism was unwarranted and not shared by other British observers. District Commissioner Andrews' replacement in Nazareth reported a mixed reaction from Galilee. Villagers were 'tired of the unrest caused by these ill-advised methods of ventilating grievances', such as cutting telegraph wires, arson and ineffective bombings. But, he argued, villagers still feared government punishment less than rebel vengeance and thus refused to cooperate with the authorities.[40] Of course, they were often supportive of the rebels despite the potential government response. In fact, in 1938, rebels gained control of much of central Palestine including Nablus, and, in October, they defeated British forces and took and held the Old City of Jerusalem for five days. In that month, at the height of the revolt's military success, High Commissioner MacMichael attested to a different interpretation of events: 'the Arab movement has recently become more of a national one, and it is directed as much against the Mandatory Power as against the Jews'.[41] That same month, October 1938, on the eve of the Second World War, London responded to a request by High Commissioner MacMichael to send an additional army division to Palestine to crush the revolt. This enhanced British military effort was successful, and the rebellion trickled to a halt by mid-1939.[42]

There were two common interpretations of Palestinian support for the rebellion: expanded nationalist fervour among Palestinians and fear of rebel vengeance. Though contradictory, both reflect British attempts to simplify the revolt and the complexity of varied Palestinian loyalties. MacMichael's understanding of the nationalist mood was accurate for many, but between rebel groups there were clashes for both political and personal reasons.[43] The most important catalyst for Palestinian disunity was the intensity of the Husayni–Nashashibi hostilities. Shortly before the royal commission officially published its report, both Nashashibi representatives, Raghib al-Nashashibi and Yaʿcoub Farraj, withdrew from the AHC.[44] The Nashashibis, Ann Lesch concludes, were simply freeing themselves from the AHC agenda in order to take a more pragmatic approach to the conflict.[45] Many assumed, however, that al-Nashashibi was responding to a call from the ruler of Transjordan, Amir Abdullah, for the opposition to unite in support of the commission's suspected call for partition.[46] The AHC itself was an arena for Nashashibi–Husayni bickering even though it served as the unified front of the revolt,[47] but while political posturing took place when both parties were in the AHC, the Nashashibi withdrawal led to a more violent interfamilial conflict. When the revolt reignited in

1937, the rift produced a downward spiral of violent factionalism. Both to prove loyalty to the British and for self-protection, the opposition sought financial assistance from the Zionists to create counter-insurgency 'peace bands' to fight the rebels.[48] By the end of the revolt, Arab attacks on fellow Arabs were nearly as common as attacks on British and Zionist forces.

Late in 1938, the high commissioner reported that villagers feared government repression more than rebel vengeance, a turning point which opened the door to Arab assistance in tracking rebel bands.[49] By then there were ten times as many British troops as Arab rebels, and much of the country had been brought back under firm British control.[50] The British had succeeded in ending the Palestinian revolt prior to the outbreak of war in Europe. To placate the Palestinians and prevent further rebellion, the British offered an important concession: the White Paper of 17 May 1939. The White Paper set forth a new British policy based on the premise that the notion of a Jewish homeland as outlined in the Balfour Declaration had been fulfilled. The White Paper eliminated partition, limited Jewish immigration and accepted Arabs as the majority community in Palestine. Al-Husayni rejected the proposal in favour of the immediate creation of an Arab state and a complete end to Jewish immigration.[51] The Jewish community reacted strongly against the new British policy, but Tom Segev writes that Ben-Gurion had been personally informed by British Prime Minister Chamberlain that the White Paper was to be a short-lived policy, to last for the duration of the Second World War as a way of quieting the Arabs.[52] This allowed British troops to return to Europe on the eve of the war knowing that the Zionists would support Britain in its war against Germany regardless of its policies in Palestine.[53]

Religion and Politics in the Great Revolt

Three features of the revolt are essential to understanding Christians' relationship to the nationalist effort. First, a new type of political action drove the revolt: rather than accepting political direction from a handful of elite politicians who were increasingly split along factional lines, the uprising was spontaneous, organised by the leaders of rural rebel bands and connected only loosely, and only eventually, to the traditional Arab political leadership. Secondly, while some Muslims were clearly uncomfortable with their Arab Christian brethren, this was not necessarily a widely-held perspective. In fact, other self-proclaimed Islamists worked very hard to counter signs of communalism and sought to maintain strong relationships with Christians. Finally, Christians were anything but 'aloof' in their relationship to the revolt, or at least they were no more inclined towards aloofness than their Muslim neighbours. They participated in a variety of ways, ranging from armed rebellion to political organisation. The conclusion that Christians were inactive was based on a narrow view of participation in the revolt, misinterpretation of statistics, limited sources and a failure to see diversity and variation among Christians and Muslims alike.

Most evidence of anti-Christian behaviour arises from rebel bands operating outside traditional hierarchies of Palestinian leadership, although as was the case in the 1920s, factionalism also turned communalist at times. The shifting centres of political decision-making meant that long-standing relationships between various segments of society could no longer be taken for granted, and it is undeniable that this shift led to sometimes serious anti-Christian attitudes and even intercommunal violence.

Historians often cite ʿIzz al-Din al-Qassam, a regionally important religious leader living near Haifa during the 1920s and early 1930s, as playing a primary role in fomenting the uprising.[54] During his time serving as the Imam of the al-Istiqlal Mosque in Haifa, al-Qassam articulated an interpretation of Islam that demanded Muslim opposition to British and Zionist colonialism in Palestine. He advocated armed revolt and encouraged the lower classes to become fully engaged in the nationalist struggle. Al-Qassam was successful in harnessing Palestinian anger by organising landless peasants, who had flocked to Haifa's impoverished shanty towns, into cells of armed resistance, and urging them to fight against their oppressors. Palestinians were fed up with Zionist immigration, empty British promises of political change and their leadership's inability to gain concessions from the mandatory government that had been given control of the country by the League of Nations following the collapse of the Ottoman Empire in the First World War. An increase in provocative Zionist activities served as a rallying point for Palestinian nationalists who were particularly alarmed when, in October 1935, authorities discovered a shipment of illegal weapons in cement barrels at the Jaffa port.[55] Al-Qassam's death at the hands of the British in November of that year solidified rebel resolve and created a martyr around whom the resistance could rally. Arab peasants responded angrily, rising spontaneously against those who they believed were responsible for their landlessness and poverty. The Husaynis and Nashashibis put aside their differences in an effort to catch up to and assert control over the movement. Such a dramatic protest could not have been demanded by the elite leadership, who suffered financially from the six-month strike, but instead grew directly out of lower-class frustrations.

While the revolt ostensibly targeted Zionist and British interests in Palestine, violence was often directed at fellow Arabs who rebels deemed threatening to their cause. Historian Ann Lesch notes three categories of Arabs targeted for assassination: first, those deemed supportive of the Zionists or British, and even those lukewarm in their support of the revolt; secondly, Arabs who assisted the British courts in cases against rebels; and thirdly, the exacerbation of inter-familial rivalry between the Husaynis and Nashashibis (whose Higher Committee power-sharing quickly faltered) led to all leaders of the other faction being added as rebel targets.[56] Because of British and Zionist views of the power of communal identification, which have been reinforced by Porath and others, attacks on a Christians are often interpreted as communalist in nature instead of fitting into Lesch's categorisation.

While it is true that anti-Christian violence was not hard to find, correlation does not equal causation. Historians, it seems, have engaged in the fallacy of *cum hoc, ergo propter hoc*, 'with this, therefore because of this'. Other forms of conflict stemming from class struggles, urban–rural tensions and the Husayni–Nashashibi rivalry were often the real reasons for such attacks. For instance, Bethlehem mayor ʿIsa Bandak was targeted for assassination twice during the revolt, but it is uncertain if the attacks were communalist in nature. British reports do not clarify who carried out the attacks, but other sources suggest that by the mid-1930s Bandak was openly questioning the Husayni-led nationalist leadership.[57] Likewise, the Christian mayor of Ramallah, Salme Zarour, was asked to resign by the Central Committee because 'his presence as a Mayor will hinder our work', a rebel proclamation explained.[58] But in 1936, during the same week that Christian newspaper editor ʿIsa al-ʿIsa's home was invaded by armed men, the Muslim mayor of Hebron was shot and killed for his lack of support for the strike, and 'other leaders and notables' received warnings.[59] Muslim Nashashibi supporters Sulaiman Tuqan, the mayor of Nablus and Ahmad Shakʿa, a soap manufacturer from the same city, fled the country out of fear of assassination.[60] And while Christian police were common targets of rebel attack, Muslim police were as well.[61] A detailed account of such violent incidents suggests that there were many tensions at play in Palestinian Arab society, and violence against a Christian was not necessarily due to his or her religious identification.

The rebels imposed social restrictions on the population as a whole, though it is commonly assumed that such restrictions were more onerous for Christians than Muslims. In August 1938, for example, rebels forbade Palestinian men to wear the *tarbush* (fez), demanding that they instead don the *kaffiyeh* and ʿ*agal*, traditional headwear worn by rural Muslims. Yet Ghassan Kanafani, author and leader of the Palestinian Front for the Liberation of Palestine (PFLP) who was killed by the Israelis in Lebanon in 1972, argued that 'the revolutionary spirit that prevailed throughout the whole of Palestine led to everyone in the towns wearing the peasant headdress (*keffiya* and *agal*) so that the countryman coming into the town should not be subjected to oppression by the authorities'.[62] A photograph of the resistance army of the Christian village of Beit Jala, near Bethlehem, shows most members of the Christian group wearing the *kaffiyah*, as many older Palestinian Christian men continue to do so to this day.[63] Kanafani, a secular nationalist, argued that the *tarbush* ban was imposed for the benefit of the rebels, and was directed more at city-dwellers in general than specifically at Christians, although he agrees that Christians were disproportionately affected since most of them were urban. This suggests, however, that the restrictions were not anti-Christian, but signify a conflict between rural and urban Arabs.

British treatment of some Christians also added to Muslim scepticism of their Christian neighbours. For example, the British believed that Christians Shibley Jamal and Ya᷄coub Farraj were moderating influences on Arab politics, seeking their participation in an Arab negotiating team in autumn 1938.[64] At other times, perception of how the British treated Christians was just as important. In Jaffa, Muslims reportedly believed that the British were only targeting Muslim homes during military raids on Arab cities, so they moved in among the Christians for protection. 'This idea is held by all Muslims, not only in Jaffa, but in all other cities', Najib, an Arab informant, declared in his report to the Zionist leadership in August 1936.[65] The same informant also described an army raid on Rafidiyya, a village near Nablus:

> When the army arrived at it the residents started to raise the cross sign in front of them and when the army saw these signs they returned to Nablus without doing anything in the village, and they were very happy about that. In the Christian villages now, they started to do the cross sign on the doors of their homes.[66]

Just as any stereotype develops, the positions of a few British-leaning Christians quickly convinced some Muslims that, in the words of one Zionist intelligence report from November 1938, 'Christians [were] lying – their hearts [were] not at one with the movement'.[67] Instead, the report alleged, Christians were trying to increase hatred between Arab Muslims and Jews in order to benefit economically.[68] Indeed, British reports also suggested that a few Christian merchants exploited the revolt for economic gain.[69] While such incidents did occur on a small scale, the long-held British belief that Christians were opposed to Zionism because they feared marketplace competition enhanced their focus on the few Christians who sought to enrich themselves at the expense of their Arab neighbours. Christians' half-hearted nationalism, one district commissioner suggested, was why Muslims complained that Christians supported the revolt with 'great demands, no performance' and why there were so few Christians in prison.[70] Despite the inaccuracy of this interpretation, the sentiment was born out of a Muslim sense of Christian economic and political privilege, anger Muslim peasants also harboured towards privileged Muslims.

Unfortunately for Arab Christians, even if rebels were really frustrated with wealthy urbanites, the fact that many Christians fitted that description meant that some Muslim rebels developed religiously-based biases which led to some violence against Christians. Arabs were also prone to accept logical fallacies and generalised stereotypes just as much as British officials and historians. Such ideas were also fuelled for some by the more militant teachings of al-Qassam which overrode the moderate ones of al-Husayni, and the merger of Islamic fervour and Palestinian nationalism occasionally became a cause for anti-Christian action.

The AHC-led boycott of Jewish goods continued and even grew stronger when the general strike ended in October 1936, and Zionist intelligence reported that some rebel leaders sought to expand the boycott to include Christian goods and services as well. In November, Zionist intelligence described a 'secret boycott' against Christians with 'Muslim youth . . . standing near Christian shops encouraging shoppers to go to Muslim stores'.[71] In December, Muslim drivers called for a boycott of the National Bus Company, specifically pointing out in the boycott announcement that 'in all [the Company's] works it favours the Christians over the Muslims'.[72] And, of course, the 'Carriers of the Banner of al-Qassam' described at the beginning of the chapter issued a boycott statement at the same time.

Others who blamed Christians sought to induce full Christian support by giving plenty of warning of the disaster that would follow from failure to support the revolt. In an open letter to the Maronite Youth (*al-Shabaab al-Maruni*), which had apparently published a communally-tinged proclamation, an unknown group warned that Maronite communalist tendencies were dangerous:

> We want to tell you frankly that it's not for your God to set the fire of sectarian conflict in the country because if you succeed in infuriating the Muslims and driving them to clearly being your rivals and show you their animosity, the result would be bad for you.[73]

The letter continued, praising the pro-Islamic efforts of other Christians, such as Najib al-Nassar and ᶜIsa al-ᶜIsa, who used the pages of their newspapers to call for unity. Al-ᶜIsa, the letter claimed, argued that 'saving Palestine ... through an Islamic path, is closest to [saving it] through a national road'.[74] Indeed, even prior to the revolt al-ᶜIsa argued that both the Nebi Musa procession and Easter services should be converted 'into national demonstrations which shall prove to our opponents the power of the Arabs in Palestine'.[75] (Al-ᶜIsa's nod to the Islamic nature of Palestinian nationalism could not hide his pro-Nashashibi sentiments, however. At one point the Husayni–Nashashibi conflict became so serious that he, too, was attacked, though likely for strictly political as opposed to communal reasons.[76])

Anti-Christian sentiments continued throughout the revolt, although variations in demands on Christians suggest striking differences between the loosely connected rebel groups. One example, in December 1937 from Zionist intelligence reported that rebels had adopted a new policy concerning Arab civil servants: 'Christians will be killed without warning. Muslims will be warned and required to resign. If not, they'll be killed.'[77] The report claimed that rebels 'killed a Palestinian Christian police officer as the initiation of their new policy concerning those who worked for the government'.[78] Another policy aimed at government employees, and presumably emanating from a different rebel group, was a demand that Arabs continuing their work as government clerks had to give an increasing percentage to rebel groups. Late in 1938, rebels insisted on receiving 30 per cent of an Arab's pay (presumably it was raised from 10 to 20 per cent at some time earlier in the year), a measure rejected by all in the government service, though Christians held the majority of such posts.[79] Despite the differences in the particular demands, both reported policies reflect the growing frustration of the rebels at the lukewarm support they received from certain segments of the population. The increased extortion from governmental employees also suggests a decline in rebel income as the revolt neared its end.

Some Christians certainly believed that they were targeted because of their religious identification. Labour leader George Mansur lamented the difficulties he faced, 'first because [he was] a Christian and most workers are Muslim', and also because of the bad economic situation.[80] In Acre, Zionist intelligence reported that Christians had even founded a Christian Defence Force to protect themselves during the revolt, though this is the only reference available to such a force.[81] Such reports, particularly given the tendency of British and Zionist intelligence to assume Arab communalism, cannot conclusively demonstrate the existence of widespread Christian communal fear. Still, they do highlight the rising importance of the religiously charged nature of revolt-era internal Palestinian politics.

Despite AHC directives to support interreligious unity, some among the rural revolt leadership were prone to engaging in anti-Christian activity. While it is difficult to isolate religious tensions from those emanating from class differences, urban–rural tensions and factional politics, the religious language occasionally used by rebels led some Christians to believe that they were targeted because of their religion.

Muslims against Communalism

Along with the assumption about Arab Christians' fears of Muslims during the revolt is a parallel assumption that all Muslims were prone to communalism. In fact, Muslims at various levels of society actively argued for unity between Christians and Muslims. If the leaflet calling for a boycott of Christians was written by followers of al-Qassam, it is damning indeed, suggesting that those at the helm of the revolt were hostile towards Arab Christians. But a conclusion based on scant evidence is insufficient. As discussed below, al-Husayni went to great lengths to maintain strong connections with elite Christians, but it was not only among politicians that such relationships remained important. A self-declared member of The Brotherhood of al-Qassam (*Ikhwan al-Qassam*), Palestinian poet Nuh Ibrahim, published a booklet of poetry during the revolt reflecting at least one Islamist's desire for intercommunal cooperation and acceptance. In the introduction, Ibrahim described himself as a 'popular [*sha'bi*] Palestinian poet who serve[d] his country as a representative of the successful call in martyrdom', and claimed that his collection of poems, despite being banned by the government, was in its second printing. The booklet's dedication quotes al-Qassam's last words: 'God is great. We won't submit, for this is jihad in the way of God and the Nation'.[82]

Despite this introduction, Ibrahim specifically argued against communalism in a poem titled, 'Indeed, the Nation is for all'. In the poem's introduction, Ibrahim explained that he wrote the poem to bring the issue to the attention of the AHC, in the hope that the national leadership would take the growing problem seriously. The poem opened with a blunt confirmation of religious unity and a paraphrase of a common slogan from elsewhere in the Arab world: 'The Christians and the Muslims / Their unity is strong and invincible / and the religion and the *mathab* [denomination, religious creed] is God / Indeed, the Nation is for all.'[83] From a member of *Ikhwan al-Qassam*, the secular Arab nationalism driving this poem is remarkable. While al-Qassam's protest against European colonialism had reached across national boundaries by appealing to a shared

Figure 4.2 Nuh Ibrahim, Popular Palestinian
poet and student of ʿIzz al-Din al-Qassam.
Courtesy of the Central Zionist Archive

religion, Ibrahim's goal (and the goal of al-Qassam, Ibrahim claimed) was 'nationalism; our search is for honour and freedom'. The central argument is an Arabist one: all Palestinians, Christian and Muslim alike, are Arab, Ibrahim argued, and as such are equal. Ibrahim spoke directly to the government and international powerbrokers as well:

Oh West, you must know us   our unity is strong and invincible,
May the efforts of the conspirators   and may the Muslim–Christian union
    fail   live. [84]

This appeal served two purposes. First, for his Palestinian audience it highlighted the importance of a unified front before Western powers. It also attested to his solid understanding of the interaction between internal Palestinian unity and diplomatic efforts among the elite. He was a poet of the people who used his poetry to spread elite-level political concerns to a broader audience.

Over-simplifications of Muslim–Christian relations are often based on assumptions about the essential importance of communal identification to Arabs. Religious identity was static, complete and unified, an interpretation supported by Mandate-era British and Zionist intelligence reports. While such thinking was common among administrators throughout the Middle East, Africa and Asia, it should not be accepted as a fact of Palestinian life, but rather as an unconfirmed, or even erroneous, colonial assumption. Among the reasons for pushing the idea of a monolithic religious community was that both the British and Zionists would benefit politically, since a united Christian community would have been easier to interpret, penetrate and control. This mindset ensured that the British and Zionists interpreted violence against Christians as anti-Christian, despite the variety of other factors at play during the revolt. Nuh Ibrahim was certainly not the only Arab Muslim calling for religious unity at this time, and his poetry undermines the notion of fixed religious identification, confirming instead the presence of a debate about the nature of religion and nationalism.

Accepting either Ibrahim's poems stressing the desirability of religious unity or a single leaflet calling for a strike against Christians as conclusive of Christian actions during the revolt is insufficient and irresponsible. Instead, it is important to develop a nuanced picture of the role of Christians in the revolt in order to understand the multiple ways they engaged in, and struggled with, revolt-era actions and politics.

Christian Participation in the Revolt

Contrary to essentialist claims of communal unity, Christians' level of participation in the revolt varied from individual to individual. Some Christians were deeply involved while others were not fully invested in the uprising. The same, of course, can be said of Arab Muslims at that time. When Christians did participate, they did so in a wide variety of ways, although statistics on how widespread such activity was are impossible to assess. Early in the rebellion, when street protests were still common, the British highlighted Christian participation at intercommunal rallies. At one Nablus event in late May 1936, Christians began a demonstration in a church while the Muslim *fellaheen* began at the opposite edge of town, meeting in the middle for a joint rally.[85] Later that week in Gaza, women and girls organised an event during which 'girl students delivered speeches in front of the Orthodox Church, and later the demonstration proceeded to the Mosque where the crowd was again addressed by the girls'.[86] A few days later a joint Muslim–Christian rally was held in conjunction with a memorial service at an Orthodox church in Jaffa, with a procession leading to the Orthodox Club.[87]

Individual Christians were often noted in intelligence reports as supportive of the rebellion. An Arab wrote to the Jewish Agency telling them that 'Mr. George Abou Alice, a native of Bethlehem and a resident of Ramle is dealing in the smuggling of arms, ammunitions, etc., for the rioters in the districts of Ramle and Jaffa',[88] and Jews from Galilee and the Jordan Valley wrote to the assistant district commissioner of the northern district to complain about the Arab Christian district officer, Hanna Bulus, who 'justifie[d] the actions of armed Arab gangs and demand[ed] the stoppage of Jewish Immigration to [their] Home-land'.[89] When a Christian clerk was appointed to the department of customs at Allenby Bridge, Zionists were concerned that he had received bribes from 'border smugglers (terrorists arriving from Syria or Iraq) and weapons smugglers to Eretz Israel'.[90] Yaᶜcoub ᶜIsa Hishme of Ramallah was arrested after firing shots at a Jew who also had a shop in the Ramallah market,[91] and a Jaffan doctor, Amin Awad, was listed as organising an 'anti-British movement, especially among the Christian population'.[92] Even the Christian mayor of Nazareth, a Zionist leader complained, was 'helping the Mufti's men and pressing the Christians to assist the terrorists'.[93]

Occasionally Christian religious leaders also spoke out in favour of the rebellion. In August 1936, Nicola Khuri, an Orthodox priest originally from Birzeit who worked for the church in Jerusalem, began planning a conference of priests to protest against the British, but was exiled back to Birzeit when the government heard of his plans.[94] That same month Christian leaders from across Palestine appealed to the Christian world to recognise the danger of Zionist control of Palestine, expressing concerning that a Jewish government would establish foreign laws, fix oppressive taxes and bring socialism and anarchy to the Holy Land. These Palestinian Christian leaders used traditional arguments to insist that the international Christian community should prevent Jewish immigration, stop them from defiling the Church of the Nativity in Bethlehem, and prevent the neglect of the holy sites that would occur under Jewish rule. An impressive list of Christian leaders, including important nationalist leaders from the Orthodox, Catholic, Protestant, Anglican and Maronite communities signed the appeal 'to save the holy places from the Zionist danger'.[95] In a more local show of interdenominational support, Acre's Christians united to demand that the government disarm the Zionists. Along with Muslim leaders, Archmandrite Bulus Shuᵓayd, acting metropolitan of the Roman Catholic community in Palestine; Khuri Antonios Sadr, priest of the Maronite community in Acre; and P. Galmo Martin, a Latin priest, all signed the statement.[96]

Christian women played an increasingly public role in Palestinian national politics through their support of the revolt. Ellen Fleischmann argues that 'women's militancy reached new heights' during the revolt, 'and their participation in the nationalist movement underwent a trans-formation and radicalization commensurate with that of the rest of the country'.[97] Elite women, whose 'participation in the revolt has been described as more "passive" than peasant women's', joined their male counterparts in writing petitions, raising money and leading demonstra-tions.[98] Matiel Mughannam, the secretary of the Women's Committee and wife of the noted Protestant lawyer, Mughannam Mughannam, was among the most active women. She helped to distribute money collected for families of those killed in the violence, as well as for wounded rebels.[99] Another leader among Palestinian women was Sadji Najib Nassar, wife of Najib Nassar, who joined a group of women smashing the windows of a bakery that was not observing the strike.[100] She was in contact with rebel commanders in Damascus and publicly demanded that German troops be sent to control Palestine. The British believed her to be so dangerous that they arrested her in the spring of 1939.[101] While most Christian women did not gain the notoriety of Mughannam and Nassar, Fleischmann lists Katrin Shukhri Dib, Mary Bulus Shihada and Melia al-Sakakini (as well as Mughannam) among the members of the Arab Women's Executive Committee.[102] Unfortunately, the involvement of Christian women at the non-elite level is impossible to assess due to a lack of documentation.

Sadji Najib Nassar's actions were radical compared with other members of the Arab elite. Khalil al-Sakakini's form of protest was likely to be more common for upper-class Palestinians, whether Christian or Muslim. He admired the rebels tremendously. In a letter to his son, who was study-ing in the United States at the time, al-Sakakini wrote about gunmen who shot Jewish moviegoers as they left the cinema. He wrote, 'there is no other heroism like this, except the heroism of Sheikh al-Qassam'.[103] Yet at the same time he confessed, 'I feel the pain of the troubles, whether they fall on Arabs or on the English or on the Jews.'[104] He both deplored acts of violence and honoured Palestinians willing to fight for their cause. His personal form of rebellion did not require the risks of those on the front lines, only refusing a dinner invitation from the high commissioner and the opportunity to speak on the government's Arabic radio station, since it used the common Hebrew name for Palestine: 'The Land of Israel'.[105] When visiting his upper-class friends, he insisted on drinking Arabic coffee and smoking a *nargila* instead of sharing in the European (and upper-class Arab) habit of tea and cigarettes.[106] And he sent a scathing editorial to *Filastin* titled, 'The Jewish People are Insane', in which he outlined psychological evidence of paranoia among the Jews.[107] Like their father, al-Sakakini's teenage daughters, Hala and Dumya, maintained the strike out of a sense of idealism, even denying themselves the pleasure of watching *Gone with the Wind* in order to support the nationwide economic boycott.[108]

While Arab Christians upheld the spirit of the revolt in a variety of ways, they also retained their importance in nationalist political circles. Al-Husayni, in particular, pushed for an even greater Christian presence in Arab delegations visiting London. Indeed, most Arab interaction with European leaders was carried on by Christians. One well-documented trip taken by al-Husayni supporters, Emil al-Ghuri and priest Nicola Khuri, sought Christian assistance in Greece and other Orthodox countries. Khuri explained in his memoir that Adil Arslan, a Lebanese-born Muslim intellectual living in Geneva and editor of *La Nation Arabe*, pressured al-Husayni into sending a Christian delegation to Orthodox countries.[109] Despite Orthodox Christian Yaᶜcoub Farraj's affiliation with the Defence Party, al-Husayni wrote to Farraj asking that he recommend someone for such a mission. After initially sidelining the project (Khuri suggested that Farraj did not want to be overshadowed by other Christians taking on important roles in the political realm),[110] Farraj called upon Khuri and al-Ghuri to make the trip. Following stops in Damascus and Istanbul, the two Orthodox Christians travelled to the Balkans in September 1937.[111] They met church leaders, newspaper editors and politicians in Sofia, Belgrade and Bucharest among other Eastern European cities.[112] Though his trip failed to produce the desired impact, Khuri recalls that upon his return Muslim Palestinians were more likely to show appreciation for his efforts than were Christians.[113] Khuri does not explain the reason for this discrepancy, and whether accurate or not, he assured his readers that Muslims were supportive of Christian efforts on behalf of the nationalist cause.

Christians also maintained a leadership role within the labour movement and played an important role in perpetuating the general strike. Michel Mitri was the leader of the Arab Labour Society in Jaffa until his assassination by an unidentified attacker in 1936, at which time George Mansur, also a Christian, took his place.[114] Like those in the political elite, Arab labour leaders acted on multiple levels. They were moved not only by class considerations, but also a strong sense of Arab nationalism. Mansur was arrested in 1936 and wrote to the secretary of state complaining about the deplorable conditions of the prison camp.[115] In his letter he declared a hunger strike, explaining that the prisoners were willing to die for their cause: 'We die in order that Arab Palestine may live.'[116]

One arena in which Christians did not play a large role was within the rebel leadership. Such leaders were, Porath has shown, mostly 'Muslim villagers of the lower strata'.[117] The lack of Christian commanders was notable for communally-minded observers, including Porath. He cites only three Christians among revolt 'officers' (that is, people with some form of organisational responsibility): Hanna Bulus of Ramah in central Galilee; Fu°ad Nassar of Nazareth, a communist who apparently led a band composed mostly of Christians in the Bethlehem area; and Butrus al-Sayigh of Gaza.[118] In addition to those cited by Porath, Hanna °Isa Khalaf was a rebel band treasurer and George Jabr of Jifna (near Ramallah) was a 'minor rebel leader'.[119]

Of Porath's list of rebel commanders, only 1.5 per cent were Christian. He compares this number with the percentage of Arab Christians as a whole (approximately 9 per cent) to display what he sees as their tendency to refrain from direct participation.[120] Certainly, compared with the composition of the Arab leadership in the 1920s, at which time Christians were perhaps over-represented, the number of Christians was greatly diminished. But Porath's comparison is faulty for two reasons. First, his list of commanders suggests that they were most often Muslim and that they were lower-class villagers. In urban areas, Christians represented more than 25 per cent of the Arab population, while in rural areas their representation was less than 4 per cent. That is, among villagers Christians were a tiny minority.[121] There is no data concerning the comparative economic status of Christian and Muslim villagers, but scholars have generally described the Christian population as a whole as being wealthier than its Muslim counterpart.

In addition to this important recalculation of Christians' representation among rural Palestinians, it is unreasonable to suggest that members of a religious minority would be represented equally among the revolt leadership. Porath himself notes that many of the rebel commanders were trained by the Brotherhood of al-Qassam, a specifically Muslim organisation created from the remnants of al-Qassam's original followers, suggesting that the core of the rebel leadership came from an exclusively Muslim source.[122] In political circles as well, Christians often participated in important organisations and committees, but only rarely served in top leadership positions. Indeed, the presence of even a single Christian commander is surprising, particularly given the standard legitimation of Palestinian leaders, which included personal charisma as well as religious, tribal and familial elements.

Of the many references to rebels, most are not labelled by religion, or even mentioned by name, complicating efforts to gauge levels of Christian participation accurately. The British did, however, compile comprehensive casualty statistics for the first stage of the revolt, from its outbreak in April 1936 until the appointment of the Peel Commission (a British commission assigned to look into the reasons for the increased violence) in October of that year. During that period, Christians sustained approximately 5 per cent of Arab injuries and deaths. While this percentage is lower than their percentage of the national population, it is higher than Porath's assessment would suggest, and still does not prove a lack of Christian participation. Given that most Christians were urban-dwellers, while most of the armed rebellion was conducted by rural *fellaheen*, a low percentage of casualties would have been possible even with proportional participation.[123]

Porath's most egregious error is his interpretation of the low percentage of Christian rebel leaders as evidence of universal Arab Christian apathy towards the revolt. Universal it was not, even if some Christians were wary of the rebellion and its impact on their place in Palestinian society. Like their Muslim counterparts, some Christians were supportive of the rebellion, some remained distant from the political upheaval, and still others, despite the revolt, continued to seek a negotiated solution to the Palestinian problem. A few even turned against the nationalist movement and supported the British or Zionists outright.

Most reasons for the varied level of support for the revolt were the same for Christians and Muslims: economic uncertainty, fear of government reprisal, and the like. Of course, at least some Christians were also afraid of the rebels and the threat of anti-Christian violence. Selim Ayyub, a Christian, in a 1936 letter to a Zionist leader, explained Christian participation in the revolt 'on the grounds that 80 to 85% of them were motivated by fear. They lived in mixed . . . quarters and were afraid of the Moslems, but they really had nothing against the Jews.'[124] He argued that Christians were better off under the British, having once suffered under Muslim rule. (This opinion was, however, quite uncommon.) Aziz Khayat, who had delivered money to al-Husayni in Beirut earlier in the revolt, approached the district commissioner of Haifa in September 1939 to express his willingness to work more closely with the government and for 'healing the unreal association in politics between Christians and Moslems'.[125] He informed the district commissioner that Christians of various denominations were organising a committee to represent Christians.[126] That same month, because the revolt had largely subsided, the British pulled troops out of Bethlehem, but British reports suggested that Christian residents feared that the withdrawal would lead to a resumption of rebel raids.[127] A murder in that town coincided with the announcement of the troop withdrawal, adding to their fears.[128] Later that year the mayor, opposition supporter Hanna Kawas, resigned when he discovered that his name was on an assassination list.[129]

Other Christians seemed less afraid of rebel attacks and more concerned about their economic status. Such individuals sought a quick end to the strike in order to stave off further hardship. Others went even further. Intelligence reports from November 1936 cited a meeting in Nablus during which Christians argued in favour of Jewish immigration, since stopping it 'would bring a terrible economic crisis'.[130] Economic considerations frequently led both Christian and Muslim merchants to open their shops despite the national strike, and the rebel response was often severe. In particular, as discussed above, many Arabs working for in the British government did not strike, and the high percentage of Christians in this position sometimes translated into anti-Christian sentiments stemming from complaints that such employees did not support the revolt.[131]

What is clear from this account of Christian rebels and revolt supporters is that a broad range of Christians were involved: government employees; religious figures; doctors; residents of Jaffa, Ramallah, Haifa, Bethlehem and Tiberias; members of well-known families; and those from families that appear nowhere else in the historical record. Christian elites joined in the rebellion in varying capacities, remaining important on the front lines of all diplomatic efforts. Likewise, there were a variety of reasons that some Christians did not support the revolt, and those Christians also acted in a variety of ways, some adopting a quietist approach and others actively assisting the British.

The Impact of the Revolt on Arab Christian National Identity

The relationship of Arab Christians to the rest of the Palestinian population was more complex in the revolt period than in the previous decades for a number of reasons. Shifts in Palestinian society during nearly twenty years of British rule led to new social divisions, new forms of leadership and an increasingly important role for non-elite Palestinians in the workings of the national movement. The language of religious unity, with standard references to 'both Muslims and Christians' as used by the Muslim Christian Association in the early 1920s, was largely dropped by nationalist organisations such as the AHC, yet Christians refrained from communal demands, instead maintaining their status as important segments of every political party, movement and committee. The educated, wealthy Christian elite continued to participate in politics as they had in previous years. Even as the Mufti of Jerusalem and President of the Supreme Muslim Council, Hajj Amin al-Husayni took a strong and personal interest in preserving a Christian presence in leadership circles.

Elite Christian leaders were probably less influenced by the rise in communalist tendencies among some Muslim *fellaheen* than were other Christians. Tannus, Farradj, Shihada and others associated mostly with other elite Christians and, occasionally, with elite, well-educated Muslims as well. Their actual contact with rebel leaders and members of rebel groups was minimal. For Christians living in Christian towns or villages, such as Ramallah, Birzeit, Bethlehem and Beit Sahour, the presence of armed rebel bands on the outskirts of town was frightening. The impact of rebel-imposed demands on Christians, however uneven, and whether based on religious or other reasons, induced among some Christians a fear of Muslim domination.

The threat of communalist violence was important to the Christian population, even if such actions were only perpetuated by a small segment of rebels, and even if a sizable segment of the Christian population supported the revolt. Interreligious conflict also troubled nationalist and revolt leaders. Three indicators highlight this concern: Christians met to discuss their relationship with Muslims; al-Husayni issued statements designed to reduce tensions between the two religions; and the new revolt leadership also sought to quell interreligious conflict.

Christian elites met often to discuss their community's relationship to Muslims and the national movement. In Haifa, leaders of the Melkite community met in May 1938, and Bishop Hajjar sent Priest Bardawil 'to lodge a protest [with al-Husayni] on behalf of the Arab Christians of Palestine'.[132] Similarly, a group of Nashashibi-supporting Christians met at the home of Ya'coub Farraj in early November 1938, while later in the month a different Christian group met in the Talbieh neighbourhood of Jerusalem. At the latter meeting, they decided to send Priest Maramurah to meet with the Mufti.[133] If these reports, one British, the other Zionist, are true, they suggest that Christian elites were worried about their position vis-à-vis the national movement.

Al-Husayni's response to Christian demands for protection from rebel harassment also suggest potential problems arising from communal tensions. The British and Zionists assumed that al-Husayni did not really believe in Muslim–Christian brotherhood and was simply using Christians as political pawns.[134] Al-Husayni may have attained his leadership position by harnessing religious sentiments and tapping into British beliefs about the religious structure of Arab society, yet again and again during the revolt he proved to be an important champion of Christian rights. His support for that minority may have been ultimately responsible for maintaining a viable and active Christian community into the 1940s. Often when Christian–Muslim tensions were reported in Zionist and British intelligence, the reports conclude by noting that al-Husayni was active in trying to end such divisions. On at least one occasion, he reportedly 'directed mosque preachers throughout the country to preach for peace and brotherhood among Muslims and Christians'.[135] The Jewish Agency also received reports in November 1936 that the AHC had sent a delegation to Lebanon to help calm Muslim–Christian tensions there, for fear that open violence could spread to Palestine.[136]

The third indicator is the response of the rebel Central Committee for the Arab Revolt, a Damascus-based, AHC-affiliated effort to organise revolt activities, to any sign of anti-Christian behaviour among rebel groups. A boycott of Arab Christian interests and the December 1936 proclamation highlighted by Porath and discussed above did suggest serious intercommunal tensions. The rebel leadership was decentralised, however, and it is clear that while some rebel groups were indeed spreading anti-Christian propaganda, the Husayni-controlled AHC and the rebel leadership in Damascus were not in favour of such activities. The Central Committee published a proclamation alerting rebels that special permission had been granted to Christians to keep their shops open on Fridays.[137] More explicitly, the Central Committee found it necessary in September 1938 to forbid rebel forces from disturbing 'Churches, Convents, Patriarchate Priests, Monks, Nuns, foreign Consuls and their foreign or Arab subjects, either by collecting money or by trespassing upon their personal or religious liberty'.[138] This communiqué suggests that some rebels had been harassing Christians and trespassing on Christian property,[139] but it also reconfirms that such activity was not universally accepted.

British and Zionist observers took note of these tensions. As one British official put it, the British were convinced that the Christian community 'view[ed] the prospect of being included in an Arab or Jewish state with equal apprehension' and preferred a continuation of British rule.[140] The Zionists, on the other hand, argued that 'if Christians could be sure of non-maltreatment, they would have left the Muslims and joined with the Zionists, because what they most want is to keep their religion'.[141] This interpretation, however, overestimated the importance of religious community, while simultaneously underestimating the importance of the national identity that had grown in importance over the previous decades.

In 1938, the district commissioner of Haifa reported that the Christians were concerned about their future and were preparing to share their views with the British Peel Commission. Rather than speak individually, he wrote, Bishop Hajjar, with the help of Wadi al-Bustani, had prepared a statement to be read on behalf of 'all Arab Christians' because 'none of them dare[d] speak for themselves'.[142] This British interpretation of events may have exaggerated Christian fears, and it is plausible that Christians simply felt that a communal response would be more powerful than an individual one. Indeed, Bishop Hajjar spoke highly of the Arab nationalist leadership in his testimony to the Commission.[143] Khalil Totah, principal of the Friends School in Ramallah, also advocated greater SMC control over public schools and an Arab government for an independent Palestine.[144] Still, the tendency to seek a unified Christian voice foreshadowed Christian efforts in the 1940s to rely on communal politics to further their national aims.

The British had an alternative answer for such Christian political stances. The district commissioner of Jerusalem, Edward Keith-Roach, strongly believed that Christians were only supportive of Arab nationalism out of self-preservation. 'The community is following the policy of Brer Rabbit,' he explained in July 1939, alluding to the folkloric rabbit famous for using his quick wits to escape from dangerous situations.[145] Keith-Roach was convinced that the Christians (presumably unlike the Muslims) were 'able to distinguish between nationalism and Religion', but were 'obliged to adopt publicly the policy of the Moslems'.[146] When he received a letter demanding that the government guarantee the permanent appointment of a Muslim mayor, he feigned surprise that the two signatories were George Khader and Shibley Jamal, 'both Christian Protestants!'[147] Christian support for the Muslim leadership would have fit clearly into his interpretation of Christian behaviour as self-preserving: as trying to buttress nationalist credentials by supporting the Muslims. What Keith-Roach failed to understand was that Arab Christians feared the loss of many things: their religious freedom; their position of importance in Arab society; their lucrative jobs both within and without the government; their access to and control over Christian holy places; their land; and their national identification. At no point during the Mandate did Arab Christians care only about religious identification.

There is no doubt that some Arabs sought self- or communal preservation at all costs. Some hedged their bets and worked with the British or even the Zionists, either openly or behind the scenes. Much of the Druze population actively assisted government efforts to crush the revolt, a decision that caused a serious rift between the Druze and Christian minorities who often inhabited the same villages and towns in the Galilee.[148] Both Christians and Muslims sometimes assisted government troops on an individual basis as well, and the Nashashibi-led 'peace bands' provided a public organisation for those willing to work alongside the British to stifle the revolt. But, by and large, the Christian community maintained its support for the Palestinian Arab cause despite anti-Christian sentiments and incidents, and a fear of intercommunal violence.

Despite holding fast to nationalist ideals, Christian communal identification was altered by the revolt. At the elite level, and particularly among the older generation, little had changed. Important Christian participation continued throughout the end of the Mandate. But with the end of the revolt in 1939 and the start of the relatively quiet 1940s, much of the Christian community turned inwards. Palestinians were tired of the unrest, and the new decade saw a number of new social organisations across the country. But rather than insist on joint Muslim–Christian activities, the emerging generation of leaders after the revolt focused on developing large and active social organisations within their own religious communities.

There was no concerted national effort to attack Christians or Christian interests in Palestine, or specifically calling for severing relations with them. Still, Christians sensed a rise in communalist tensions and developed a new relationship with nationalism. The traditional Christian elite continued to participate at the highest levels of the Palestinian leadership, yet most Christians were more likely to pursue nationalist goals with religious affiliation as a primary label instead of a secondary one. British and Zionist assumptions about religious divisions, anti-Christian policies perpetuated by some rebels, and the fear instilled in some Christians were not fully inaccurate, though the outcome was not at all like that of Muslims in India or sectarianism in Lebanon. Arab Christians in Palestine were still fully committed to the same nationalist programme as their Muslim counterparts, but with a reinvigorated attachment to Christian communal identification.

Notes

1. CZA S25/3875, Zionist Intelligence Report, Jaffa, 17 August 1936.
2. CZA A113/20, Nuh Ibrahim, *Jihadi Palestine*, 'The Nation is for All', n.d.
3. CZA S25/9350, Memorandum from the 'Carriers of the Banner of al-Qassam', dated Shuwaal 1355 (December 1936).
4. Porath, *Palestinian Arab National Movement*, pp. 269–70.
5. See, for instance, Matthews, *Confronting an Empire*, p. 8; Swedenburg, 'The Role of the Peasantry in the Great Revolt (1936–9)'. in Ilan Pappé (ed.), *The Israel/Palestine Question*, 2nd edn (New York: Routledge, 2007); and Mustafa Kabha, 'The Courts of the Palestinian Arab Revolt, 1936–1939', in Amy Singer, Christoph Neumann and Selçuk Akşin Somel (eds), *Untold Histories of the Middle East: Recovering Voices from the 19th and 20th Centuries* (New York: Routledge, 2010), pp. 197–213.
6. CZA S25/3875, Najib from Jaffa, apparently to Zionist officials, 17 August 1936.
7. CZA S25/22192, Intelligence of the Arab Office, 3 January 1937.
8. Helena Lindholm Schulz, *The Reconstruction of Palestinian Nationalism:*

Between Revolution and Statehood (New York: Manchester University Press, 1999), p. 28.

9. CZA S25/22765, 'The Murder of Chazan and Danenburg', no author, no date.

10. Porath, *Palestinian Arab National Movement*, p. 162. Porath writes that Farhan al-Saᶜdi was the leader of the band.

11. *Report of the Palestine Royal Commission Report* (Peel Report) (London: HMSO, 1937), p. 70.

12. Porath, *Palestinian Arab National Movement*, p. 165. The Arabic name for the group, *al-lajna al-ᶜarabiyyah al-ᶜulya*, is perhaps best translated as The Supreme Arab Committee, although Lesch follows the AHC's own rendering of its name, the version most commonly used by the British as well. Porath, on the other hand, refers to the group as the AHC.

13. *Palestine Royal Commission Report*, p. 70.

14. Porath, *Palestinian Arab National Movement*, p. 164.

15. Porath, *Palestinian Arab National Movement*, p. 177.

16. CZA S25/22710; 'Government Apathy to the Jewish National Home and its Reactions on the Arab Policy', no author, no date. See also *Porath, Palestinian Arab National Movement*, p. 165. Porath describes Rok as a Greek Catholic, but most scholars agree that he was Latin.

17. Lesch, *Arab Politics*, p. 116.

18. Lesch, *Arab Politics*, p. 117.

19. Lesch, *Arab Politics*, pp. 218–19.

20. *Palestine Royal Commission Report*, p. 75.

21. CZA S25/22741, CID, Weekly Intelligence Summary, 7 September 1936.

22. Porath, *Palestinian Arab National Movement*, p. 261.

23. Porath, *Palestinian Arab National Movement*, p. 181.

24. H. M. Wilson, *School Year in Palestine, 1938–1939* (Oxford: St Antony's Documentation Centre, 1939), p. 1.

25. Lesch, *Arab Politics*, p. 119.

26. Musallam, *Yawmiyat Khalil al-Sakakini*, vol. 5, p. 177. Entry from 4 November 1933.

27. Porath, *Palestinian Arab National Movement*, pp. 172–3.

28. Porath, *Palestinian Arab National Movement*, p. 212.

29. Quoted in Porath, *Palestinian Arab National Movement*, p. 221.

30. Porath, *Palestinian Arab National Movement*, p. 218.

31. Annual Report by His Majesty's Government in the United Kingdom to the League of Nations for 1937, 'Public Security', UNISPAL, available at: unispal.un.org/UNISPAL.NSF/0/7BDD2C11C15B54C2052565D100572 51E, accessed 5 July 2012.

32. *Palestine Royal Commission Report*, pp. 77–81. Hajjar was cut off by one member of the commission when he began speaking of the situation of the *fellaheen*. The British official insisted that they had heard plenty about them already, though peasant concerns were not addressed in the section

of the report titled, 'Underlying Causes': PRO 733/343/6, *Palestine Royal Commission: Evidence of Bishop Hajjar*, 2 February 1937.

33. *Palestine Royal Commission Report*, pp. 285–96.
34. See CZA S25/22763, OAG to Secretary of State, 11 October 1937.
35. Lesch, *Arab Politics*, pp. 221–2.
36. Porath, *Palestinian Arab National Movement*, p. 233.
37. Porath, *Palestinian Arab National Movement*, pp. 242–3.
38. Lesch, *Arab Politics*, p. 225.
39. PRO 733/332/12, Wauchope to Cosmo, 21 December 1937; CZA S25/22763, HC to Advisory Council, 21 December 1937.
40. CZA S25/22768, DC Galilee to HC, 1 November 1937.
41. CZA S25/22761, MacMichael to Secretary of State, 24 October 1938.
42. Porath, *Palestinian Arab National Movement*, p. 239.
43. Porath's detailed account of Palestinian in-fighting remains the most thorough; see Porath, *Palestinian Arab National Movement*, p. 9.
44. Basheer Nafi, *Arabism, Islamism and the Palestine Question: A Political History* (Reading: Ithaca Press, 1998), p. 250.
45. Lesch, *Arab Politics*, p. 120.
46. Porath, *Palestinian Arab National Movement*, p. 225; Nafi, *Arabism*, p. 251.
47. Porath, *Palestinian Arab National Movement*, p. 169.
48. Porath, *Palestinian Arab National Movement*, p. 251; Nafi, *Arabism*, pp. 262–3.
49. PRO 733/398, HC to Colonial Secretary, 26 November 1938.
50. Lesch, *Arab Politics*, p. 226.
51. Walter Laqueur and Barry Rubin (eds), *The Israel–Arab Reader: A Documentary History of the Middle East Conflict*, rev. edn (New York: Penguin, 1995), pp. 54–5.
52. Segev, *One Palestine*, p. 449.
53. Segev, *One Palestine*, p. 450.
54. See Nafi, 'Shaykh ʿIzz al-Din al-Qassam', pp. 187–215 and Abdullah Schleiffer, 'The Life and Thought of ʿIzz-id-Din al-Qassam', *Islamic Quarterly*, 23(2) (1979), pp. 61–81.
55. Matthews, *Confronting an Empire*, p. 237.
56. Ann Mosely Lesch, 'The Nationalist Movement Under the Mandate', in William B. Quandt, Fuad Jabber and Ann Mosely Lesch (eds), *The Politics of Palestinian Nationalism* (Berkeley, CA: University of California Press, 1973), p. 39, ff 55.
57. PRO 733/370/9, 'Outstanding Examples of Rural Gang Activity During 1937, and 1938 to Date, 2/28/38 incl'. See also, in the same file, 'Terrorist Crimes Against the Person in Jerusalem City and Rural Area from 1/1/37–2/28/38'. While Porath suggests that at this time Bandak was leaning towards the Nashashibi faction, he provides no documentation of Bandak's shift, and *Sawt al-Shaʿb*, Bandak's newspaper continued to publish articles highly supportive of al-Husayni throughout the period.

58. CZA S25/22731, CID Daily Intelligence Summary, 11 July 1938.
59. CZA S25/22741, Weekly Summary of Intelligence, 21 August 1936.
60. CZA S25/22761, MacMichael to Secretary of State, 19 January 1938.
61. PRO 733/370/9, 'Assassinations, and Attempted Assassinations of British, Jews, and Others, by Arabs', from 1 January 1937 to 28 February 1938.
62. Ghassan Kanafani, *The 1936–1939 Revolt in Palestine* (English edition published by the Committee for Democratic Palestine, New York, 1972). Citations from the unpaginated version found at: http://www.newjersey solidarity.org/resources/kanafani/kanafani4.html, accessed 5 July 2012.
63. See cover photograph, Beit Jala Army.
64. CZA S25/22729, HC to Secretary of State, 13 November 1938.
65. CZA S25/3875, from Najib in Jaffa (an informant), 17 August 1936.
66. CZA S25/3875, 17 August 1936.
67. CZA S25/22191, 'The Sharp Edge of Relations between Muslims and Christians', 13 November 1938.
68. CZA S25/22191, 13 November 1938.
69. PRO 733/398/10, District Commissioner, Southern District to Chief Secretary, 11 March 1939.
70. PRO 733/398/10, 11 March 1939.
71. CZA S25/6390, 26 November 1936.
72. CZA S25/9350, 24 December 1936.
73. CZA S25/9350, to *al-Shabaab al-Marouni* and those affiliated 24 December 1936.
74. CZA S25/9350, 24 December 1936.
75. Translated in CZA S25/10007, from *Filastin*, 2 April 1936
76. Porath, *Palestinian Arab National Movement*, p. 206.
77. CZA S25/22192, Intelligence Report, 22 December 1937.
78. CZA S25/22192, 22 December 1937.
79. CZA S25/22191, Intelligence Report, 30 November 1938. In police force statistics from 1939, for instance, among the Arab rank and file, 20 per cent were Christians, while among inspectors, 30 per cent were Christian. Of the eleven Arab Superior Police Officers enlisted in the British force, seven (64 per cent) were Christian; CZA S25/22747, Security Committee meeting minutes, 19 August 1939.
80. CZA S25/22192, Intelligence Report, 23 September 1937.
81. CZA S25/22227, Intelligence Report, 1 January 1937–1 July 1937.
82. CZA A113/20, Nuh Ibrahim, *Jihadi Palestine*, 'What a Pity Oh ʿIzz al-Din', n.d., although Ibrahim makes it clear that the book is a revolt-era publication.
83. A113/20, Nuh Ibrahim, *Jihadi Palestine*, 'Indeed, the Nation is for all'.
84. Ibrahim, *Jihadi Palestine*, 'Indeed, the Nation is for all'.
85. CZA S25/11297, 'Attacks, Demonstrations, Incendiarism, Destruction of Trees, etc.', 1936.
86. CZA S25/11297, 1936.

87. ISA M566/6, 'Palestine Riots, Official Communiqués', No. 84/36, 1 June 1936.
88. CZA S25/9783, Sassoun to Joseph, sharing letter written by Khalil Yusif Rizk, 1936.
89. CZA S25/4368, Jewish Colonies of Kevuzoth of Galilee and the Jordan Valley to Blackburn, DO Northern District, 15 July 1936. It is unclear if this Hanna Bulus is the same as the officer cited by Porath.
90. CZA S25/22192, Zionist Intelligence Report, Intelligence of the Arab Office, 11 April 1937.
91. PRO 733/370/9, 'Assassinations, and Attempted Assassinations of British, Jews, and Others, by Arabs', from 1 January 1937–28 February 1938.
92. CZA S25/22226, Zionist Intelligence Report, n.d.
93. CZA S25/3574, Dr Kohn to Dr Joseph, 31 October 1939.
94. CZA S25/3875, 17 August 1936.
95. 'Call of Palestinian Christians to the Christian World to Save the Holy Places from the Zionist Danger', 19 August 1936 (in ʿAbd al-Wahhab Kayyali, *Wathaaʾiq al-muqʾawamah al-Filastiniyah dudd al-ikhtilal al-Baritani wa-al-siyuniyah 1918–1939* (Muʾassasat al-Dirasat al-Filastiniyah), pp. 430–2).
96. CZA S25/22793, Muslim and Christian leaders to HC, 6 August 1938.
97. Fleischmann, *The Nation and its 'New' Women*, p. 124.
98. Fleischmann, *The Nation and its 'New' Women*, p. 128.
99. CZA S25/22732, CID Daily Intelligence Summary 58/38, August 1938.
100. Fleischmann, *The Nation and its 'New' Women*, p. 131.
101. CZA S25/22793, High Commissioner to Secretary of State, 1 April 1939; see also CZA S25/22714, CID report, 30 March 1939, for the announcement of her arrest.
102. Fleischmann, *The Nation and its 'New' Women*, pp. 213–17, Appendix II.
103. Segev, *One Palestine*, p. 365.
104. Segev, *One Palestine*, p. 373.
105. Segev, *One Palestine*, p. 369.
106. Segev, *One Palestine*, p. 372.
107. ISA P350/27, 'The Jewish People are Insane', 9 December 1936.
108. Fleischmann, *The Nation and its 'New' Women*, pp. 130–1.
109. Al-Khuri Nicola Khuri, *Memoirs of the Jerusalem Priest: Birzeit 1885–Beirut 1954* (no publication information available), p. 24. For more on Adil Arslan, see Stéphane A. Dudoignon, Hisao Komatsu and Yasushi Kosugi (eds), *Intellectuals in the Modern Islamic World: Transmission, Transformation and Communication* (London: Routledge 2006).
110. Khuri, *Memoirs*, p. 24.
111. CZA S25/4153, Aliahu Epstein, 'Activities of the Arab Office in Washington', 5 November 1945.
112. Khuri, *Memoirs*, pp. 24–35.
113. Khuri, *Memoirs*, p. 39.
114. Zachary Lockman, *Comrades and Enemies: Arab and Jewish Workers*

in Palestine, 1906–1948 (Berkeley, CA: University of California Press, 1996), p. 250; Ghassan Kanafani argues that Mitri was assassinated by al-Husayni's men (Kanafani, *The 1936–1939 Revolt in Palestine*).

115. PRO 733/310/1, Mansur to Secretary of State, 23 July 1936.
116. PRO 733/310/1, 23 July 1936.
117. Porath, *Palestinian Arab National Movement*, p. 264.
118. Porath, *Palestinian Arab National Movement*, pp. 388–403, Appendix B; Additional information on Fuᶜad Nassar, CZA S25/22732, Deputy Inspector of CID, Intelligence Summary, 'Armed Gangs', 3 November 1938.
119. CZA S25/22644, Zionist Intelligence Report, 11 June 1943; PRO 733/398/11, District Commissioner, Jerusalem to Chief Secretary, 5 November 1939.
120. Porath, *Palestinian Arab National Movement*, p. 269.
121. Extrapolated from McCarthy, *The Population of Palestine*, pp. 35 and 159.
122. Porath, *Palestinian Arab National Movement*, pp. 182–4.
123. Casualty statistics compiled from CZA S25/22723, CZA S25/22764, CZA S25/22765, PRO 733/310/1-5 and PRO 733/311/1.
124. CZA S25/10093, Ayyub to Joseph, 24 June 1936
125. PRO 733/398/11, J. Pollock, District Commissioner, Haifa to Chief Secretary, 21 September 1939.
126. PRO 733/398/11, 21 September 1939.
127. PRO 733/398/10, Jerusalem District Commissioner to Chief Secretary, 18 May 1939.
128. PRO 733/398/10, District Commissioner, Jerusalem to Chief Secretary, 5 May 1939.
129. PRO 733/398/11, District Commissioner, Jerusalem to Chief Secretary, 1 September 1939.
130. CZA S25/6397, 25 November 1936.
131. Porath, *Palestinian Arab National Movement*, p. 170.
132. CZA S25/22731, Daily Intelligence Summary, CID, 17 May 1938.
133. CZA S25/22191, Intelligence Report, 30 November 1938.
134. PRO 733/425/18, J.E.S. to Sir G. Gater, 10 April 1940.
135. See CZA S25/22227, Intelligence report for 1 January 1937–1 July 1937; CZA S25/10097, R.Z to Arab Office of ZO, 3 January 1937.
136. CZA S25/22193, 22 November 1936.
137. CZA S25/22191, Zionist Intelligence Report, 28 December 1938; CZA S25/9332, Announcement for the Central Committee to 'Our Arab Brothers in Holy Jerusalem', approximately December 1938.
138. CZA S25/22732, Abdel Rahim Hajd Mohd., 22 September 1938.
139. In April 1938, the Mukhtar of Iqrit, a Melkite village near Acre with a population of about 500, was murdered by unknown assassins. That same day, 'an armed gang entered Turan village and stole a sum of money form the Christian Priest and other members of the village'. PRO 733/366/4, CID Bulletin, 11 April 1938. The population statistics come from the *Iqrit*

Heritage Society, available at: www.iqrit.org/?LanguageId=1&System=
Category&MenuId=11&PMenuId=11&MenuTemplateId=1&Categor
yId=8, accessed 15 July 2012.

140. PRO 733/332/12, Battershill to Shuckburgh, 21 November 1937
141. CZA S25/22192, Intelligence Report, 4 November 1937.
142. CZA S25/22793, District Commissioner, Haifa and Samaria, May 1938 Monthly Report.
143. PRO 733/343/6, *Palestine Royal Commission: Evidence of Bishop Hajjar*, 2 February 1937.
144. CZA S25/4442, evidence of Dr Khalil Totah to the Peel Commission, 18 January 1937.
145. PRO 733/398/10, District Commissioner to Chief Secretary, 4 July 1939.
146. PRO 733/398/10, District Commissioner, Jerusalem to Chief Secretary, 1 June 1939.
147. PRO 733/398/10, District Commissioner, Jerusalem to Chief Secretary, 18 July 1939.
148. PRO 733/398/10, District Commissioner, Galilee and Acre to Chief Secretary, 2 February 1939.

5

1940–1948: National Strength through Communal Unity

We are the army of the nation

Our course is straight	our symbol is unity
Arab is in our core	brothers in the jihad
From ancient times	our blood is for the country

The Sacrifice and the Cost

The Union Club	sends us: Forward March!
For the success of the revolt	under the protection of unity
For the progress of the nation	it sends us in peace

From the Anthem of the Orthodox
Union Club, Jerusalem, 1942[1]

In 1944, the Union of Arab Orthodox Clubs (UAOC) set out to adopt a logo for the club's various publications. Nearly a dozen options were considered, all including a gold cross and a black, green, red and white Palestinian flag. The artist who drafted the samples must have been shocked by the ensuing debate in which the majority of Union committee members rejected the cross logo 'under the pretext that [if] an emblem with a symbol of the cross is adopted . . . [their] Arab Muslims brothers [would] become angry'.[2] Jiryis Hanna Butrus of Ramallah wrote to the Union headquarters sharing his concern over this development. Citing a local anecdote about a Christian who raised a cross during a public gathering, he concluded that the man 'wasn't paid any notice of disgust from our Muslim brother, rather the opposite: they gave him all respect'.[3] The UAOC was, after all, an umbrella organisation representing Arab Orthodox clubs through-out Palestine and, as such, was a specifically communal group. Perhaps the Union abandoned the search for a logo due to the cross controversy. Throughout the decade, there is no logo on the club's monthly newsletter, standard letterhead or literary journal. The majority opinion hints at the tensions present in the Orthodox Clubs' efforts to identify as both a religious community and part of the national movement. Yet that is exactly the balance that a new generation of Arab Christians sought through communal organisations in the 1940s.

Two major factors contributed to a notable change in Christian political identification during the 1940s. First, Palestinian leaders exiled during the revolt established new centres of nationalist activity outside Palestine, creating a gap between the Arabs of Palestine and their spokespeople abroad.[4] Histories of the 1940s invariably describe the Palestinian national leadership's failure to secure a Palestinian state, while completely ignoring the lives and activities of Arab Palestinians in Palestine. Secondly, the absence of a nationalist leadership from their daily lives allowed for a new generation of leaders to emerge who moved Palestinian society in new directions. These new leaders, often younger and part of a new middle class, had not been active during the late Ottoman constitutional days or the early years of the Mandate, so their ideological and societal influences were different to those of their predecessors. Christians of all denominations witnessed the increase in sectarian violence and communal identification during the revolt, and even the Orthodox community, whose members had generally insisted on their Arabness, was shaken by the increased anti-Christian sentiments.

In that sense, revolt transformed the relationship between Arab Christians and the wider Palestinian Arab community. Even if Christians were very active in the revolt and if instances of anti-Christian behaviour were limited to small groups of people, Christians had long sought affirmation as full members of society, not evidence that they were unwelcome. The new Arab Christian leadership in Palestine changed its tactics. Rather than insisting on a secular Arab identification, they reorganised along communal lines in an effort to reassert their importance in Arab circles, to establish a unified denominational voice and to protect their communal interests. In one sense, then, they embraced communalism. Yet Arab Christians did so in addition to their national identification, not at its expense.

The Union of Arab Orthodox Clubs stands out for its efforts to establish a strong Orthodox community as a way to reassert communal influence within the context of the nationalist movement and continued colonial occupation. The UAOC was not the only Christian organisation to enhance communal structures, but as the central committee of the largest Christian denomination, it serves as a strong example of the tendency towards reinvigorating Christian nationalism with a stronger sense of religious identification.

The 1940s Social and Political Atmosphere

Among the most pressing reasons for the British to subdue the Arab revolt were the rising tension and the expected outbreak of war in Europe. With the exception of a series of bombings of coastal cities by Italy in 1940, Palestine avoided direct combat in the Second World War. Despite this, the war played an important role in the political atmosphere of the early 1940s. Most importantly, Palestine was an important centre of British military activity, which led to a period of rapid economic growth.[5] While economic prosperity was enjoyed by many Palestinians, some among the nationalist leadership sought help from Germany, either secretly or openly, adhering to the theory that an enemy's enemy is a friend. As a result, Zionist accusations of pro-German political activity by Arabs were common.

Hajj Amin al-Husayni was the most famous Palestinian to seek German support in his fight against the British and Zionists, though that relationship is muddied by the obvious politicisation of research on the Mufti's war years.[6] Still, al-Husayni was not the only Palestinian who saw Hitler as a potential ally against Zionism. Khalil al-Sakakini's children attended a German school in Jerusalem and learned the Nazi anthem there. Al-Sakakini himself was an admirer because, he wrote, Hitler 'opened the world's eyes' to the true position of the Jews.[7] Mary Wilson, a teacher at Birzeit throughout the revolt, also noted that most of her students were pro-Nazi and approved of Hitler.[8] Zionist intelligence files cite numerous specific Arab Christians who supported Germany and suggested that the Latin community was generally in favour of the Italians.[9] Segev notes that the British believed

> the Arab tendency was to support whoever was going to win. At the beginning of the war, the high commissioner reported to London that fortune-tellers in Jerusalem were predicting Hitler's death. As the German army advanced, Hitler's popularity increased, and at the height of his success he was being described as an Arab hero.[10]

Yet the *Palestine Post* reported in August 1945 that both Arab priests and laity participated in 'Thanksgiving services for victory in the war'.[11] In reality, Arab Christians had a complex relationship with the Germans, the Italians and the Second World War. Like all Palestinians who supported the Axis, their support was based on their trust in al-Husayni and desire for international help in defeating the British and the Zionists.

Despite the end of the revolt and the beginning of the Second World War, Muslim–Christian tensions did not dissipate immediately or fully, though relations between Muslims and Christians did seem to improve over previous years. Occasional anti-Christian sentiments did arise, but the decrease in violence on a national level also reduced the intercommunal tensions that threatened Palestinian unity in the late 1930s. In May 1940, Zionist intelligence reported an attack on a church in Lydda, followed a day later by a similar attack on a mosque. Five Muslims were arrested in the former case, and five Christians in the latter.[12] But such instances of open hostility were far rarer than during the revolt.

Still, an underlying sense of unease remained between some Christians and Muslims. Zionist observers reported a number of cases in which prominent Muslims privately shared concerns about Arab Christians. In an anonymous report titled 'Several Days with Aref al-Aref', a Jew who spent a few days with al-ᶜArif reported that he was 'surprised to hear how he speaks sharply against Arab Christians'.[13] Al-ᶜArif was a strident nationalist and was sentenced *in absentia* to ten years in prison for his part in the 1920 Jaffa riots. He returned to Palestine in 1929 after being pardoned by the British and was appointed as district commissioner in Beersheba. He remained a Palestinian government official until the end of the Mandate and later worked for the Jordanian regime as well. Throughout the 1936–9 revolt, al-ᶜArif prided himself on maintaining the peace in his district.[14] Al-ᶜArif, the Zionist report asserted, complained about Christians holding too many government jobs, even while they 'have the YMCA and lots of communal and church institutions', and he blamed them for 'cheating' the Muslims, for putting on 'the national cloak as an excuse', but in reality shying from open revolt or sacrificing anything important.[15] 'The Christians,' al-ᶜArif was reported as saying, 'are the servants of the British and fill the offices of the secret service'.[16] Another Zionist intelligence worker reported that Ahmed Salmeh al-Khalidi, a member of the prominent Jerusalem family, 'spoke with terrible unhappiness about the Christians', arguing that Muslim hatred for Christians far outweighed their hatred of Jews. He, too, raised the long-simmering issue of Christians in government jobs.[17]

Zionist intelligence also claimed that Arab Christians were fearful of Muslims: 'Jews who are close to the Christian circles', a 1941 report suggested, say that 'Christians are starting to fear that the Muslims will inflict punishment on them when the opportunity arises.'[18] A report from Tiberias in the same year attributed Christians' 'lack of loyalty' directly to Muslim pressure on that community, suggesting that the two ideas are directly connected, without revealing which one drove the other. An informant recounted a conversation he had with a Christian *mukhtar* in Bethlehem about recent 'cases of theft by Muslims'.[19] As he spoke, the report explains, 'one could sense the fear in which Christians live because of Muslims. Although [Christians] are a majority in Bethlehem, in the region they're a minority and that puts them under constant fear.'[20] In addition, the issue of governmental positions once again became a sticking point between the two communities. Even while the real issue was British policy, Muslims complained about preferential treatment for Christians, while Christians argued that they were being released from government positions in favour of less qualified Muslims.[21]

The economic boycott against the Jews remained in effect throughout much of the 1940s and occasionally exposed anti-Christian sentiments. When two store owners in Shefaᶜamr were found guilty of selling Jewish products in their stores, Hillel Cohen writes that the Christian 'was humiliated in public and forced to pay a fine to the local boycott committee. No action was taken against the Muslim.'[22] A resident of the Christian-majority town complained to the AHC demanding steps to reduce Muslim–Christian tensions. In a similar case, a series of thefts from Christian shops was blamed on their selling of Jewish goods.[23] As was the case during the revolt of the 1930s, Christians were no more likely than Muslims to support the Zionists, but the entire Christian community was far more likely to be blamed for the actions of one or two individuals. The reduction in direct hostility and open violence confirms that while the actions of rebel groups were directly responsible for sectarian hostilities, intercommunal unease was still a common sentiment in various segments of society.

Politically speaking, the first half of the 1940s was as quiet for Palestinians as the revolt years were explosive. Because of this, many histories of the Mandate end in 1939 and ignore the last decade altogether.[24] Studies of the Jewish community are more common since Jews revolted against the British (particularly the White Paper of 1939) once the Second World War had ended.[25] The few books that examine the last decade of the Palestine Mandate focus on the British failure to establish either a unified state or an acceptable partition plan. Issa Khalaf, in his study of 1940's Palestinian factionalism, explains that the political scene 'was characterized by diplomacy more than anything else and the activist radical nationalism of the thirties was largely missing or largely quiescent'.[26] Diplomacy was carried out by the British and leaders of the neighbouring Arabs states, with the Palestinian leadership pushed out of the political limelight.[27] The shift towards external diplomacy was the result of the failed Palestinian rebellion. Many non-elite rebel leaders were killed in the harsh British response at the end of the revolt, some politicians were forcibly exiled, and others fled out of fear due to factional infighting among the Husayni and Nashashibi clans.[28] Remaining notables were forced to operate in a new political field with a Palestinian populace that had been worn down by three years of strikes and open rebellion. In addition, factionalism, 'a manifestation of traditional, largely agrarian societies dominated by vertical cleavages, identities and divisions', which had marked Palestinian politics during the Mandate in general, became even more prominent in the 1940s.[29]

While the lower stratum of society had been heavily involved in political action in the late 1930s, by 1940 the population was worn out. Peasants also witnessed the political elite embracing a more radical agenda, leading peasants to believe that their active involvement was no longer fully necessary or, perhaps, useful.[30] Yet despite sharing political goals, the factionalised Palestinian leadership was much less effective due to 'distrust and cynicism' than it had been in previous decades.[31] In fact, during the 1940s, the Arabs lost the Jerusalem mayor's office to a Jewish mayor, failed to end Jewish immigration, unsuccessfully tried to dismantle the Tel Aviv port that had been built in response to the Arab strike, and were unable to challenge the United Nations proposal for the partition of Palestine effectively.

Khalaf's explanation of Palestinian factionalism, which focuses on vertical divisions based on family, kinship and clan, helps to explain the political failures of the 1940s. Yet he pays no attention to the communal repercussions of such rifts even though kinship naturally includes a religious element. To be certain, religion was not always the most salient factor, but as described in the previous chapter, violent times increased the focus on communal differences and occasionally led to communalist tensions and violence. In addition to intercommunal rifts, a division appeared within Christian communities as well. Within the Orthodox community in particular, and the Christian community in general, a newly emergent Christian leadership displaced the old guard. Some prominent Christians continued to work at the national level, but a very active group of new leaders began organising local Christians at the communal level. The Christian community's leaders of the 1920s and 1930s were the political elite: ʿIsa al-ʿIsa, Najib Nassar, Bulus Shihada, ʿIsa Bandak, Khalil al-Sakakini and others. In the 1940s, a whole new cast of Christian figures emerged who were not affiliated with the political parties and movements of the 1920s and 1930s, and who represented a rising middle class of educated and moderately wealthy Christians.

While the Arab political leadership was decimated by imprisonment and exile, the war provided a tremendous economic boost to the Palestinian economy. The country had been ravaged by the First World War, but in the Second World War, Palestine saw little fighting, and instead became Britain's second most important base in the region, after Egypt. Allied troops were stationed in Palestine, even taking over a large portion of the Jerusalem YMCA for some time.[32] The troops needed everything from food to gear, which, following a brief economic scare at the outbreak of war, helped the local economy grow during the first half of the 1940s. Many peasants who had become heavily indebted throughout the Mandate were able to improve their standard of living due to the money pouring into the wartime economy; the Arab farm price index rose 500 per cent between 1938 and 1943.[33] Ilan Pappé concludes that 'Palestine in 1946 was quite different from at the beginning of the mandate. Thousands of cars, buses and trucks appeared on the new network of asphalt roads, where previously horses and carriages had transported passengers in a slow and haphazard manner.'[34] The British had introduced some modern technologies into Palestine, though they remained unsuccessful in finding a solution to the Jewish–Arab conflict.

Economic growth triggered a number of important changes in Palestinian Arab society. Rapid urbanisation was one such result. Even though agriculture was booming, Zionist land policies of the previous decade had left thousands of Palestinians landless. Employment in light industry increased dramatically in cities, and migrant and landless peasants flocked to urban areas to fill those positions. In addition to the major cities of Haifa, Jaffa and Jerusalem, the population of mid-size cities such as Tulkarm, Nazareth and Majdal increased dramatically throughout the 1940s.[35]

Many scholars argue that the new economic structures and urbanisation did not upset the 'traditional patronage networks' on which Arab society was built.[36] Others disagree. Khalaf argues that:

> the war economy and the relative prosperity it brought to villagers, generational change and changes in social structure, were factors which influenced a change in village perceptions of authority, in some regions more than others. Younger and more educated men began to complain about the illiteracy, incompetence, or corruption of some of the *mukhtars* and domination by single families.[37]

Ylana Miller agrees, citing Arab villagers' demands for a more active role in local politics as evidence of their newly critical view of the traditional elite.[38] The latter argument is defensible. Throughout the 1940s a new elite was busy forming labour unions, religious organisations, women's committees and other such groups, even while the political trajectory of Palestine was determined largely by Arab leaders outside the country.

Rather than view the nascent alternative elite as unsuccessful in bidding for political power, it is more appropriate to view their successes as short-lived, terminated by the rupture that occurred in 1947/8. Khalaf provides a number of reasons for the notables' success in maintaining political power (as opposed to the new notables' control of the political economy), the most important of which is that the older families maintained strong connections to the countryside, ties that the new generation of leaders had not developed prior to the 1948 war.[39] Thus, the scope of the influence of the new elites was limited to urban centres and smaller circles of influence than that of the most important national clans such as the Husaynis, Nashashibis and Khalidis.

Still, the emergent leadership was politically and socially active in a number of ways. In addition to urbanisation, economic prosperity among Arabs enhanced various forms of social organisation. Labour unions grew tremendously, and the Palestine Arab Workers Society, which had just 2,000 members in 1940, boasted a membership of over 9,000 by the end of 1943.[40] Nor did labour unions distance themselves from the nationalist movement, although they pursued their own agendas rather adhering to one faction or another. For instance, the National Liberation League (NLL), which advocated Jewish–Arab worker cooperation within the context of a unified democratic Palestine, emerged in the mid-1940s following the collapse of the Palestine Communist Party.[41]

Some Arabs responded to the communalist tensions of the 1930s by embracing more radical versions of secular ideology. For some Christians, the Arab communist movement provided the perfect opportunity to engage at all levels of the organisation since the movement was necessarily non-religious in nature. The mouthpiece of the movement, *al-Ittihad*, was founded in 1944 by Emil Toma, a Christian from Haifa. He, along with Christians Emil Habibi, Tawfiq Tubi, Hanna Naqara and others not only joined the ranks of the Communist Party, but were among its most important leaders during the 1940s, with members of the Arab Orthodox community comprising more than 50 per cent of the party well into the 1950s and 1960s.[42] Ilana Kaufmann suggests that Christian leadership among communists was a response to the difficulties of entering the traditional Muslim elite, since the communist movement provided Christians with a unique opportunity, ideologically unconnected to religious identification.[43] This conclusion seems likely, and while the growth of religious organisations was on assertion of communal identity, alternatives remained, including those who sought to erase religious identification completely.

In addition to a growth in organised labour, the economic boom was accompanied by other forms of social organisation, such as sport and literary clubs, theatre productions, lectures and concerts.⁴⁴ As Fleischmann notes, this cultural renaissance was not divorced from the political realities of the day, and a strong nationalist tone remained present in most activities of this sort. Like other social groups, women's organisations did not pursue direct political negotiations with British officials as they had in earlier decades of the Mandate, but instead 'continued to work on residual problems from the revolt', such as supporting the families of prisoners, petitioning the government for their release, and educating revolt-era orphans.⁴⁵ Like organised labour and the women's movement, specifically Christian organisations also emerged at this time and challenged the traditional power structures of their individual denominations.

The Christian Elite

Due to the exile and displacement of many among the Arab Christian elite, harsh wartime press regulations and the natural ageing of the Christian notables, the traditional class which had been prominent in Palestinian politics since before the Mandate was replaced by a new set of Arab Christian leaders. Some younger Christians did join the ranks of the political elite, but there was a deep generational gap between the traditional leadership and those who came of age under the British.

Many among the leadership fled along with Hajj Amin al-Husayni in the late 1930s and were unable to return. In addition, many Christians who did remain in politics travelled to London or New York to pressure the British and the League of Nations (and later the United Nations) to side with the Palestinians. As a result, they were distant from the day-to-day activities of their respective communities in Palestine and were uninvolved in the emerging communal organisations. Emil al-Ghuri was a champion of Arab Orthodox rights, but spent little time on the issue in the 1940s. Instead, he served as the secretary of the Husayni-controlled Arab Party, was a member of the AHC, represented Palestinians at the Arab League in Cairo, and spent the last two years of the Mandate in London and New York. Henry Kattan, a Jerusalem lawyer, began the decade as a chairman of the Orthodox Community Council, but by 1946 was fully entrenched in national politics, spending the end of the Mandate in Paris and the United States working in the AHC's propaganda office, and was a representative to the United Nations. Other newly prominent Christians spent equally little time in Palestine. ʿIsa Nakhleh, a Jerusalem lawyer, appeared in 'law-suits of a national character' in the early 1940s before departing for the United States, and Izzat Tannus, a Christian physician from Jerusalem, spent most of the 1940s in London, South America and the United States.[46]

Wartime politics also led to a decreased role for the Arabic press, a traditional realm of Christian control. Newspaper editors such as ʿIsa al-ʿIsa, Najib Nassar and ʿIsa Bandak, whose efforts were instrumental in rallying Palestinians against the Zionist cause in the early years of the Mandate, were silenced as a result of the government's emergency laws which, among other things, severely limited the freedom of the press.[47] The government imposed strict 'Newspaper Publishing Regulations' in 1945 and 'required newspaper publishers to acquire a licence from the district commissioner, who may refuse to issue the licence without giving any reason whatsoever'. Once granted, a licence could be revoked at any time.[48] In addition, there was a shortage of paper, decreased national fervour and economic hardship, all of which decreased the Arab readership.[49] Finally, when restrictions were lifted in the latter half of the 1940s, a proliferation of smaller weekly and monthly papers challenged the primacy of the traditional press.[50]

Such changes meant that the editors who had been so important in the 1920s and 1930s became less influential. ʿIsa al-ʿIsa was arrested during the revolt, and later fled to Egypt and Cyprus.[51] Ultimately he settled in Beirut where he lived for most of the 1940s until he died in 1950. He continued to write for *Filastin*, and his son, Raja al-ʿIsa, published the paper throughout the decade and into the Israeli period.[52] ʿIsa Bandak turned from the national political scene to the local and become mayor of Bethlehem in 1946. With the exception of a 1947 article in *al-Minbar*, the UAOC's monthly journal, not much was heard on the national level from the once prominent Orthodox politician.[53] After a turbulent 1930s in which he was threatened with assassination, arrested and deported, Bandak may have sought a quiet tenure as Bethlehem's mayor. That he was able, as a member of non-Husayni-oriented parties, to live peaceably in Bethlehem attests to the reduced level of internal Arab tensions in the late 1940s. Ultimately, Bandak also left Palestine, settling in Chile where he died in 1984.

Other Christian leaders simply faded from political importance or passed away. George Antonius, a Lebanese Christian who had long been interested in the Orthodox issue and also in the Palestinian problem in general, died in Jerusalem in 1942. A charismatic and brilliant thinker according to his contemporaries, he began his career in Palestine working in various government posts; in fact, he generally supported the British. Eventually, however, he broke relations with the mandatory government because he felt that he was never given full respect or fair opportunity as an Arab.[54] Yaʿcoub Farraj also died during this decade. Long an important notable in Jerusalem, he was viewed by some as a relic of a past era of the politics of notables. Sari al-Sakakini highlighted Farraj's obsession with being a notable in a memo to Lowell C. Pinkerton, the American Consul General: 'You say to Faradj three times "Nakhleh Katan [a member of the new Christian middle class] is a Christian notable" and he will faint', al-Sakakini explained.[55] When Farraj resigned from the Jerusalem municipal council in February 1944, the Arab Orthodox Club responded a week later with a hand-delivered letter to the council president asking that he appoint another Christian to take Farraj's place, suggesting his importance to the community as its spokesman in governmental affairs.[56] Farraj died a month later.[57]

Of Christians active in national politics, only Shibley Jamal, a Protestant active in the nationalist movement during 1920s, was also a member of the YMCA. He wrote a 'Prayer of Peace for Jerusalem' in the association's newsletter in 1934 and remained a member into the 1940s.[58] Zionist intelligence reported in 1943 that Jamal was appointed to the 'committee for the reduction of living costs' in Jaffa, and that Muslims objected to the appointment on religious grounds.[59] Despite this appointment, Jamal's role in the national movement waned even before the revolt, and he too died near the end of the Second World War.

Due to death, political pressures and the broader shift of the Palestinian leadership away from local influence, the once prominent Arab Christian leadership virtually disappeared from the Palestinian Christian community in the early 1940s. While some remained active abroad in the upper echelons of the Husayni-dominated political organisation, the leadership void in Palestine itself made space for a new Christian elite.

Arab Orthodox Organizations

The void left by the Christian notables was quickly filled by the rise of a new generation of Christian leaders who had played no significant part in earlier communal or national debates. Due to their specific place in history, they opted against advocating secular Arab nationalism as had the preceding generation of Christians. Instead, and contrary to the theory that nationalism and communalism contradict one another, the new leadership embraced communal organisation while simultaneously fully embracing Palestinian nationalism. While there is evidence to this effect from various Christian communities, the Orthodox community provides the best example of this two-pronged approach because of its status as the largest denomination and the extensive documentation of various organisations' activities.

Orthodox clubs had long been present in Palestine, although mostly on a small, local scale. The Orthodox Philanthropic Foundation was established in Jaffa in 1879, and the beginning of the Mandate gave rise to an increased number of clubs and organisations of all sorts.[60] The conflict with the patriarchate was an important trigger for the establishment of the initial Orthodox clubs. At the First Arab Orthodox Congress in July 1923, the attendees 'advocated . . . the establishment of new societies and clubs throughout Palestine and Transjordan' as a way to provide Arab leadership in the community. The community responded, and in 1924 Arab Orthodox leaders in Jaffa founded the first Orthodox Club, soon to be followed by Orthodox clubs in Jerusalem (1926), Acre (1929, although some sources list 1934 as the founding date), Beit Sahour (1930), Lydda (the Young Men's Orthodox Club, 1932) and Haifa (1937).[61] Yet while the groups were occasionally engaged in Orthodox issues, there is no evidence that they had much impact in national circles, or that their influence was felt outside their immediate communities. Instead, throughout the 1920s and 1930s, the Christian community identified itself more fully with the wider Palestinian Arab community.

After the Orthodox laity failed to influence the election of the new patriarch in the early 1930s, the community turned its attention away from the conflict with the Orthodox patriarchate. This shift was marked by better organisation of Orthodox clubs as well as increased importance on both a communal and national level, and available statistics suggest that the newly formed clubs were well attended. The Arab Orthodox Labour Society of Haifa quickly gained 100 members when it was founded in 1941.[62] In 1946, the Jaffa Orthodox Club reported almost 900 members, including those with full voting privileges (166), associate members (465) and women (155).[63] At that time there were less than 17,000 Christians of all denominations in Jaffa. That nearly a thousand participated in the Orthodox Club is telling of its popularity.

Of all the Christian organisations that emerged as social and political entities during the 1940s, the UAOC was the most important. As an umbrella organisation, it pulled together a number of Orthodox clubs from around Palestine and transformed them from groups with local influence into a national conglomerate that served as a new mouthpiece for Arab Orthodox Christians. The Orthodox Union Club of Jerusalem (OUC-Jerusalem) was founded in early 1942 and by early March it boasted 200 members, with the stated hope of doubling in size by the end of the year.[64] The club soon began its effort to unite Orthodox groups from around the country, and the UAOC was officially founded at the Second Conference of Arab Orthodox Clubs, held in Jerusalem in October 1943. The conference

Figure 5.1 The Orthodox Society of Bethlehem, 1948. Seated (left to right): ʿIsa Bandak, Tawfiq Kattan. *Courtesy of Fayez (Frank) Nasser*

brought representatives of ten clubs together under a single umbrella; clubs from Jerusalem, Jaffa, Haifa, Acre, Lydda, Beit Jala, Ramallah, Ramle, Gaza and Nazareth joined, with Jerusalem given the role of heading up the central leadership of the UAOC.[65] The creation of a national Orthodox organisation triggered the establishment of new groups in other Palestinian towns such as Ramle and Bethlehem, which joined in 1944. By 1947, the UAOC comprised fourteen clubs.[66] Hanna Salameh (often rendered as John in English), president of the OUC-Jerusalem, was elected UAOC president, and Michel Cotran, also of the OUC-Jerusalem, was named secretary.

The absence of any nationally known Orthodox leaders from the UAOC's leadership was emblematic of the changing face of the Arab Orthodox leadership. In addition to these officers, many others are listed as attendees, yet none had participated openly in the MCA, the Husayni or Nashashibi factional politics of the 1920s, or the various political parties of the 1930s. The only well-known Orthodox figure (and Husayni supporter) to participate in any capacity with the UAOC was al-Khuri Nicola Khuri, who served as spiritual guide and religious educator for the group. ʿIsa Bandak does appear in one 1948 photograph of the Bethlehem branch, though his name does not appear in any of the groups documents.

The UAOC took on more responsibility as the decade progressed, and its leadership became widely accepted within the Orthodox community, by the mandatory government and within nationalist political circles. However, because the OUC-Jerusalem was an independent club as well as the central leadership for the UAOC, it is often difficult to tell where one group's actions end and the other's begin. Further confusion arises from Hanna Salameh's many roles. He was founder and president of the OUC-Jerusalem, the UAOC and the Orthodox Community Council. He eventually took on the presidency of the YMCA as well. Likewise, Michel Cotran served as secretary of the OUC, UAOC and OCC at some point during the decade. Little is known about Salameh and Cotran, but their absence from British correspondence is telling, since al-Sakakini, Antonius, Farraj and others from among the traditional elite had been well-acquainted with the British government.

The UAOC's role as a national support network for other Orthodox clubs was at times very clear. In 1945, the UAOC donated £200 to help construct a new building for the Acre Orthodox Club. A thank you from Acre closed by declaring the UAOC as 'the main artery of the Orthodox movement in Palestine'.[67] Likewise, in 1947, upon learning of the UAOC's support for the Holy Cross Girls' School, the principal wrote to Secretary Cotran commending the Union's generosity and success in creating a central leadership for the denomination.[68] By 1945, the Jerusalem office of the UAOC was recognised by the British as the body responsible for distribution of government benefits to the wider Orthodox community. When the president of the Ramle Orthodox Club wrote to the district officer asking for its government-issued wireless set, he was told to contact the UAOC.[69] Thus, by the mid-1940s, the UAOC was known to Christian organisations, the British government and AHC as the most important Orthodox organisation in Palestine.

The UAOC was aware of the important gap it filled and was not hesitant to seek government assistance when, for instance, it sought to care for the poor. In August 1943, the Charity Committee wrote to the British adviser on social welfare seeking a grant to help the committee 'continue its activities in helping the poor and destitute persons of our Community in these difficult and abnormal times, where it is mostly needed'.[70] The budget for the previous year, £520, was spent on New Year and Easter food distribution, monetary donations to impoverished families and charcoal distribution in the winter months.[71] In May 1947, Salameh and Cotran wrote to the chief secretary asking that the government supplement the efforts already made by the UAOC in relieving Arabs in the southern districts of Palestine from the effects of drought.[72] Correspondence between the UAOC and various other groups verifies its importance in establishing connections and building communal ties between a wide variety of establishments, filling the void left by a poorly functioning patriarchate and a mandatory government with the Arab–Zionist conflict on its hands.

The role of the Orthodox Community Council (OCC) is more difficult to define. The OCC's basic rules were very similar to those of the UAOC, with a focus on the social, religious and cultural betterment of the Orthodox community. The founding members were also largely the same as those of the UAOC, although they stepped aside within a couple years. The OCC was, like the UAOC, a respected organisation in government circles. In April 1945, the Jerusalem district commissioner wrote to the president of the OCC asking for his help in 'eliminate[ing] some of the rowdyism and irreverence which have been a characteristic feature of [the Easter Holy Fire ceremony] in the past'.[73] The OCC complied and met with the district commissioner later in the month.[74] One noticeable difference is that OCC correspondence often took on a more political tone concerning both the Orthodox patriarchate and the national movement, although other Orthodox groups also adopted a political tone from time to time.

The official regulations of all Palestinian Orthodox clubs, like all recognised social groups in Palestine, claimed to not participate in politics, and in general the UAOC and its member clubs did seem to steer clear of officially joining the political realm.[75] Instead, they focused on religious, social, charitable and cultural aspects of Orthodox life in Palestine. Underlying the work of the Orthodox clubs was a new approach to the old Arab Orthodox conflict with the patriarchate. Whereas in the first two decades of the Mandate Orthodox leaders sought changes in the patriarchate by petitioning both the church and the government, the UAOC simply distanced the Arab community from the patriarchate and created an alternative Orthodox leadership. The new Orthodox clubs, particularly under the leadership of the UAOC, sought to alleviate Arab Orthodox suffering itself, enhance the Arab Orthodox religious establishment and improve the lives of all Orthodox Palestinians. While this goal was not made explicit in the foundational aims of the organisations, the shift away from political manoeuvring by Orthodox leadership towards a new generation of socially active leaders was clear. By the end of the decade, the Orthodox issue had once again emerged as a primary concern. Professor ʿIsa al-Sifri of Jaffa, a member of the executive committee of the Arab Orthodox Congress, wrote regularly about Orthodox demands in *al-Minbar* in the late 1940s.[76] Yet even when the UAOC took up the traditional Orthodox issue, it did so as one element of a much broader programme. In this way,

Arab Orthodox Christians distanced themselves from the church hierarchy while developing a more closely-knit lay community.

The OUC even distanced itself from the church hierarchy on religious education. The organisation's founders stressed the importance of a religion committee even prior to the official establishment of the organisation. In 1943, for example, the committee sponsored a lecture series by Nicola Khuri on the history of the Orthodox Church.[77] Khuri, who had written a history of the church in 1925 at the request of the First Arab Orthodox Congress, was an obvious candidate to present the series.[78] The committee report noted that the lectures were a success 'because of the importance of the topic and the ignorance that many had'.[79] In addition, the OUC opened a religious school that year and translated the Holy Divine Service into Arabic for the first time. In 1944, Khuri continued weekly religious lectures and also led a regular Bible study at the club.[80]

The UAOC also sought to enhance its religious training and established scholarships to send young men to study at theological schools abroad as the local Orthodox seminary had closed early in the Mandate. In 1947, Salameh wrote to an Orthodox seminary in Paris seeking information in the hope that the UAOC could sponsor a student to attend the following year. He wrote:

> We have now seven scholars in the Palestine Secondary schools and one of them will receive his degree this year. Since there are no more ecclesiastical institutes here in which to prepare these young men to dedicate their services to the Almighty, we think of sending them to you.[81]

The patriarchate had failed to nurture young Arabs who were interested in serving the church, so the laity bypassed the church hierarchy and actively pursued educational opportunities for such men.

In addition to enhancing religious education, after three years of violence and strikes, the Orthodox clubs sought to provide opportunities that had been absent during the revolt years. Orthodox clubs had been involved in such efforts before the revolt, but the importance of rebuilding Palestinian life after three years of hardship gave added impetus to social offerings. The president of the Jaffa Orthodox Club wrote to the AHC in 1946 describing the club's activities. Among the committees was the 'Party Committee' that 'organise[d] harmless parties for enjoyment of the members'.[82] Likewise, festivals and dances were held at the OUC building in the Upper Baqᶜa neighbourhood of Jerusalem's new city, and other cities' clubs also hosted social gatherings.

One of the most visible ways in which the Orthodox community mixed with the non-Orthodox community was through sports. Orthodox clubs had earlier been involved in the 1931 founding of the Arab Palestinian Sports Federation (APSF: *al-Ittihad al-Riyadi al-ʿArabi al-Filastini*), an umbrella group designed to organise sports events in Palestine between all Arab organisations.[83] The federation was created as an Arab response to the Jewish-led Palestine Sports Federation (PSF), and, according to Issam Khalidi, was one of the 'new tactics [that] were required to handle Zionist expansion and control'.[84] He notes the importance of nationalism in the relationship between Jewish and Arab sports clubs in Palestine and describes how, by 1931, the Zionist movement dominated the PSF to the point where only Jewish teams represented Palestine at international level.[85] Rather, sports clubs were popular among all segments of society, and the relative calm of the 1940s stimulated a resurgence of interest. By 1948, there were sixty-five Arab sports clubs in Palestine, fifty-five of which were members of the APSF. In Jerusalem alone there were eighteen, half of which had been established during the last decade of British rule.[86] Christians were heavily involved, offering the building of the Jaffa Orthodox Club for federation meetings and supplying players to the first 'national' team. George Musa of the Jaffa Orthodox Club was elected as secretary of the club.[87]

The APSF fell apart in the early months of the revolt, with some Arab teams joining the PSF despite its Jewish leadership, while others organised competitions at a local level. Despite his argument that sports were considered a fully political tool, Khalidi also suggests that the revolt actually led to an increase in Jewish–Arab tournaments due to the lack of Arab leadership and 'the perception that sports were not political'.[88] It is true that some sports teams, including Orthodox clubs, did compete against Jewish teams during the revolt years.[89] There was also a stronger effort put forth by Jewish teams 'to hold sporting contests in football, swimming, water polo and hockey against the army units, in an attempt to bring British soldiers closer to the Zionist settlement in Palestine'.[90] Arab clubs also occasionally played against British teams, both during and after the revolt.[91]

The first years of the 1940s offered the most opportunities for Jewish–Arab competition, and Orthodox clubs were among the first to join the Jewish-run leagues. Such intercommunal competition must have been somewhat rare. In March 1940, the Zionist-run *Palestine Post* reported on the first post-revolt match between a Jewish and Arab club which was held in Nazareth. The report, while not specifically addressing the political importance of the event, specifically noted that both sides played cleanly and that Arab fans gave the Jewish club a 'right royal welcome'.[92] In the months following the revolt, sports enthusiasts quickly re-established organised events in Palestine. The Zionist leadership was particularly successful in building strong athletic organisations.

In competitive soccer there was a general Arab–Jewish division, though the boundary between the two was not always present. The Jerusalem Football League was established in 1940 and comprised of six teams: four Jewish, one Armenian and the sixth from the YMCA, a team including Arab and British Christians as well as some Jews.[93] Both the YMCA, which had remained politically neutral throughout the Mandate and was run by a mix of British and Arab individuals,[94] and the Armenians were on the margins of mainstream Arab society, the former because of its mixed membership and avowed apolitical nature, the latter because of its unique ethnicity. Still, these two teams were later accepted as members in a rejuvenated Arab-only APSF in the mid-1940s. Despite this Christian participation in the Jerusalem division, in 1940 neither the Armenian nor the Jerusalem YMCA teams participated in the nationwide (Jewish) Palestine League, which comprised thirty-two Jewish and British teams in five divisions. Most teams in that league adopted names that were either overtly Jewish (Macabbis and Balfourians, for example) or represented government-affiliated clubs, such as police teams from various districts. In 1941, the Christian Club of Jerusalem joined the Jerusalem league, notably the only Arab team listed in league standings, and lost to Jerusalem Maccabbi in the semi-finals for the district cup. In July of the same year, the *Palestine Post* expressed surprise that the newly established Jaffa Orthodox Club basketball team beat Tel Aviv Maccabi.[95] In 1943, the *Palestine Post* highlighted the OUC-Jerusalem's debut match in the Jewish-run Association Football versus the Armenian team, and after the first match between the Orthodox and Armenian clubs, the clubs gathered at the Orthodox Club, and an Orthodox representative called for the establishment of a joint Orthodox–Armenian 'select team'.[96] During this period, the YMCA, Orthodox and Armenian teams were the only non-Jewish teams covered by the *Palestine Post* under the heading of 'Association Football', suggesting that Muslim teams were slower to join the Jewish-led league.

It is unclear if this trend also applied outside Jerusalem, where Arab teams organised by various religious and social organisations competed against Jewish teams as early as March 1942. At that time, the Haifa Cup was established with six teams, three Arab and three Jewish. At least one club was specifically affiliated with the Islamic club, while the others do not have clear communal affiliations.[97]

Palestinians were frustrated by Jewish control over sports leagues, though they did eventually join those as well.[98] Arab athletes from neighbouring countries were aware of these tensions and supported Palestinians. In 1940, a Lebanese team came to Tel Aviv to play against a Jewish Palestinian team, but five Lebanese players sat out the game in solidarity with the Palestinians.[99] In addition to frustration at not having control of their own league, Palestinian Arabs looked to the pre-revolt APSF as a model, although it was not until September 1944 that the federation was re-established. This time the club rules 'stipulated that no member club was to have any relationship with Jewish organizations', with the one exception of the YMCA.[100] At least one Christian, Rok Farraj, was on the federation's Central Committee.[101] Apparently, the federation also banned play against non-member teams; in December 1945, the OUC-Jerusalem refused to play against the Catholic Club of Beit Jala for that reason.[102] This also suggests that Orthodox clubs eventually joined the federation rather than continue to play against Jewish teams.

In addition to athletic cooperation, the communally-centred Orthodox clubs and Muslim Palestinians showed mutual interest in supporting each other. When the Orthodox Club at Acre held a festival in honour of its sixteenth anniversary, the invitation included a note of congratulations from Shawkat Ali, the India writer and *Khilafat* movement activist, whose brother, Muhammad Ali, was buried at the al-Aqsa Mosque in Jerusalem.[103] Ali signed the note 'servant of the Ka‘ba and guardian of al-Aqsa mosque and *al-Buraq*', and it read: 'It is announced with great happiness the heart-felt solidarity between the Muslims and the Christians in this holy country.'[104] Ali's statement of support suggests that the international pan-Islamic movement also accepted the continued participation of Christians in the local Palestinian movement. The OUC-Jerusalem also expressed its nationalist stance during a contentious debate about whom the British should appoint as Jerusalem governor, declaring in 1945 that 'both Moslems and Christians stand together as Arabs nationally, and [a] Moslem should therefore be appointed Mayor'.[105] To avoid the appointment of a Jewish mayor, Arab councillors in Jerusalem renewed the concept of communal representation and suggested a yearly rotation between an Arab Muslim, an Arab Christian and a British mayor.[106] Later, the Arabs agreed to a similar rotation, but with a Jewish mayor replacing the British representative in the rotation.[107] The plan was a classic example of the willingness to adapt the identity of Arab Christians as necessary to meet political demands.

In the same way many Orthodox Christians were wary of including a cross in their logo, the anthem of the OUC-Jerusalem did not betray the group's communal identity. Rather, the words were extremely nationalistic, praising all Arabs, advocating militancy and never mentioning

Orthodoxy or Christianity.[108] The Youth Orthodox Club of Lydda was also more openly Arabist than some other UAOC branches. A 1946 address from the club's president was read at a club festival praising the strength and valour of the *shabaab* [youth] in the times of difficulty faced by the nation. He commended them for their leadership, their willingness to face danger and adversity, their energetic support of the country, and their exemplary role as the 'pillar and strong tower of the nation'. Not once in the nationalist salute to the youth did the speaker mention religious identity, despite the fact that the speech was given at an Orthodox Club event.[109]

The Haifa Arab Orthodox Club also presented itself as fully pan-Arab at times, particularly in its July 1944 celebration of a meeting of Arab governments in Alexandria. In honour of that event, the Arab Orthodox Club of Haifa sent out an invitation that read: 'We honour this kinship by inviting you to attend the *shabaab*'s celebration, which will hold a party on this great day ... of Arab hope.'[110] An illustration of an unbroken chain held by seven hands labelled Lebanon, Syria, Yemen, Egypt, Iraq, the Saudi Kingdom and Transjordan adorned the cover, while an eighth hand, Palestine, was in the centre of the chain holding a flag reading 'Arab Unity'.[111]

In 1945, the Palestinian Arab Party (PAP) contacted the OCC to assure the Christian group of its continued support for the Orthodox issue, which had 'always been considered part of the general Arab issue'.[112] The OCC responded positively, thanking the PAP for its support and acknowledging that their communal concerns were indeed part of the greater national issue.[113] Likewise, the Jaffa Orthodox Club confirmed its support for the national cause and its willingness to 'advocate any work prescribed as the national duty for our great nation' in a letter to the AHC in 1946.[114] As these examples illustrate, the supposed non-political nature of the Orthodox clubs was breached at times, an unsurprising turn at a time when, despite the end of the revolt, national sentiments ran high and political efforts were still underway to defeat the Zionist programme.

Despite these examples of support for Palestinian political aims, the UAOC also hedged its bets; when Union president Salameh wrote about his satisfaction with the publication of the first issue of *al-Minbar*, the UAOC journal, he used language resembling nationalist rhetoric, yet vague enough to be acceptable to British observers. The journal, he wrote, was simply one more way for the UAOC to further its aim of strengthening 'the intellectual, cultural, communal, and religious connections' among Orthodox Arabs.[115] Salameh's statement epitomises the UAOC's careful approach to all political matters. The UAOC maintained a balance between enhancing its communal, denominational credentials, on the one hand, and ensuring its nationalist credentials, on the other, while simultaneously treading carefully around British policies. The UAOC spent time and money bolstering the Arab Orthodox religious experience, encouraging Palestinians to study for the priesthood abroad, and seeking to 'explore [the] cultural and religious relationship' between the worldwide Orthodox churches.[116] At the same time, the UAOC and other Orthodox clubs ended competition against Jewish soccer teams, adhering to nationalist demands. They petitioned their own patriarch as well as that of the Latin Church when they felt that the foreign Christian leadership was ignoring Arab Christians' interests. More than any other Christian group at this time, the UAOC represented a strong effort to empower the Orthodox lay community as a way of preparing it for a greater influence on the national and international scene.

Other Denominations

Although the Orthodox community emerged as the most active denomination at this time, others went through similar processes of communal reorientation in the 1940s. Latin (Roman Catholic) Arabs had never been as well organised as the Orthodox community because they had little need. In the early years of the Mandate, Patriarch Barlassina had been known for his strong pro-Arab views and had also kept a tight rein on his small Arab congregation. Even when Barlassina stepped back from politics for fear of being reassigned, he still worked hard to isolate the Arab Latin community from the rest of Arab society. And while Barlassina would be remembered as a champion of Arab rights long after his death in 1947,[117] many Palestinians were less certain of his pro-Arab stance.

In a 1947 UAOC newsletter, Father Albert Rok al-Francisi challenged a proclamation issued by the OUC-Jaffa as 'heaping rebuke upon the Patriarch Louis Barlassina' because the Latin leader demanded that his parishioners stay clear of nationalist organisations. On the contrary, al-Francisi argued, 'in this country there is not Muslim and not Catholic and not Orthodox and not Protestant', but it was clear to the Orthodox community that Barlassina was interested in bolstering Latin identification at any cost.[118] The AHC was unconvinced that the Latin patriarchate was abiding by nationalist demands to avoid land sales to Jews. Barlassina's secretary wrote to the AHC in February 1947 denying such accusations, assuring the council that 'the Latin Patriarch has announced repeatedly that it would never consider, no matter what, selling a plot of its land if the result were that this land would slip into non-Arab hands'.[119]

The UAOC's organisational successes did not go unnoticed by the Arab Catholic laity. In May 1946, the UOC-Jerusalem received a letter from a newly established Latin organisation, the Arab Catholic Union, which followed the UAOC's lead 'in an effort to unite Catholics from around the country'.[120] Even while the organisation did not emerge as a major social player like the UAOC, the shift towards increased communal organisation is unmistakable.

The Melkite (Greek Catholic) community faced the loss of its charismatic and well-connected leader, Bishop Hajjar, in a car accident in November 1940, but remained an important denomination in Palestinian politics. The *Palestine Post* reported that 'one of the most impressive funerals ever witnessed in Haifa was held today when the Archbishop Mgr Gregorios Hajjar was laid to rest in St Elias Church in the Suq Quarter, with crowds estimated to exceed 25,000 lining the streets and following the cortege.'[121] George Hakim, the new bishop of Galilee, immediately sought to fill Hajjar's role, speaking out strongly against Zionism and publicly declaring the Old Testament 'annulled' as a way of undermining God's covenant with the Jews.[122] He appealed to the British in 1945 for help in ending what he said were anti-Melkite activities in some villages in the Galilee in which their community was only a small minority. The bishop blamed the British occupation for increased hostilities between Muslims and Christians (who had lived 'for hundreds of years past in perfect harmony'), and demanded that the government step in to protect the Christian population.[123] He had, he wrote, worked with the Muslims of the area to alleviate anti-Christian behaviour, and had even paid a large sum to settle false accusations against an elderly Melkite man, but his efforts were in vain.[124] In an internal document the British acknowledged the difficulties in mixed villages, but insisted (in an odd reversal of their long-standing insistence on communal identification) that the tensions were the result of 'rivalries of wealth [rather] than in ill-feeling between Moslems and Christians'.[125] Despite this issue, there is no evidence that the Melkite community diverged from its consistent support for the national project. Bishop Hakim continued to present the Melkite position as identical to that of the rest of the Palestinian community.[126]

The Anglican Church faced serious problems balancing its status as part of the Church of England and as the church of a growing local Arab congregation.[127] Arab Anglicans pushed a strong nationalist agenda throughout the 1940s, and British Anglican leaders in Palestine were concerned that 'the Palestinians might try to form a pan-Arab non-Roman church together with American Presbyterian Arabs in Syria and German Lutheran Arabs and discontented Arab Orthodox in Palestine'.[128] The

Anglican bishop, Weston H. Stewart, feared that 'their nationalist spirit is both strong and wrong', although he did advocate for the Palestinian cause.[129] For Stewart, as head of the Anglican Church in Palestine, the perpetuation of the Mandate, particularly if it opposed a Jewish state, and a strong British presence in Palestine was best for the church and the Arab Anglican laity alike. However, in 1947 when the mandatory attorney-general and the Archbishop of Canterbury both accepted a proposal to grant Palestinian Anglicans full recognition as a part of the Anglican Church, the Palestinian council rejected the proposal, demanding recognition as an independent indigenous Arab organisation.[130]

Christians across Palestine watched with interest as the Orthodox Union established itself as a denominational leader, and they sought to do the same. But due to the small size of the other denominations and the continued strength of their foreign-born clerical leadership, effective organisation was limited. Still, efforts of Arab Christians who sought to establish lay organisations outside the control of the church hierarchy parallels movements by other political, social and religious groups at this time. Mandate policies, changes in economic and social structures, the destruction of the notable leadership during the revolt, all contributed to this movement, and the intercommunal tensions of the period ensured that some minority communities would reorganise along communal lines.

Like the revolt in the late 1930s, rising political tensions leading up to the war of 1948 once again exacerbated interreligious tensions. Communal stereotyping and accusations over national loyalties between Muslims and Christians tore Palestinian communities apart. Hillel Cohen writes that the situation 'reached the point that the Christians in Haifa were accused by the local national committee of treason, and a battalion commander in the Arab Liberation Army ordered that only Muslim volunteers be allowed into his unit'.[131] In February 1948, a Muslim leader of a national committee formed during the war called all Christians 'traitors and pimps for the Jews'; Christian members threatened to leave the committee if such accusations continued.[132] Arab Orthodox residents of Jerusalem 'declared their preference for forming their own guard and purchasing weapons with their own funds', while in Nazareth, Christians also formed a communally-based defence force under the leadership of Naᶜif Zuᶜabi.[133] In May 1948, the *Palestine Post* reported that 'the so-called Arab National Committees [had] placed their spies and agents in all the Christian quarters . . . and in the religious institutions'.[134] Cohen suggests that fear of outright sectarian violence following an Arab victory kept many Christians and Druze from joining the resistance.[135]

Yet as Arab Christians show over and over throughout the Mandate, fears of intercommunal violence did not lead Christians to aid Zionists during the war. Rather, the Christian community rallied against Zionist aggression. In March 1948, the heads of the Christian churches in Jaffa wrote to the high commissioner complaining about violent acts perpetrated against them by Zionists.[136] In June, shortly after the declaration of Israeli statehood, the newly-established Christian Union, an organisation 'composed entirely of Arab Clergy who identified themselves completely with the aims of the Arab Higher Committee', accused Jewish forces of killing three priests and demanded that Israel take responsibility for the destruction of Christian institutions in Jerusalem.[137] In towns and villages throughout Palestine, local Christians organised defence forces against Zionist incursions, such as the Defenders of Beit Jala, a group made up of local Christians (see cover photograph).

But religion did matter at times, and Christians did sometimes 'remain distant'. Benny Morris notes that Christian villagers were both less likely to flee and more likely to be allowed to stay in their homes. For instance, during *Mivtza Dekel* (Operation Palm Tree) in June and July 1948, a pattern emerged throughout the Galilee. The Druze population made a communal decision to sever ties with the Muslim and Christian population and to remain out of the fight.[138] Christians, 'in less uniform and organized fashion', also leaned towards avoiding resistance and staying in their homes even if that meant submitting to Jewish rule.[139] In Shefaᶜamr, for instance, the Muslim minority fled, while the Christian and Druze populations, under the encouragement of their Christian mayor, remained in the village.[140] A number of Israeli officials specifically noted this difference and encouraged better treatment of Christians than Muslims. When Ben-Gurion ordered the conquest of Nazareth (whose Christians reportedly surrendered peacefully to protect local holy sites[141]), he 'issued warnings against the desecration of "monasteries and churches" (mosques were not mentioned) and against looting. Soldiers caught looting should be fired upon, "with machine-guns, mercilessly."'[142] Of course, the concern was not for the Arab Christian inhabitants, but for maintaining good religions with Christians elsewhere. The day after the Israel Defence Force (IDF) occupied Nazareth the front commander of the newly created organisation issued an expulsion order. The newly installed military governor refused and took the issue to Ben-Gurion, who agreed to let Nazareth's Arabs stay.[143]

Likewise, in Operation Hiram of October 1948, Morris concludes that the Palestinians' fate was often based on their religious affiliation and that 'the demographic upshot of the operation followed a clear, though by no means systematic, religious–ethnic pattern: Most of the Muslims in the pocket fled to Lebanon while most of the pocket's Christian population remained where they were.'[144] He found that 'no clear guidelines were issued ... about how to treat each religious or ethnic group', but that both the conquered communities and the Israeli forces followed similar instincts. Christians, then, were less likely to resist occupation and to flee at this time (as were Druze and other minority populations), but they were also less likely to be forcibly expelled by the IDF. The residents of ͨEilabun, a largely Christian village which defied the trend and put up a strong resistance, were even allowed to return to their village after initially being expelled, an option not given to Muslim villagers who also chose to resist.[145]

Villages with mixed populations were often depopulated and destroyed or occupied, but on at least two occasions, Christians and Muslims were dealt with in a different manner by Israeli forces. Reverend Naim Ateek recalls that his family, along with other Christians from the village of Beisan, were sent to Nazareth, while Muslims were bussed to Jordan.[146] Likewise, when al-Bassa (Acre subdistrict) was depopulated in mid-May, 'about 100 old people and Christians', from an original population of around 4,000, were transferred from al-Bassa to Mazraͨa, an Arab town on the coast that received many Palestinians expelled from other parts of Galilee.[147] At other times, Israel's political concerns trumped such religious profiling. At least two Christian villages were among the many Palestinian towns destroyed along the Lebanese border: Iqrit was home to nearly 500 Christians, mostly Melkite, and thirty Muslims.[148] According to Morris, the village was too close to the border, so the IDF had decided definitively that the border region must be Arab-free.[149] Kafr Birͨim, another Christian town, was also among those villages destroyed along the border.[150] In Jerusalem as well, Christians fared no better than their Muslim neighbours.[151]

Conclusion

Tsimhoni argues that Christians' dependence on the Muslim majority led to their 'decline as a distinct group towards the end of the Mandate'.[152] This conclusion is based largely on research from the first half of the Mandate. Nearly all of her sources are from the 1920s, and she does not broach the subject of Christian organisations in the 1940s, failing to address the revolt's lasting impact on Arab Christians. The rise of inter-communal tensions brought old fears of minority oppression into the open, and the national leadership was in no position to stem those fears. It had failed to stop Jewish immigration or secure any meaningful concessions from the British government. In the lull following the revolt, Christian communities organised on a communal basis under the guidance of new community leaders in an effort to enhance their national position through communal strength. For Arab Christians, however, communal organisation was not at odds with their nationalist endeavours. It was simply a new, or renewed, way of understanding their role as a minority community.

While the focus of this chapter has been the UAOC and its role in organising the Orthodox community, it is important to reiterate that other denominations also saw an increased reliance on communal organisations run by lay leaders rather than foreign clergy. As mentioned above, a group of Latin laity founded a communal organisation in the mid-1940s, and Arab Anglicans sought independence from the Anglican Church.

This movement was part of the wider shift away from centralised national leadership among other Arab groups as well. Women's committees, labour organisations, rural advocates, alternative political parties and even the growth of social and religious organisations' sports clubs reflects the growth of alternative forms of social organisation following the reduction of elite power after the revolt. But to interpret Christian communal organisation solely as part of this trend would be incorrect. Palestinian Arab Christians' place in society was challenged to varying degrees and at various times throughout the Mandate, and the fear of intercommunal violence during the revolt, whether real or imagined, led Christians to reassess the relationship between their communal and national identification.

Communal organisation has been overlooked in Palestinian historiography for a number of reasons. First, there are actually very few histories that include the 1940s. If they do, the focus is usually on the diplomatic efforts of the elite class. The British were concerned with war in Europe, the Zionist insurgency began in full before the war even ended, and the mandatory government was seeking a way out of its failed Palestinian experiment. Scholars writing about the 1940s have had a difficult enough time explaining these issues. The social history of the 1940s, let alone a study of communal organisation among a minority group, has been overlooked.

While Arab diplomats continued their work outside Palestine, life went on for Palestinians. After the revolt ended, Arabs were generally ready to pick up where they had left off three years earlier. Resuming 'normal life' was not easy for communities that had been influenced by the intercommunal tensions of the revolt, and the cessation of violence led immediately to greater levels of Christian communal organisation than in the past, even while those same groups openly declared their allegiance to the goal of an independent Palestine.

Zionist and British sources continued to highlight moments of intercommunal tension and express surprise that Christians considered themselves both fully Arab and fully Christian. With the colonial belief that communal identification was a primary element of Arabs' self-identification, it was difficult to accept both communal and national labels as inclusive of one another. Such Christians, European observers often argued, must have been frightened into maintaining their nationalist credentials (by fear of Muslim retribution) or, alternatively, have been motivated by economic self-interest (in preparation for either Jewish or continued British rule).

Contrary to these views, it is clear that the general trend among Christians was to be both communally and nationally oriented for the same reasons that Muslims relied on a combination of identifiers in determining their relationship to the national movement. Strengthening communal organisation provided Christians with that opportunity. Even in 1948, Christians continued to publicly state their support for the Palestinian national cause and to condemn Zionist and later Israeli actions, though many also showed a willingness to surrender peacefully to Israeli conquest of their villages. This dual approach was explained by British officials throughout the Mandate as an example of Christians supporting the 'Muslim position' out of fear. A better assessment is that Christians were fully connected to both their national and religious labels and never abandoned one for the other.

Notes

1. ISA P-3061/50, Anthem of Orthodox Union Club, Jerusalem, 1942.
2. ISA P3061/3, Jiryis Hanna Butros, Ramallah, to UAOC, 28 October 1944.
3. ISA P3061/3, 28 October 1944.
4. David Waines, 'The Failure of the National Resistance', in Ibrahim Abu-Lughod (ed.), *The Transformation of Palestine: Essays on the Origin and Development of the Arab–Israeli Conflict* (Evanston, IL: Northwestern University Press, 1971), p. 234. Similar summaries can be found in many histories of the Mandate prior to a focus on external political matters.
5. Roza El-Eini, *Mandated Landscape: British Imperial Rule in Palestine, 1929–1948* (New York: Routledge, 2006), p. 27.
6. Mattar, *Mufti of Jerusalem*, p. 107. The famous picture of al-Husayni and Hitler together has been used repeatedly by anti-Palestinian groups to tie Palestinians to Hitler and the Holocaust.
7. Segev, *One Palestine*, p. 411.
8. Wilson, *School Year in Palestine*, p. 65.

9. CZA S25/22341, Zionist Intelligence Report, 'To the Office', 20 April 1941; S25/22340, 22 May 1941; S25/22338, 'Fifth Column in Beisan', 1 August 1942; S25/22341, Zionist Intelligence Report, 5 August 1942.

10. Segev, *One Palestine*, p. 411. For more on the relationship between Arabs and Germany in the 1930s, see Basheer M. Nafi, 'The Arabs and the Axis: 1933–1940', *Arab Studies Quarterly*, 19 (1997), pp. 1–24.

11. *Palestine Post*, 20 August 1945.

12. CZA S25/22312, Zionist Intelligence Report, 6 March 1940; other conflicts between Muslims and Christians were reported in November 1940 (S25/22317, 12 November 1940), June 1941 (S25/22842, 7 June 1941) and August 1942 (S25/22338, 21 August 1942).

13. CZA S25/22340, 'Several Days with Aref al-Aref', 30 April 1941.

14. Bernard Wasserstein, '"Clipping the Claws of the Coloniser": Arab Officials in the Government of Palestine, 1917–48', *Middle Eastern Studies*, 13(2) (1977), p. 182.

15. CZA S25/22344, to Sassoun, 30 November 1941.

16. CZA S25/22344, 30 November 1941.

17. CZA S25/22344, 30 November 1941.

18. CZA S25/22476, Zionist Intelligence Report, 8 May 1941; see also 30 April 1941.

19. CZA S25/22344, G.D., 'Visit to Bethlehem', 6 November 1941.

20. CZA S25/22344, 6 November 1941.

21. CZA S25/22634, Zionist Intelligence Report, 12 September 1941.

22. Cohen, *Army of Shadows*, p. 223.

23. Cohen, *Army of Shadows*, p. 224.

24. Porath's standard work covers only until 1939, at which point he continues with a pan-Arab political study, *In Search of Arab Unity, 1930–1945* (London: Frank Cass, 1986); Lesch (*Arab Politics*, 1979) ends her study of the nationalist movement in 1939, while Bernard Wasserstein's study only covers until 1929 (*The British in Palestine: The Mandatory Government and Arab–Jewish Conflict, 1917–1929*, 2nd edn (Oxford: Blackwell, 1991).

25. A variety of works written over the past half century cover this period in Jewish history. See, for example, Cohen, *Palestine to Israel*; Joseph Heller, *The Birth of Israel, 1945–1949* (Gainesville, FL: University of Florida Press, 2000); Yehuda Bauer, *From Diplomacy to Resistance: A History of Jewish Palestine 1939–1945* (Philadelphia, PA: Jewish Publication Society of America, 1970); and Menacham Begin, *The Revolt: Story of the Irgun* (New York: Henry Schuman, 1951).

26. Issa Khalaf, *Politics in Palestine, Arab factionalism and Social Disintegration, 1939–1948* (Albany, NY: SUNY Press, 1991), p. 1.

27. R. Khalidi, *The Iron Cage*, p. 125.

28. Khalaf, *Politics in Palestine*, p. 1.

29. Khalaf, *Politics in Palestine*, p. 1.

30. Khalaf, *Politics in Palestine*, pp. 3–4.

31. Khalaf, *Politics in Palestine*, p. 240.
32. ISA P201/32, YMCA Report of the Acting General Secretary, January 1939.
33. Khalaf, *Politics in Palestine*, p. 37. Concerning the booming wartime economy, see also James Gelvin, *The Israel–Palestine Conflict: One Hundred Years of War* (Cambridge: Cambridge University Press, 2005), p. 121; Ilan Pappé, *A History of Modern Palestine: One Land, Two Peoples* (Cambridge: Cambridge University Press, 2004), p. 117.
34. Pappé, *History of Modern Palestine*, p. 117.
35. Khalaf, *Politics in Palestine*, pp. 37–8.
36. Glenn Robinson, *Building a Palestinian State: The Incomplete Revolution* (Bloomington, IN: Indiana University Press, 1997), p. 5.
37. Khalaf, *Politics in Palestine*, p. 40.
38. Ylana N. Miller, 'Administrative Policy in Rural Palestine: The Impact of British Norms on Arab Community Life, 1920–1948', in Joel S. Migdal (ed.), *Palestinian Society and Politics* (Princeton, NJ: Princeton University Press, 1980), p. 140.
39. Khalaf, *Politics in Palestine*, p. 59.
40. Khalaf, *Politics in Palestine*, p. 38.
41. Lockman, *Comrades and Enemies*, pp. 268, 323–4.
42. Ori Stendel, *The Arabs in Israel* (Brighton: Sussex Academic Press, 1996), pp. 92 and 103. See also Musa Budeiri, *The Palestine Communist Party, 1919–1948: Arab and Jew in the Struggle for Internationalism* (London: Ithaca Press, 1979; rev edn Chicago, IL: Haymarket Books, 2010).
43. Ilana Kaufman, *Arab National Communism in the Jewish State* (Gainesville, FL: University of Florida Press, 1997), p. 26.
44. Farsou and Aruri, *Palestine and the Palestinians*, p. 80; Fleischmann, *The Nation and its 'New' Women*, p. 177.
45. Fleischmann, *The Nation and its 'New' Women*, p. 191.
46. For each of the people discussed above, see CZA S25/22255, Zionist intelligence-produced biographies of prominent Palestinians. See also Izzat Tannus, *The Palestinians: A Detailed Documented Eyewitness History of Palestine under British Mandate* (New York: IGT, 1988) for a full account of Tannus' life during the Mandate. See Robson, *Colonialism and Christianity*, pp. 121–6, for an account of his activities in London.
47. Najjar, 'The Arabic Press', pp. 169–70.
48. The text of this law is found in David Kirshbaum, 'Emergency Regulations List. Law of the State of Israel, Number 94', available at: http://www.israellawresourcecenter.org/emergencyregs/essays/emergencyregs essay.htm, accessed 5 July 2012.
49. Najjar, 'The Arabic Press', pp. 169–70.
50. Najjar, 'The Arabic Press', p. 179.
51. See ISA P333/2 for information on his arrest and travels to Egypt.
52. R. Khalidi, *The Iron Cage*, p. 99.

53. See *al-Minbar*, vol. 2, February 1947.
54. Wasserstein, 'Clipping the Claws', pp. 182–5.
55. CZA S25/9226, Sari al-Sakakini to Pinkerton, n.d.
56. JMA 832, Orthodox Arab Society to President of the Municipal Council, Jerusalem, 10 February 1944.
57. JMA 832, Mayor of Jerusalem to Nicola Farradj (son of Yaᶜcoub Farraj), 20 March 1944.
58 ISA P300/4, *Jerusalem Red Triangle*, Nov. 1934; ISA P201/32, Membership list, 1943.
59. CZA S25/22635, 30 August 1943.
60. CZA S25/9226, Sari al-Sakakini to Pinkerton, 22 May 1944.
61. Al-Sifri, *Filastin al-ᶜarbiyyah*, pp. 184–7.
62. *Palestine Post*, 15 April 1941.
63. ISA P3219/13, President, Jaffa Orthodox Club to Vice-President of the AHC, 14 November 1946.
64. ISA P3061/34, Cotran to Deputy Controller of Supplies, 9 March 1942.
65. *Filastin*, 18 October 1943.
66. ISA P3062/15, ISA P3061/45, OUC to Patriarch Barlassina, March 1947.
67. ISA P3062/15, Acre Orthodox Club to President, UAOC, 13 July 1945.
68. ISA P3062/1, Holy Cross Girls' School to Cotran, 12 April 1947.
69. ISA P3062/6, Ramle District Officer to President of Orthodox Club, Ramle, 4 January 1945.
70. ISA P3062/15, Chairman of the Charity Committee to W. Chinn Esq., Adviser on Social Welfare, 28 August 1943.
71. ISA P3062/15, Chairman of the Charity Committee to W. Chinn Esq., Adviser on Social Welfare, 28 August 1943.
72. ISA P3062/34, Cotran and Salameh to Chief Secretary, 1 May 1947.
73. ISA P3061/21, DC Pollock to President, OCC, 16 April 1945.
74. ISA P3061/21, Vice-president, OCC to DC Pollock, 25 April 1945.
75. In the generalised discussion that follows, the clubs listed above, as well as the various branches in other Palestinian cities and towns, are discussed as 'Orthodox Clubs', except where specific exceptions and differences arise.
76. ᶜIsa al-Sifri, 'The New Patriarchal Law', *al-Minbar*, No. 5, May 1947.
77. ISA P3061/7, List of OUC committees, 3 August 1943.
78. Khoury and Khoury, *Survey*.
79. ISA P3061/7, List of OUC committees, 3 August 1943.
80. ISA P3061/49, 'Religious Studies', 4 February 1944.
81. ISA P3061/6, Salameh to Revd Arch. Kiprian, L'institut de théologie, Paris, 22 August 1947.
82. ISA P3219/13, President, Jaffa Orthodox Club to Vice-President of the AHC, 14 November 1946.
83. *Palestine Post*, 5 December 1932 and 15 February 1934.
84. Issam Khalidi, 'Body and Ideology: Early Athletics in Palestine (1900–1948)', *Jerusalem Quarterly*, 27 (2006), p. 48.

85. I. Khalidi, 'Body and Ideology', p. 48.
86. I. Khalidi, 'Body and Ideology', p. 44.
87. I. Khalidi, 'Body and Ideology', pp. 48–9.
88. I. Khalidi, 'Body and Ideology', p. 50.
89. *Palestine Post*, 18 November 1937, report of a match between the Acre and Haifa soccer teams.
90. H. Harrif and Y. Galily, 'Sport and Politics in Palestine, 1918–1948: Football as a Mirror Reflecting the Relations between Jews and Britons', *Journal of Soccer and Society*, 4(1) (2003), pp. 41–56.
91. *Palestine Post*, 23 February 1938, 12 June 1942.
92. *Palestine Post*, 22 March 1940.
93. *Palestine Post*, 22 March 1940, 26 February 1940.
94. I. Khalidi writes that the YMCA had refused to participate in the Maccabiah Athletic Games that were held in Tel Aviv in 1932 and 1935 in compliance with 'Arab Palestinian requests that it not share in the games' (p. 57, ff. 22).
95. *Palestine Post*, 18 July 1941.
96. *Palestine Post*, 24 February 1943.
97. *Palestine Post*, 16 March 1942.
98. I. Khalidi, 'Body and Ideology', p. 52; concerning Christian participation in largely Jewish leagues, see, for instance, *Palestine Post*, 12 February 1941.
99. I. Khalidi, 'Body and Ideology', p. 58, ff. 35.
100. I. Khalidi, 'Body and Ideology', p. 52.
101. I. Khalidi, 'Body and Ideology', p. 58, ff. 33.
102. ISA P358/20, Catholic Club to OUC, 18 December 1945 and OUC to Catholic Club, 20 December 1945.
103. Gudrun Kramer, *A History of Palestine: From the Ottoman Conquest to the Founding of the State of Israel* (Princeton, NJ: Princeton University Press, 2008), p. 237.
104. ISA P3061/21, Orthodox Club of Acre festival invitation, 6 May 1945.
105. *Palestine Post*, 25 March 1945.
106. *Palestine Post*, 18 July 1945.
107. *Palestine Post*, 13 June 1946.
108. ISA P3061/50, UOC-Jerusalem Anthem, 1942.
109. ISA P3061/44, Speech from President of the Youth Orthodox Club of Lydda, 6 March 1946.
110. ISA P3062/15, Festival of Arab Unity, invitation for 25 July 1944.
111. ISA P3062/15, 25 July 1944.
112. ISA P3061/21, PAP to OCC, 5 June 1945.
113. ISA P3061/21, OCC to PAP, 9 June 1945.
114. ISA P3219/13, President, Jaffa Orthodox Club to Vice-President of the AHC, 14 November 1946.
115. Hanna Salameh, 'A Letter from the President of the Arab Orthodox Union to the Readers of *al-Minbar*', *al-Minbar*, vol. 1, January 1947.
116. ISA P3062/8, Minutes from UAOC meeting, 11 May 1947.

117. *Palestine Post*, 27 November 1947.
118. ISA P238/9, UAOC newsletter, 21 October 1947.
119. ISA P3222/22, Ibrahim ᶜIyaad to Director of Land for the AHC, 12 February 1947.
120. ISA P3062/15, Arab Catholic Club to President of UOC-Jerusalem, 20 May 1946.
121. *Palestine Post*, 4 November 1940.
122. *Palestine Post*, 24 March 1946; see also ISA M4310/49.
123. ISA M4311/1, George Hakim to HC, 12 February 1945.
124. ISA M4311/1, 12 February 1945.
125. ISA M4322/1, Response of District Commissioner Evans, 8 June 1945.
126. Haim Levenberg, *Military Preparations of the Arab Community in Palestine, 1945–1948* (London: Frank Cass, 1993), pp. 104 and 112.
127. See Robson, *Colonialism and Christianity*, ch. 5 for a more detailed account of Palestine's Anglican population.
128. Pittman, 'Missionaries and Emissaries', p. 232.
129. Pittman, 'Missionaries and Emissaries', p. 232.
130. Pittman, 'Missionaries and Emissaries', p. 234.
131. Cohen, *Army of Shadows*, p. 238.
132. Cohen, *Army of Shadows*, p. 255.
133. Levenberg, *Military Preparations*, p. 181.
134. *Palestine Post*, 10 May 1948.
135. Cohen, *Army of Shadows*, p. 238.
136. ISA P3220/26, Heads of Christian Community, Jaffa to HC, 31 March 1948. The petition is signed by Greek Orthodox, Latin, Coptic, Anglican, Melkite, Armenian and Maronite leaders.
137. *Palestine Post*, 3 June 1948.
138. Benny Morris, *The Birth of the Palestinian Refugee Problem Revisited* (Cambridge: Cambridge University Press, 2004), p. 416.
139. Morris, *Birth of the Palestinian Refugee Problem*, pp. 416–17.
140. Morris, *Birth of the Palestinian Refugee Problem*, p. 417.
141. *New York Times*, 14 July 1948.
142. Morris, *Birth of the Palestinian Refugee Problem*, p. 418.
143. Morris, *Birth of the Palestinian Refugee Problem*, p. 419.
144. Morris, *Birth of the Palestinian Refugee Problem*, p. 474.
145. Morris, *Birth of the Palestinian Refugee Problem*, p. 474.
146. Naim Ateek, *Justice and Only Justice: A Palestinian Theology of Liberation* (Maryknoll, NY: Orbis Books, 1989), pp. 7–10.
147. Walid Khalidi, *All that Remains: The Palestinian Villages Occupied and Depopulated by Israel in 1948* (Beirut: Institute for Palestine Studies, 1992), p. 8; Morris, *Birth of the Palestinian Refugee Problem*, p. 253.
148. W. Khalidi, *All that Remains*, p. 16.
149. Morris, *Birth of the Palestinian Refugee Problem*, pp. 505–36.
150. W. Khalidi, *All that Remains*, pp. 460–1.

151. Nathan Krystall, 'The Fall of the New City, 1947–1950,' in Salim Tamari (ed.), *Jerusalem 1948: The Arab Neighborhoods and their Fate in the War* (Jerusalem: Institute of Jerusalem Studies, 1999), pp. 100–1.
152. Daphne Tsimhoni, 'The Status of the Arab Christians', pp. 185–6.

Conclusion: Nationalism and Communal Identification – Conflicting Identities?

Arab Christians in Palestine constantly renegotiated their place in society and the meaning of their religious identification during the British Mandate. They shaped their relationship to Palestinian nationalism in debates among themselves as well as with the British, Zionists and other Arab communities in Palestine. The Arab Christian story is neither simple or linear, nor is it even one story. Contrary to generalised accounts of Christians during the Mandate, religion was neither insignificant nor essentially determinant, and its relationship to society and politics varied from Christian to Christian based on a wide range of influences. Certainly, the politics of the Mandate played a very important role; as Palestine changed, so too did intercommunal relationships among Arabs. Variations among Christians, hardships brought about by the First World War, the collapse of the Ottoman Empire, the arrival of British troops, the consolidation of British control as a League of Nations-appointed mandatory power, the growth of the Zionist movement, and developments within the Palestinian national movement all contributed to drastic shifts in Arab society.

The two historiographical trends commonly found in the study of Palestinian Arab Christians share an assumption of communal homogeneity even while arriving at drastically different conclusions. That is, the discussion of Christian–Muslim relations is often based on the assumption that religious affiliation meant the same thing to most, if not all, Christians, and that Christians comprised a single group. Tsimhoni, for instance, maintains that the of failure Christians to embrace communalism through accepting British efforts to establish a 'viable Christian body' (along the lines of the Zionist Agency or the Supreme Muslim Council) led the government to treat them with 'growing disregard'.[1] Such a conclusion fails to acknowledge the importance of most Christians' nationalist inclinations and judges their societal position by British instead of Arab standards. Such interpretations often over-emphasise the importance of Muslim–Christian tensions, ignoring other possibilities for inter-Arab strife.

Conclusion

Nationalist historians take the opposite approach and assume that reli-gious identification was unimportant for all Palestinian Arabs, Muslim and Christian alike, arguing that the basic ethnic conflict between Jews and Arabs drove political and social identification. In their view, the Palestinian–Israeli conflict was, and remains, a conflict in which religion is unimportant. Instead, tensions between Zionists and Arabs stem from economic, territorial and political disputes. While the source of the con-flict is impossible to blame on religious differences, religious identifica-tion became an important element of Jewish–Arab and Muslim–Christian relations as a result of the changing political climate in Mandate Palestine.

Both narratives contain elements of truth, though their narrow scope limits understanding the role religion played in the conflict, particularly in this case as it affected the minority Arab Christian population. Broad trends are clear in the chronological narrative; publicly strong in the early 1920s, the aura of Muslim–Christian unity weakened throughout the 1920s and 1930s, although more as a result of the increased importance of Islam than any sort of intercommunal tension. The declining power of the elite nationalist leadership, the broadening field of political voices in the 1930s, and the radicalisation of the Arab populace during the 1936–9 revolt increased fears of communalism and even led to violence. In response, some Arab Christians in the 1940s sought security in newly strengthened communal organisation. Despite this general trend, it is also true that Christians most often downplayed their religion in favour of non-religious ethno-national identification, even during periods of increased interreligious tension and in the 1940s while embracing their religious community. The claim that efforts towards Muslim–Christian unity were abandoned after the implementation of the Mandate is simply counterfac-tual, even if the language of the nationalist movement was less overt in pointing out interreligious cooperation.

While this sweeping summary of the role of Christians in Mandate Palestine is important, such a summary threatens to overshadow impor-tant forms of diversity within the community. Denomination, geography, economic status, educational level and social class all played a role in determining individual perspectives on communal issues. Rather than awkwardly squeeze all Christians into a single category, it is more insight-ful to explore the meaning of religious identification in varied social and political climates, and to examine how various Christians sought to either protest against or submit to general trends.

At first blush, this conclusion seems only slightly different than the argument that there was a steady trend towards intercommunal tension. But Christians' relationship with nationalism is quite different to their

197

relationship with Muslims, though the two are related. Despite social tensions, nearly all Arab Christians maintained their dedication to the nationalist cause despite differences in opinion concerning the challenges facing them as individuals and as a religious community. Some Christians accepted a more Islamically enhanced form of Palestinian nationalism, while others insisted that the movement remain non-religious. Reasons for this disagreement included the influence of foreign denominational leaders, the view of the traditional Christian elite, the rising middle class, generational differences and regional variations.

While it is impossible to fully describe a religious minority's relationship to the majority in generalised terms, religious identification still mattered. The lack of Christian unity does not undermine the fact that Christians often approached political matters from their perspective as members of a religious minority. They simply answered that challenge in divergent ways. 'Christian' may have been among the most important labels for members of the community at that time, but other factors were certainly influential as well. In the first decade of British rule only elite Christians had a public voice. Yet even among the elite, factors such as denomination, geographic location and previous interactions with Western cultures affected the way individuals formulated their political stance. Christians such as ᶜIsa Bandak, ᶜIsa al-ᶜIsa, Khalil al-Sakakini, Najib Nassar and others held a wide range of views. Later on, the traditional elite were increasingly pushed aside by a growing newly educated middle class who brought with it new ideas concerning its role in society and the best way to protect that role.

The role of Zionism in Arab political imagination and in encouraging early formulations of intercommunal unity must not be under-estimated. The shift from the *millet*-structured society of the Ottoman era to early Mandate manifestations of non-religious nationalism was consistent with the Ottoman constitutional movement, but was also enhanced by fears of Zionist encroachment in Palestine. Other Arab countries also witnessed a surge of nationalist sentiment, but the Muslim Christian Association's chief purpose was to challenge the Balfour Declaration. Internal MCA correspondence makes it clear that they had a political motivation for religious cooperation. The leadership believed that European powers would respond positively to a unified Muslim–Christian voice emanating from the Holy Land and would prevent the League of Nations from supporting the British plan for a Jewish homeland in Palestine. Even while fear of Zionism brought Arabs together, Zionists worked to drive a wedge between elements of Palestinian Arab society. Some Zionists focused on religious divides, although their more successful efforts involved exacerbating factionalism. Still, Zionists did influence the Druze decision to segregate itself from the greater Arab community, though with Arab Christians they were less successful.

Like the Zionists, the British influenced communal relations in multiple ways. First, their policy of supporting the Zionists brought many Palestinians together in protest against British rule. Even during periods of severe factional violence, various parties came together to protest the anniversary of the Balfour Declaration. Yet the government also implemented policies that made full intercommunal cooperation impossible. The British dedication to the status quo, the use of religious courts, the allocation of council seats based on religious communities, and a deeply ingrained belief in the fundamental difference between Christians and Muslims all drove Christians and Muslims apart. At times a divide-and-rule policy may have been intentional, but more often British policies seem to have been less deliberate, though equally damaging to national unification.

Among the most interesting developments concerning British beliefs about communal identity is that British and Arab Christian sentiments both reversed over the course of the Mandate. In the earliest years of British rule, when Muslim and Christian notables were advocating non-religious nationalism from within the Muslim–Christian Association, the British approached Arab society as if Muslims and Christians were two distinct communities. With this belief in mind, Mandate authorities adopted the overarching theory of the *millet* system: Christians and Muslims were separate and distinct communities. Moreover, they actively sought 'balanced' communal representation on both elected and appointed councils and advisory boards. By the 1930s, it became clear to most British officials that the Christian community was, in fact, fully part of greater Arab society. The evidence had been present since the British occupation began, but the colonial imagination rejected evidence of Christian participation in the national movement. Once the British administration accepted the unity of Arab society, it sought, in the run-up to the 1934 municipal elections, to undo the communal allocation, although even then it failed to adopt fully non-communal electoral policies.

Finally, the Palestinian case challenges conventional wisdom about the exclusionary nature of communalism. Arab Christian communal development in Palestine provides an example in which national and communal identification were not at odds with one another. Such a conclusion is often accepted for a majority religious group, but the minority group is expected to divorce religious and national identification for the betterment of the national movement. The alternative is to adopt a communalist attitude which divides the nation. Christians first supported non-religious nationalism, maintaining the traditional role of the notable class as social and political leaders. But later, when Christians' traditionally strong role in society was threatened by changing social, economic and political circumstances, some Christians sought strength in communal reorganisation, hoping it would lead them to greater societal influence as it had in Ottoman times. However wary or unsatisfied they were with their shifting position in Palestinian society, Arab Christians did not abandon the national movement, request special protection from the British or even establish specifically Christian political organisations (at least not long-lasting or powerful ones), although such developments were suggested from time to time. Instead, the more prominent voices encouraged Christians to embrace their Arab-Islamic roots, remain devoted to the national cause, and maintain a strong role in all nationalist parties rather than form their own. There were multiple reasons for this. First, it is clear that Arab Christians understood themselves as fully Arab. This most basic element of Christian identification was the hardest for the British to see. In addition, Christians wanted to retain their importance in elite national circles as a way of protecting both their individual and communal positions. Because the British (and some historians) question the legitimacy of Christian claims of Arabness, they sought alternative explanations. They argued, for instance, that Christians supported Arab nationalism out of fear of the Muslim majority or that the Zionists would harm them economically. While such arguments were certainly true for some Christians at some times, they fail to explain the entrenched nationalism held by nearly all Arab Christians of all denominations.

The situation has changed dramatically in the years since the end of British rule in Palestine, but the variety of Christian responses to their circumstances has not. In Israel, the position of Christians as a religious minority has been compounded by the fact that they are also part of the subordinated ethnic minority. Meanwhile, in recent years the population of Christians in the Palestinian territories has declined to below 2 per cent. Commentators continue to make much of Christians' religious identification, and Christians continue to differ on how to interpret their own situation. Some specifically highlight the struggle faced by Palestinian Christians, while others insist that their situation is no better or worse than that of Palestinian Muslims. Some call for Christian unity, while others join secular political parties; the Islamic party Hamas even fielded a Christian candidate in a 2006 election.

Too much emphasis is often placed on religion, but so too is it often ignored. Religious identification, like so many other elements that contribute to an individual's worldview and sense of belonging, must neither be essentialised nor overlooked; rather, it must be examined as a site of contestation and debate. Confronting the relationship between religious and national identification was a constant challenge for Arab Christians in Mandate Palestine. Dissecting such debates highlights the variety of ways in which individuals and communities understood, and continue to understand, their competing affiliations. Such an analysis also contributes to a deeper and fuller understanding of the nature of religious communal identification.

Note

1. Tsimhoni, 'The Status of the Arab Christians', pp. 185–6.

Bibliography

Archival Sources

ᶜAdnan Ayyub Musallam's Collection on Bethlehem, The Holy Land, University of Michigan, Ann Arbor, Michigan
Central Zionist Archives (CZA), Jerusalem
Christ Church Archive, Jerusalem
Haifa Municipal Archives (HMA), Haifa
Israel State Archives (ISA), Jerusalem
Jerusalem Municipal Archives (JMA), Jerusalem
Lambeth Palace Library, London
Latin Patriarchate Archives, Jerusalem
National Archives, Public Records Office (PRO) Kew
St Antony's College Archive, Private Papers Collection, Oxford

Newspapers

Filastin, Jaffa
Al-Jamiᶜa al-ᶜArabiyya, Jerusalem
Al-Jamiᶜa al-Islamiyya, Jaffa
Al-Karmil, Haifa
Al-Minbar, Jerusalem
Mirat al-Sharq, Jerusalem
New York Times, New York
Palestine Post, Jerusalem
Sawt al-Shaᶜb, Bethlehem
Suriyah al-Janubiyah, Jerusalem
Al-Yarmuk, Haifa
Al-Zuhour, Haifa

Published Primary Sources, Memoirs and Diaries

Bertram, Sir Anton and Harry Charles Luke, *Report of the Commission Appointed by the Government of Palestine to Inquire into the Affairs of the Orthodox Patriarchate of Jerusalem.* New York: Oxford University Press, 1921.
Bertram, Sir Anton and J. W. A. Young, *Report of the Commission Appointed*

by the Government of Palestine to Inquire into the Affairs of the Orthodox Patriarchate of Jerusalem. New York: Oxford University Press, 1926.

Great Britain, Colonial Office, *Palestine Royal Commission Report* (Peel Report). London, 1937.

'Great Britain, Palestine and the Jews', *Jewry's Celebration of its National Charter*. New York: George H. Doran, 1918.

Ingrams, Doreen, *Palestine Papers, 1917–1922: Seeds of Conflict*. New York: Braziller, 1973.

Jarman, Robert (ed.), *Palestine and Transjordan Administration Reports, 1918–1948*, vols 1–16. Slough: Archive Editions, 1995.

Jarman, Robert L. (ed.), *Political Diaries of the Arab World: Palestine and Jordan*, vols 1–3. Slough: Archive Editions, 2001.

Kayyali, ʿAbd al-Wahhab (ed.), *Documents on the Palestine Arab Resistance to the British Mandate and Zionism (1918–1939)*. Washington, DC: Institute for Palestine Studies, 1988.

Keith-Roach, Edward, *Pasha of Jerusalem: Memoirs of a District Commissioner under the British Mandate*. London: Radcliff Press, 1994.

Khoury, al-Khoury Nicola, *Muthakarat kahin al-Quds (Memoirs of the Jerusalem Priest: Birzeit 1885–Beirut 1954)* No publication information available.

Kisch, Frederick Herman, *Palestine Diary*. London: Victor Gollancz, 1938.

Laqueur, Walter and Barry Rubin (eds), *The Israel–Arab Reader: A Documentary History of the Middle East Conflict*, rev and updated edn. New York: Penguin, 1995.

Link, A. S. (ed.), *The Papers of Woodrow Wilson, vol. 45: 1917–1918*, Princeton, NJ: Princeton University Press, 1984.

Mills, E., *Census of Palestine, 1931*. Alexandria: Whitehead Morris, 1933.

Musallam, Akram (ed.), *Yawmiyat Khalil al-Sakakini: yawmiyat, rasaʾil wa-taʿammulat*, vols 1–8. Ramallah: Markaz Khalil al-Sakakini al-Thaqafi, 2003–2008.

Nassar, Najib al-Khuri, *Al-Sihyuniyya: Tarikhuha, gharaduha, ahamiyyatuha (Zionism: Its History, Objective and Importance)*. Haifa: Al-Karmil Press, 1911.

Newton, Frances E., *Fifty Years in Palestine*. London: Britons Publishing Society, 1948.

Priestland, Jane (ed.), *Records of Jerusalem 1917–1971*, vol. 2. Oxford: Archive Editions, 2002.

Al-Sakakini, Khalil, *Kadha ana ya dunya (Such am I, Oh World)*. Jerusalem, 1955.

Sabbagh, Karl, *Palestine, A Personal History*. New York: Grove Press, 2007.

Storrs, Ronald, *Orientations*. London: Nicholson & Watson, 1937.

Tannous, Izzat, *The Palestinians: A Detailed Documented Eyewitness History of Palestine Under British Mandate*. New York: IGT, 1988.

United Nations Information System on the Question of Palestine (UNISPAL), available at: unispal.un.org/unispal.nsf/udc.htm.

Wilson, H. M., *School Year in Palestine, 1938–1939*. Oxford: St Antony's Documentation Centre.

Secondary Sources

Abu ᶜAmr, Ziyad, *Islamic Fundamentalism in the West Bank and Gaza: Muslim Brotherhood and Islamic Jihad*. Bloomington, IN: Indiana University Press, 1994.

Abu-Ghazaleh, Adnan, *Arab Cultural Nationalism in Palestine During the British Mandate*. Beirut: Institute of Palestine Studies, 1973.

Abu-Lughod, Ibrahim (ed.), *The Transformation of Palestine: Essays on the Origin and Development of the Arab–Israeli Conflict*. Evanston, IL: Northwestern University Press, 1971.

Ahmad, Rafiuddin, *The Bengal Muslims, 1871–1906: A Quest for Identity*, 2nd edn. Delhi: Oxford University Press, 1996.

Ali, Najar Aida, 'The Arabic Press and Nationalism in Palestine', Doctoral dissertation, Syracuse University, 1975.

Allen, Phillip C., 'The Last Despot: Ethnic Consciousness, Power Politics, and the Orthodox Church in Late Ottoman Syria', Doctoral dissertation, Princeton University, 2000.

Antonius, George, *The Arab Awakening: The Story of the Arab National Movement*. London: Arab Centre, 1939.

Ateek, Naim, *Justice and Only Justice: A Palestinian Theology of Liberation*. Maryknoll, NY: Orbis Books, 1989.

Bar-Yosef, Eitan, 'The Last Crusade? British Propaganda and the Palestine Campaign, 1917–18', *Journal of Contemporary History*, 36 (2001), 87–109.

Barlas, Asma, *Democracy, Nationalism, and Communalism: The Colonial Legacy in South Asia*. Boulder, CO: Westview Press, 1995.

Barth, Fredrik, *Ethnic Groups and Boundaries: The Social Organization of Cultural Difference*. Boston, MA: Little, Brown, 1969.

Bauer, Yehuda, *From Diplomacy to Resistance: A History of Jewish Palestine 1939–1945*. Philadelphia: Jewish Publication Society of American, 1970.

Begin, Menacham, *The Revolt: Story of the Irgun*. New York: Henry Schuman, 1951.

Ben-Dor, Gabriel (ed.), *The Palestinians and the Middle East Conflict*. Forest Grove, OR: Turtledove, 1979.

Braude, Benjamin and Bernard Lewis (eds.), *Christians and Jews in the Ottoman Empire: The Functioning of a Plural Society*. New York: Holmes & Meier, 1982.

Brown, Carl (ed.), *Imperial Legacy: The Ottoman Imprint on the Balkans and the Middle East*. New York: Columbia University Press, 1996.

Budeiri, Musa, *The Palestine Communist Party, 1919–1948: Arab and Jew in the Struggle for Internationalism*. London: Ithaca Press, 1979; rev edn Chicago, IL: Haymarket, 2010.

Budeiri, Musa, 'The Palestinians: Tensions between Nationalist and Religious Identities', in Jankowski and Gershoni (eds), *Rethinking Arab Nationalism*, pp. 191–206.

Campos, Michelle U., *Ottoman Brothers: Muslims, Christians, and Jews in Early 20th Century Palestine*. Stanford, CA: Stanford University Press, 2011.

Cassese, Antonio, *Self-Determination of Peoples: A Legal Reappraisal*. Cambridge: Cambridge University Press, 1995.

Cavert, Samuel McCrea, 'Beginning at Jerusalem', *Christian Century*, 10 May 1928.

Chacour, Elias, *Blood Brothers*. Grand Rapids, MI: Chosen Books, 1984.

Chammas, Joseph, *The Melkite Church*. Jerusalem: Emerezian, 1992.

Chatterji, Joya, *Bengal Divided: Hindu Communalism and Partition, 1932–1947*. Cambridge: Cambridge University Press, 2002.

Chevallier, Dominique, 'Non-Muslim Communities in Arab Cities', in Braude and Lewis (eds), *Christians and Jews in the Ottoman Empire: The Functioning of a Plural Society*, vol. 2, pp. 159–66.

Cohen, Hillel, *Army of Shadows: Palestinian Collaboration with Zionism, 1917–1948*, trans. Haim Watzman. Berkeley, CA: University of California Press, 2008.

Cohen, Michael J., *Palestine to Israel: From Mandate to Independence*. London: Frank Cass, 1988.

Cohen, Naomi, *The Year after the Riots: American Responses to the Palestine Crisis of 1929–1930*. Detroit, MI: Wayne State University Press, 1988.

Collins, John, *Occupied by Memory: The Intifada Generation and the Palestinian State of Emergency*. New York: New York University Press, 2004.

Cooper, Frederick, *Colonialism in Question: Theory, Knowledge, History*. Berkeley, CA: University of California Press, 2005.

Cooper, Frederick with Rogers Brubaker, 'Identity', in Cooper, *Colonialism in Question: Theory, Knowledge, History*, pp. 59–90.

Davis, Eric, 'The Concept of Revival and the Study of Islam and Politics', in Freyer Stowasser (ed.), *The Islamic Impulse*, pp. 37–58.

Deringil, Selim, *The Well-Protected Domains: Ideology and the Legitimation of Power in the Ottoman Empire, 1876–1909*. New York: I. B. Tauris, 1999.

Divine, Donna Robinson, *Politics and Society in Ottoman Palestine: The Arab Struggle for Survival and Power*. Boulder, CO: Lynne Rienner, 1994.

Dudoignon, Stéphane A., Komatsu Hisao and Kosugi Yasushieds (eds), *Intellectuals in the Modern Islamic World: Transmission Transformation and Communication*. London: Routledge, 2006.

Dumont, Louis, *Religion, Politics and History in India: Collected Papers in Indian Sociology*. Paris: Mouton, 1970.

El-Eini, Roza, *Mandated Landscape: British Imperial Rule in Palestine, 1929–1948*. New York: Routledge, 2006.

Eldem, Edhem, 'Capitulations and Western Trade', in Faroqhi (ed.), *The*

Cambridge History of Turkey: The Later Ottoman Empire, 1603–1839, vol. 3, pp. 283–335.

Faroqhi, Suraiya (ed.), *The Cambridge History of Turkey: The Later Ottoman Empire, 1603–1839*, vol. 3. Cambridge: Cambridge University Press, 2006.

Farsoun, Samih K. and Naseer Hasan Aruri, *Palestine and the Palestinians: A Social and Political History*. Boulder, CO: Westview Press, 2006.

Finkel, Caroline, *Osman's Dream: The Story of the Ottoman Empire, 1300–1923*. New York: Basic Books, 2006.

Fleischmann, Ellen, *The Nation and its 'New' Women: The Palestinian Women's Movement, 1920–1948*. Berkeley, CA: University of California Press, 2003.

Foster, Zachary, 'The Emergence of a Palestinian National Identity: A Theory-Driven Approach', *Michigan Journal of History* (Winter 2007).

Friedland, Roger, 'Religious Nationalism and the Problem of Collective Representation', *Annual Review of Sociology*, 27 (2001), 125–52.

Gelvin, James, *The Israel–Palestine Conflict: One Hundred Years of War*. Cambridge: Cambridge University Press, 2005.

Gelvin, James, 'Secularism and Religion in the Arab Middle East: Reinventing Islam in a World of Nation States', in Peterson and Walhof (eds), *The Invention of Religion: Rethinking Belief and Politics in History*, pp. 115–31.

Gershoni, Israel and James Jankowski (eds), *Rethinking Nationalism in the Arab Middle East*. New York: Columbia University Press, 1997.

Al-Ghuri, Emil, *Palestine in Sixty Years*. Beirut: Dar al-Nahar, 1974.

Hacohen, Mordechai Ben-Hillel, *The Wars of the Nations* (in Hebrew). Jerusalem: Yad Ben-Zvi, 1985.

Haddad, Robert, 'The Ottoman Empire in the Contemporary Middle East', in *Aftermath of Empire: In Honor of Professor Max Salvadori*. Northhampton, MA: Smith College, 1975, 39pp.

Hammond, Phillip E., 'Religion and the Persistence of Identity', *Journal for the Scientific Study of Religion*, 27(1) (1988), 1–11.

Hanna, Paul, *British Policy in Palestine*. Washington, DC: American Council on Public Affairs, 1942.

Harries, Patrick, 'Exclusion, Classification and Internal Colonialism: The Emergence of Ethnicity Among the Tsonga-Speakers of South Africa', in Vail (ed.), *The Creation of Tribalism in Southern Africa*, pp. 82–117.

Harrif, H. and Y. Galily, 'Sport and Politics in Palestine, 1918–1948: Football as a Mirror Reflecting the Relations between Jews and Britons', *Journal of Soccer and Society*, 4(1) (2003), 41–56.

Heller, Joseph, *The Birth of Israel, 1945–1949*. Gainesville, FL: University of Florida Press, 2000.

'History and Activities of the Latin Patriarch of Jerusalem', available at http://www.lpj.org/newsite2006/patriarch/history_patriarchate.html, accessed 5 July 2012.

Hobsbawm, Eric and Terrence Ranger (eds), *The Invention of Tradition*. New York: Cambridge University Press, 1983.

Hopwood, Derek, *The Russian Presence in Syria and Palestine, 1843–1914: Church and Politics in the Near East*. Oxford, Clarendon Press, 1969.

Hourani, Albert, *Arabic Thought in the Liberal Age, 1798–1939*. Cambridge: Cambridge University Press, 1983.

Hourani, Albert, Phillip Khoury and Mary Wilson (eds), *The Modern Middle East*, 2nd edn. London: I. B. Tauris, 2004.

Hudson, Michael, *Arab Politics: The Search for Legitimacy*. New Haven, CT: Yale University Press, 1979.

Hyamson, Albert Montefiore, *Palestine under the Mandate, 1920–1948*. New York: Taylor & Francis, 1976.

Inalcik, Halil, 'The Meaning of Legitimacy: The Ottoman Case', in Brown (ed.), *Imperial Legacy: The Ottoman Imprint on the Balkans and the Middle East*, pp. 17–29.

Iqrit Heritage Society, available at: www.iqrit.org, accessed 5 July 2013.

Jabarah, Taysir, *Palestinian Leader, Hajj Amin al-Husayni, Mufti of Jerusalem*. London, Kingston Press, 1985.

Jacobson, Abigail, *From Empire to Empire: Jerusalem between Ottoman and British Rule*. Syracuse, NY: Syracuse University Press, 2011.

Jacobson, Abigail, 'Alternative Voices in Late Ottoman Palestine: A Historical Note', *Jerusalem Quarterly*, 21 (2004), 41–8.

Jankowski James P. and I. Gershoni (eds), *Rethinking Arab Nationalism*. New York: Columbia University Press, 1997.

John, Robert, 'Behind the Balfour Declaration', *Journal for Historical Review*, 6(4) (Winter 1985/6), 389pp.

Johnson, Nels, *Islam and the Politics of Meaning in Palestinian Nationalism*. Boston, MA: Kegan Paul, 1982.

Jones, Kenneth W., 'Communalism in the Punjab', *Journal of Asian Studies*, 28 (1968), 39–54.

Kabha, Mustafa, 'The Courts of the Palestinian Arab Revolt, 1936–1939', in Singer, Neumann and Aksin (eds), *Untold Histories of the Middle East: Recovering Voices from the 19th and 20th Centuries*, pp. 197–213.

Kanafani, Ghassan, *The 1936–1939 Revolt in Palestine*. New York: Committee for Democratic Palestine, 1972.

Kaplan, Benjamin, *Divided by Faith: Religious Conflict and the Practice of Toleration in Early Modern Europe*. Cambridge, MA: Harvard University Press, 2009.

Karpat, Kemal H., *Studies on Ottoman Social and Political History*. Boston, MA: Brill, 2002.

Karpat, Kemal H., *The Politicization of Islam: Reconstructing Identity, State, Faith, and Community in the Late Ottoman State*. Oxford: Oxford University Press, 2001.

Kaufman, Ilana, *Arab National Communism in the Jewish State*. Gainesville, FL: University Press of Florida, 1997.

Kayali, Hasan, *Arabs and Young Turks: Ottomanism, Arabism, and Islamism in the Ottoman Empire, 1908–1918*. Berkeley, CA: University of California Press, 1997.

Kedourie, Elie, *The Chatham House Version and other Middle-Eastern Studies*. London: Weidenfeld & Nicolson, 1970.

Khalaf, Issa, *Politics in Palestine: Arab Factionalism and Social Disintegration, 1939–1948*. Albany, NY: SUNY Press, 1991.

Khalidi, Issam, 'Body and Ideology: Early Athletics in Palestine (1900–1948)', *Jerusalem Quarterly*, 27 (2006), 44–58.

Khalidi, Rashid, 'The Formation of Palestinian Identity: The Critical Years, 1917–1923', in Gershoni and Jankowski (eds), *Rethinking Nationalism in the Arab Middle East*, pp. 171–90.

Khalidi, Rashid, *Palestinian Identity, The Construction of Modern National Consciousness*. New York: Columbia, 1997.

Khalidi, Rashid, *The Iron Cage: The Story of the Palestinian Struggle for Statehood*. Boston, MA: Beacon Press, 2006.

Khalidi, Rashid, 'The Palestinians and 1948', in Rogan and Shlaim (eds), *The War for Palestine*, pp. 79–103.

Khalidi, Walid. *All That Remains: The Palestinian Villages Occupied and Depopulated by Israel in 1948*. Beirut: Institute for Palestine Studies, 1992.

Khater, Akhram Fouad, *Inventing Home: Emigration, Gender, and the Middle Class in Lebanon, 1870–1920*. Berkeley, CA: University of California Press, 2001.

Khoury, Shahadeh and Nicola Khoury, *A Survey of the History of the Orthodox Church of Jerusalem*. Amman: Feras, 2002.

Kimmerling, Baruch and Joel S. Migdal, *Palestinians: The Making of a People*. Cambridge, MA: Harvard University Press, 1993.

Kirshbaum, David, 'Emergency Regulations List. Law of the State of Israel, No. 94', available at: http://www.israellawresourcecenter.org/emergencyregs/ essays/emergencyregsessay.htm, accessed 5 July 2012.

Kramer, Gudrun, *A History of Palestine: From the Ottoman Conquest to the Founding of the State of Israel*. Princeton, NJ: Princeton University Press, 2008.

Kramer, Martin, *Islam Assembled: The Advent of the Muslim Congresses*. New York: Columbia University Press, 1986.

Krystall, Nathan, 'The Fall of the New City, 1947–1950', in Tamari (ed.), *Jerusalem 1948: The Arab Neighborhoods and their Fate in the War*, 92pp.

Kupferschmidt, Uri M., *The Supreme Muslim Council: Islam Under the British Mandate for Palestine*. Boston, MA: Brill, 1987.

Laqueur, Walter. *A History of Zionism*, 3rd edn. London: Tauris Parke, 2003.

Le Beau, Bryan F. and Menachem Mor (eds), *Pilgrims and Travelers to the Holy Land*. Omaha, NE: Creighton University Press, 1996.

Lesch, Ann Mosely, *Arab Politics in Palestine, 1917–1939: The Frustration of a Nationalist Movement*. Ithaca, NY: Cornell University Press, 1979.

Lesch, Ann Mosely, 'The Nationalist Movement Under the Mandate', in Quandt, Jabber and Lesch (eds), *The Politics of Palestinian Nationalism*, pp. 5–42.

Levenberg, Haim, *Military Preparations of the Arab Community in Palestine, 1945–1948*. London: Frank Cass, 1993.

Lihaam, The Metropolitan Lutfi, *Kitaab al-youbeel al-takhkari* (*The Book of the Memorial Jubilee*). Jerusalem: Amerzian Print Foundation, 1998.

Likhovski, Assaf, *Law and Identity in Mandate Palestine*. Chapel Hill, NC: University of North Carolina Press, 2006.

Lockman, Zachary, *Comrades and Enemies: Arab and Jewish Workers in Palestine, 1906–1948*. Berkeley, CA: University of California Press, 1996.

Lundsten, Mary Ellen, 'Wall Politics: Zionist and Palestinian Strategies in Jerusalem, 1928', *Journal of Palestine Studies*, 8(1) (1978), 3–27.

Makdisi, Ussama, 'Pensée 4: Moving Beyond Orientalist Fantasy, Sectarian Polemic, and Nationalist Denial', *International Journal of Middle Eastern Studies*, 40(4) (2008), 559–60.

Makdisi, Ussama, *Culture of Sectarianism: Community, History and Violence in Nineteenth Century Ottoman Lebanon*. Berkeley, CA: University of California Press, 2000.

Mandel, Neville, *The Arabs and Zionism before World War I*. Berkeley, CA: University of California Press, 1976.

Maʾoz, Moshe (ed.), *Palestinian Arab Politics*. Jerusalem Academic Press: Jerusalem, 1975.

Masters, Bruce, *Christians and Jews in the Ottoman Arab World: The Roots of Sectarianism*. Cambridge: Cambridge University Press, 2004.

Mattar, Philip, *The Mufti of Jerusalem: Al-Hajj Amin al-Husayni and the Palestinian National Movement*, 2nd edn. New York: Columbia University Press, 1992.

Matthews, Weldon C., *Confronting an Empire, Constructing a Nation: Arab Nationalists and Popular Politics in Mandate Palestine*. New York: I. B. Tauris, 2006.

Matthews, Weldon C., 'Pan-Islam or Arab Nationalism? The Meaning of the 1931 Jerusalem Islamic Congress Reconsidered', *International Journal of Middle Eastern Studies*, 35 (2003), 1–22.

Mazza, Roberto, *Jerusalem: From the Ottomans to the British*. New York: I. B. Tauris, 2009.

McCarthy, Justin, *The Population of Palestine: Population History and Statistics of the Late Ottoman Period and the Mandate*. New York: Columbia University Press, 1990.

Migdal, Joel S. (ed.), *Palestinian Society and Politics*. Princeton, NJ: Princeton University Press, 1980.

Mikesell Marvin W. and Alexander B Murphy, 'A Framework for Comparative Study of Minority-Group Aspirations', *Annals of the Association of American Geographers*, 81(4) (1991), 581–604.

Miller, Ylana N., 'Administrative Policy in Rural Palestine: The Impact of British

Norms on Arab Community Life, 1920–1948', in Migdal (ed.), *Palestinian Society and Politics*, pp. 124–40.

Milton-Edwards, Beverly, *The Israeli–Palestinian Conflict: A People's War*. London: Taylor & Francis, 2008.

Mitchell, Richard Paul, *The Society of the Muslim Brothers*. Oxford: Oxford University Press, 1969.

Morris, Benny, *The Birth of the Palestinian Refugee Problem Revisited*. Cambridge: Cambridge University Press, 2004.

Moscrop, John James, *Measuring Jerusalem: The Palestine Exploration Fund and British Interests in the Holy Land*. New York: Continuum, 2000.

Muslih, Muhammad Y., *The Origins of Palestinian Nationalism*. New York: Columbia University Press, 1988.

Musallam, ᶜAdnan, *Folded Pages from Local Palestinian History: Developments in Politics, Society, Press and Thought in Bethlehem in the British Era, 1917–1948*. Bethlehem: Wiᵓam Center, 2002.

Nafi, Basheer M., *Arabism, Islamism and the Palestine Question: A Political History*. Reading: Ithaca Press, 1998.

Nafi, Basheer M., 'The Arabs and the Axis: 1933–1940', *Arab Studies Quarterly*, (Spring 1997), 1.

Nafi, Basheer M., 'Shaykh ᶜIzz al-Din al-Qassam: A Reformist and a Rebel Leader', *Journal of Islamic Studies*, 8(2) (1997), 187–215.

Ochsenwald, William, 'Islam and the Ottoman Legacy in the Modern Middle East', in Brown (ed.), *Imperial Legacy: The Ottoman Imprint on the Balkans and the Middle East*, pp. 263–83.

O'Mahony, Anthony (ed.), *The Christian Communities of Jerusalem and the Holy Land: Studies in History, Religion and Politics*. Cardiff: University of Wales Press, 2003.

O'Mahony, Anthony (ed.), *Palestinian Christians: Religion, Politics and Society in the Holy Land*. London: Melisende, 1999.

O'Mahony, Anthony, Goran Gunner and Kevork Hintlian (eds), *The Christian Heritage in the Holy Land*. London: Scorpion Cavendish, 1995.

Ormanean, Maghakᵓia. *The Church of Armenia: Her History, Doctrine, Discipline, Liturgy, Literature, and Existing Condition*, 2nd edn. London: Mowbray, 1955.

Owen, Roger (ed.), *Studies in the Economic and Social History of Palestine in the Nineteenth and Twentieth Centuries*. Carbondale, IL: Southern Illinois University Press, 1982.

Pacini, Andrea, *Christian Communities in the Arab Middle East: The Challenge of the Future*. New York: Clarendon Press, 1998.

Pandey, Gyanendra, 'Questions of Nationalism and Communalism', *Economic and Political Weekly*, 22(25) (1987), 983–4.

Pappé, Ilan, *A History of Modern Palestine; One Land, Two Peoples*. Cambridge: Cambridge University Press, 2004.

Pappé, Ilan (ed.), *The Israel/Palestine Question*. London: Routledge, 1999.

Parsons, Laila, 'The Palestinian Druze in the 1947–1949 Arab–Israeli War', in

Schulze, Stokes and Campbell (eds), *Nationalism, Minorities and Diasporas: Identities and Rights in the Middle East*, pp. 144–57.

Peleg, Ilan (ed.), *The Middle East Peace Process: Interdisciplinary Perspectives*. Albany, NY: SUNY Press, 1998.

Peters, Joan, *From Time Immemorial: The Origins of the Arab–Jewish Conflict Over Palestine*. New York: Harper & Row, 1984.

Peterson, Derek R. and Darren Walhof (eds), *The Invention of Religion: Rethinking Belief and Politics in History*. New Brunswick, NJ: Rutgers University Press, 2002.

Pittman, Lester Groves, 'Missionaries and Emissaries: The Anglican Church in Palestine 1841–1948', dissertation, University of Virginia, 1998.

Porath, Yehoshua, *In Search of Arab Unity, 1930–1945*. London: Frank Cass, 1986.

Porath, Yehoshua, *The Palestinian Arab National Movement: From Riots to Rebellion, vol. 2: 1929–1939*. London: Frank Cass, 1977.

Porath, Yehoshua, 'The Political Organization of the Palestinian Arabs under the British', in Maʾoz (ed.), *Palestinian Arab Politics*, pp. 1–20.

Porath, Yehoshua, *The Emergence of the Palestinian–Arab National Movement, 1918–1929*. London: Frank Cass, 1974.

Powaski, Ronald E., *Toward an Entangling Alliance: American Isolationism, Internationalism, and Europe, 1901–1950*. Westport, CT: Greenwood, 1991.

Quandt, William B., Fuad Jabber and Ann Mosely Lesch (eds), *The Politics of Palestinian Nationalism*. Berkeley, CA: University of California Press, 1973.

Reiter, Yitzhak, *Islamic Endowments in Jerusalem under British Mandate*. New York: Routledge, 1996.

Ricca, Simone, Reinventing Jerusalem: Israel's Reconstruction of the Jewish Quarter After 1967. London: I. B. Tauris, 2007.

Robinson, Glen, Building a Palestinian State: The Incomplete Revolution. Bloomington, IN: Indiana University Press, 1997.

Robson, Laura, *Colonialism and Christianity in Mandate Palestine*. Austin, TX: University of Texas Press, 2011.

Rogan, Eugene L. and Avi Shlaim (eds), *The War for Palestine*, 2nd edn. Cambridge: Cambridge University Press, 2007.

Roussos, Sotiris, 'The Greek Orthodox Patriarchate and Community of Jerusalem: Church, State and Identity', in O'Mahony et al. (eds), *The Christian Heritage in the Holy Land*, p. 211.

Rowe, Paul S., 'Neo-Millet Systems and Transnational Religious Movements: The Humayun Decrees and Church Construction in Egypt', *Journal of Church and State*, 49(2) (2007), 329–50.

Rowe, Paul S., 'The Sheep and the Goats? Christian Groups in Lebanon and Egypt in Comparative Perspective', in Shatzmiller (ed.), *Nationalism and Minority Identity in Islamic Societies*, pp. 85–107.

Ruane, Joseph and Jennifer Todd, *The Dynamics of Conflict in Northern Ireland:*

Power, Conflict and Emancipation. Cambridge: Cambridge University Press, 1996.

Salvadori, Massimo, *Aftermath of Empire: In Honor of Professor Max Salvadori*. Northhampton, MA: Smith College, 1975.

Salzmann, Ariel, 'An Ancien Regime Revisited: "Privatization" and Political Economy in the Eighteenth-Century Ottoman Empire', *Politics and Society*, 21(4) (1993), 393–423.

Schleiffer, Abdullah, 'The Life and Thought of ᶜIzz-id-Din al-Qassam', *Islamic Quarterly*, 23(2) (1979), 61–81.

Schulz, Helena Lindholm, *The Reconstruction of Palestinian Nationalism: Between Revolution and Statehood*. New York: Manchester University Press, 1999.

Schulze, Kristen E., Martin Stokes and Colm Campbell (eds), *Nationalism, Minorities and Diasporas: Identities and Rights in the Middle East*. New York: I. B. Tauris, 1996.

Scott, Rachel, *Challenge of Political Islam: Non-Muslims and the Egyptian State*. Stanford, CA: Stanford University Press, 2010.

Segev, Tom, *One Palestine, Complete: Jews and Arabs Under the British Mandate*. New York: Macmillan, 2001.

Seikaly, May, *Haifa: Transformation of an Arab Society 1918–1939*. London: I. B. Tauris, 2002.

Sela, Avraham, 'The "Wailing Wall" Riots (1929) as a Watershed in the Palestine Conflict', *The Muslim World*, 84(1/2) (1994), 60–94.

Shatzmiller, Maya (ed.), Nationalism and Minority Identity in Islamic Societies. Montreal: McGill-Queen's University Press, 2005.

Shimoni, Yaacov, *Arabs of Israel* (in Hebrew). Tel Aviv: Davar Printing Press,1947.

Shlaim, Avi, 'The Debate about 1948', in Pappé (ed.), *The Israel/Palestine Question*, pp. 150–68.

Shomali, Qustandi, 'Politics, Press and Religious Identity, 1900–1948', in O'Mahony *et al.* (eds), *The Christian Heritage in the Holy Land*, pp. 225–36.

Al-Sifri, ᶜIsa, *Filastin al-ᶜarabiyyah bayn al-intidab wa al-sahyuniyyah* (*Arab Palestine between the Mandate and Zionism*). Jaffa, 1937.

Singer, Amy, Christoph Neumann and Selcuk Aksin (eds), *Untold Histories of the Middle East: Recovering Voices from the 19th and 20th Centuries*. New York: Routledge, 2010.

Smith, Charles, '"British–Zionist Alliance", Review of *One Palestine, Complete* by Tom Segev', *Journal of Palestine Studies*, 31(1) (2001), 89–91.

Smith, Donald Eugene, *India as a Secular State*. Princeton, NJ: Princeton University Press, 1963.

Stein, Kenneth, 'Review of *The Supreme Muslim Council*, by Uri Kupferschmidt, and *The Mufti of Jerusalem*, by Philip Mattar', *International Journal of Middle Eastern Studies*, 23(4) (1991), 641–2.

Stein, Leonard, *The Balfour Declaration*. London: Vallentine, Mitchell, 1961.

Bibliography

Stendel, Ori, *The Arabs in Israel*. Brighton: Sussex Academic Press, 1996.

Stowasser, Barbara Freyer (ed.), *The Islamic Impulse*. Washington, DC: Taylor & Francis, 1987.

Summers, Lawrence, America's Palestine: Popular and Official Perceptions from Balfour to Israeli Statehood. Gainesville, FL: University of Florida Press, 2001.

Swedenburg, Ted, 'The Role of the Palestinian Peasantry in the Great Revolt (1936–1939)', in Hourani, Khoury and Wilson (eds), *The Modern Middle East*, pp. 467–502.

Swedenburg, Ted, *Memories of Revolt: The 1936–1939 Rebellion and the Palestinian National Past*. Fayetteville, AR: University of Arkansas Press, 2003.

Swedenburg, Ted, 'Al-Qassam Remembered', *Alif: Journal of Comparative Poetics*, 7 (1987), 7–24.

Tamari, Salim, 'A Miserable Year in Brooklyn: Khalil Sakakini in America, 1907–1908', *Jerusalem Quarterly*, 17 (2003), 19–40.

Tamari, Salim (ed.), *Jerusalem 1948: The Arab Neighborhoods and their Fate in the War*. Jerusalem: Institute of Jerusalem Studies, 1999.

Tamari, Salim. 'Factionalism and Class Formation in Recent Palestinian History', in Owen (ed.), *Studies in the Economic and Social History of Palestine in the Nineteenth and Twentieth Centuries*, pp. 177–202.

Tessler, Mark, *A History of the Israeli–Palestinian Conflict*. Bloomington, IN: Indiana University Press, 1994.

Al-Thᵓaalbi, ᶜAbd al-Aziz. *Khalfiyat al-muᵓtamar al-islami bi al-Quds, 1350 h, 1931 m (Background of the Islamic Congress in Jerusalem, 1350 hijrah, 1931 AD)*. Beirut: Dar al-Arab al-Islaammi, 1988.

Thio, Li-ann, *Managing Babel: The International Legal Protection of Minorities in the Twentieth Century*. Boston, MA: Martinus Nijhoff, 2005.

Thursby, G. R., *Hindu–Muslim Relations in British India: A Study of Controversy, Conflict, and Communal Movements in Northern India 1923–1928*. Boston, MA: Brill, 1975.

Tsimhoni, Daphne, 'Palestinian Christians and the Peace Process', in Peleg (ed.), *The Middle East Peace Process: Interdisciplinary Perspectives*, pp. 141–60.

Tsimhoni, Daphne, *Christian Communities in Jerusalem and the West Bank Since 1948: An Historical, Social, and Political Study*. Westport, CT: Praeger, 1993.

Tsimhoni, Daphne, 'The Status of the Arab Christians under the British Mandate in Palestine', *Middle Eastern Studies*, 20(4) (1984), 166–92.

Tsimhoni, Daphne, 'The Arab Christians and the Palestinian Arab National Movement During the Formative Stage', in Ben-Dor (ed.), *The Palestinians and the Middle East Conflict*, pp. 73–98.

Tsimhoni, Daphne, 'The British Mandate and the Arab Christians in Palestine, 1920–1925', dissertation, University of London, 1976.

Vail, Leroy (ed.), *The Creation of Tribalism in Southern Africa*. Berkeley, CA: University of California Press, 1991.

Verete, Mayir, 'The Balfour Declaration and its Makers', *Middle Eastern Studies*, 6(1) (1970), 48–76.

Waines, David, 'The Failure of the National Resistance', in Abu-Lughod (ed.), *The Transformation of Palestine: Essays on the Origin and Development of the Arab–Israeli Conflict*, pp. 207–36.

Wasserstein, Bernard, *The British in Palestine: The Mandatory Government and Arab–Jewish Conflict, 1917–1929*, 2nd edn. Oxford: Blackwell, 1991.

Wasserstein, Bernard, '"Clipping the Claws of the Colonisers": Arab Officials in the Government of Palestine, 1917–48', *Middle Eastern Studies*, 13(2) (1977), 171–94.

Wells, H. G., *The Idea of a League of Nations*. Boston, MA: Atlantic Monthly Press, 1919.

Yasin, Subhi, *Al-thawrah al-ᶜarabiyah al-kubra fi filasin (The Great Arab Revolt in Palestine)*. Cairo: Dar al-Kitab al-ᶜArabi, 1967.

Index